Following his highly successful *The Man from the Alamo – Why the Welsh Chartist Uprising of 1839 Ended in a Massacre*, John Humphries again unearths an amazing story unknown to modern historians. Was Caryl ap Rhys Pryce a British secret agent or a freedom fighter? From public school he spent some time in a bank and then ten years in South Africa with the British South African Police, transferring to the Natal Police where he was decorated for his part in the Relief of Ladysmith. Service in the Imperal Light Horse and the South African Constabulary ended his ten years in conflicts in South Africa and he moved to Canada and signed up with the 6th Duke of Connaught's Own Rifles. Next, a penniless drifter in Los Angeles, Pryce eventually became *generalissimo* of the Magonista revolutionaries in Mexico, capturing Tijuana. After a trial in Los Angeles, he was a Hollywood film star before joining the Canadian Expeditionary Force in World War I, and transferring to the 38th (Welsh) Division as an artillery officer. Major Pryce was awarded the DSO, and after the war seemingly vanished for four years, quite possibly serving with the Black and Tans in Ireland, before resurfacing with many of their men in the Palestine Gendarmerie.

A native of Newport, and educated at St Julians High School, the author has been a professional journalist all his life, firstly in Wales, then as a foreign correspondent based in Brussels. As European Bureau Chief for thirteen Thomson daily newspapers, he traveled extensively, reporting on breaking news from all parts of Europe. After returning to Britain as London and City Editor for Thomson Regional Newspapers, he was appointed Editor of *The Western Mail*, the newspaper on which he began his career. John Humphries lives with his wife – and a very large garden – at Tredunnoc in the Usk Valley.

Text within the photograph:

Gen. Price.
Commanding the rebels
at Tijuana 5/9-1911.

General Pryce commanding the rebels at Tijuana.
(Pryce Family Papers).

Mexico's Baja California.

Gringo Revolutionary

THE AMAZING ADVENTURES OF CARYL AP RHYS PRYCE

John Humphries

WALES BOOKS
GLYNDŴR PUBLISHING

Published in 2005 by
Glyndŵr Publishing,
10 Mallory Close, Sain Tathan, Bro Morgannwg, CF62 4JJ
www.walesbooks.com

ISBN 1 903529 18 2

*This publication was assisted by a grant
from the Welsh Books Council.*

Cover Design: Welsh Books Council

Printed in Wales by
Dinefwr Press, Rawlings Road
Llandybie, Carmarthenshire, SA18 3YD

To
Rhys, Megan, Nathan and Juliette

Every life should be an adventure

Acknowledgements

On the fiftieth anniversary of his death, the Welsh soldier-adventurer, Caryl ap Rhys Pryce, continues to be reviled by Mexicans as the man who tried to steal their country. The failure of his bizarre coup had more to do with his accomplices than his inability to pull it off. In fact Pryce, a descendant of another revolutionary leader, Owain Glyndŵr, came within an ace of forcing his way into that pantheon of illustrious men and women who, rightly or wrongly, leave an indelible mark on our life and times. As it happened, after marching on to the world stage, and briefly pushing at the doors of the pantheon he fell back into the crowd, to be forgotten by almost everyone but never to be forgiven by the Mexicans. *Gringo Revolutionary* reconstructs a momentous six months in 1911 when 'General Pryce' and his 'Foreign Legion' took centre stage alongside Pancho Villa and Emiliano Zapata, albeit on opposing sides, during the Mexican Revolution.

This book would not have been possible without access to the back numbers of the many newspapers published at that time in San Diego, Los Angeles, San Francisco, and Mexico City. A period when newspapers were the only means of mass communication, this first golden age of newspaper production was marked by a proliferation of titles accompanied by an intense rivalry for news. Sadly, those days are over, and apart from the *San Diego Union* and *Los Angeles Times,* many of the titles from which I have pieced together the blow-by-blow account of the adventures of General Pryce and his army of insurgents, no longer exist. Fortunately, most of their back issues have survived in the public libraries in San Diego, Los Angeles, the Bancroft Library at the University of California at Berkley, and the Arizona Collection at Arizona State University, Phoenix. To their librarians and archivists I am hugely grateful for their courtesy and assistance. But for my re-construction of Pryce's revolutionary campaign to have a further ring of authenticity, I decided it was necessary to follow the trail he and his revolutionaries took through the Baja Peninsular (Lower California), accompanied as always on these expeditions by my wife. But for her presence of mind – and her rudimentary knowledge of Spanish – my research might have ended at the edge of Laguna Salada when our car began sinking into quick sands!

As I have discovered on previous occasions, the U.S. National Archives in Washington D.C. and National Archives Pacific Southwest Region always provide invaluable access to official records. Especially useful were the reports of two investigations conducted by the United States Senate Sub Committee on Foreign Relations: 'Revolutions in Cuba and Mexico' (CIS No: S40-3), probably the single most important official document from this period, followed by the Senate debate on 'Affairs in Mexico' (Congressional Record, 62-2).

Pryce's Welsh antecedents were confusing, considering he was born in India, and went to school in Scotland. Besides family descendants, I was helped with this by the National Library of Wales, Aberystwyth, which holds valuable source material regarding the Pryses of Gogerddan – the ancestral home – the family's interests and influence, and also genealogical links to feudal Welsh princes. Felicity Given, archivist at Glenalmond College, Perth, where Pryce received his public school education, filled in those early years from the school records. What followed, his ten years in Africa during the Mashonaland Rebellion and at the relief of Ladysmith during the Boer War, was an even greater challenge, requiring serious research assistance. For this, I am grateful to Ian Johnstone in Harare, and Audrey Portman in South Africa.

Inevitably, piecing together such a full life required the help of sources from across three continents. In London, the Royal Artillery Museum at Greenwich produced Pryce's War Diary from World War I, the National Film Museum in the Netherlands provided details and stills from one of the silent movies in which he starred, while Edward Horne, official historian of the Palestine Police, filled in some of the incident from the last days of Pryce's active service along the borders between Palestine and Syria, during the British Mandate.

But my research would never have been complete – if ever research can be – without the descendants of a very remarkable man, John ap Rhys Pryce, a great nephew, of Weybridge, Surrey, and his father, the late Brigadier Meyric ap Rhys Pryce, formerly of the Royal Welch Fusiliers. Pryce seems rarely, if at all, to have mentioned his Mexican adventure, but he did leave some personal papers to which the family very kindly permitted me free access. I have drawn extensively on the Pryce Papers to re-construct the life of the *Gringo Revolutionary*.

John Humphries,
Plas Cwm Coed, Tredunnoc,
Gwent   October 2005

Contents

Introduction

Sound, sound the clarion, fill the fife!
To all, the sensual world proclaim,
One crowded hour of glorious life,
Is worth an age without a name.

Sir Walter Scott

'Nobody cares tuppence,' was how Caryl ap Rhys Pryce explained to his fiancée Hattie Biggs why he left his Vancouver flat for an evening stroll, and did not return for two years. At 35, the Welshman had already seen more adventure than most men experience in a thousand lifetimes. But Pryce was hungry, 'lonely and off colour' as he made his way to the waterfront through Gas Town, a warren of narrow streets along the Burrard Inlet, crowded with taverns and brothels, reverberating with the excited babble of fortune-hunters bound for the goldfields of the Yukon. Two years in Vancouver trying, unsuccessfully, to run a towing company with his brother-in-law was about as much as Pryce could take that cold winter's night in January 1911. Wandering through Gas Town, the wanderlust that had driven him the whole of his life was about to lead to an escapade crowning even his previously astonishing exploits.

The club where he usually 'got his grub' was empty, so Pryce pressed on until he saw the Seattle ferry, the *SS Victoria,* tied up at the Canadian Pacific Railroad Wharf. 'On the spur of the moment' he boarded it, intending to return the next day. Instead, he continued travelling south, until Los Angeles where his money ran out.[1]

Perhaps the Welshman's state of mind had something to do with the efforts of Miss Biggs to wean him off the opiate of adventure. Born on the Feast of St Jeremy at Vizianagram, Madras, India, in 1876, the life of this public school educated son of the British Raj, who claimed descent from Gwaethfod, Lord of Cardigan, a Prince of Wales, had been one long wooing of adventure.[2]

Within a few years of leaving Glenalmond College in Perth-shire, he had enlisted in the British South Africa Police, the para-military force recruited by the empire-builder Cecil Rhodes to suppress rebellious Mashona tribesmen, by blasting them from their redoubts in the caves beneath the granite hills along the Bulawayo-Salisbury road. Wriggling on their stomachs to the lip of the deepest crevices, the para-militaries dropped pipes stuffed with dynamite on to the natives and their families huddled below. Each time a bunch of "kaffirs" was flushed into the open, stag-gering dazed and bleeding through clouds of smoke pouring from the cave entrances, the dynamiters were cheered to the blue skies of the *veldt* by comrades crouching among rocky outcrops, *kopjes*, waiting, fingers wrapped around the triggers of their Winchesters, to deal with any native who escaped the chattering machine gun. Even among Victorians besotted by the invincibility of a British Empire on which the sun would never be allowed to set, such measures caused a public outcry.

After twelve months of this, the Mashonas once again pacified and submissive, Pryce transferred to the Natal Police as a police trooper, a crack shot from the saddle, able to drop a man at the gallop from fifty paces. With such accomplishments, it was per-haps inevitable that when the Boer War broke out a year later on 11 October 1899 and the Natal Police were mobilised, Pryce set his sights on enlisting in the Imperial Light Horse, whose enthusiasm for retaliating against the families and property of the Afrikaner farmers earned it the sobriquet of 'Imperial Light Looters.'

Ten years after arriving in South Africa, he suddenly left to join his sister Gladys and brother-in-law Kenwyn Hodges in the ship-ping venture in Vancouver, where, in more settled conditions, the relationship with Miss Biggs blossomed to the point at which there was talk of a wedding. But the push in the back from a compelling lust for adventure was to prove far stronger than Hattie's ardent endeavours to nudge Pryce into a more orthodox life. Either that, or he was just another man to do a runner when confronted by the door of the church and a life of boring conven-tionality.

Boarding the *SS Victoria* at the Canadian Pacific Railroad Wharf, he never dreamed he was embarking on a journey that would end in Mexico and with his vilification as one of that country's most hated men. He had probably left Vancouver with nothing more in mind than to seek the comradeship of the sort that existed in the company of other men, usually soldiers, wandering in foreign lands, because Pryce was one of that curious legion of British who, scenting a battle from afar, always happened to be on the spot when the fighting started. Wherever he travelled, he always bore arms, and when there was no battle to be fought, enlistment in the local militia ensured he would never be far from any future action. The very first thing he did on arriving in Canada in 1907 was to enlist in the 6th Duke of Connaught's Own Rifles.

Despite all the efforts of his family and friends, Caryl had failed on leaving Glenalmond College to obtain a scholarship to Sandhurst Military Academy, unlike his elder brother, Henry, later General Sir Henry ap Rhys Pryce, who, during World War I was entrusted by Prime Minister Lloyd George with raising the Welsh Army Corps to fight in France. Nonetheless, Caryl remained loyal to the family tradition, and while not following his father, Colonel Douglas Davidson Pryce, and brother Henry into the Indian Army, his entire life would revolve around 'soldiering', either as a policeman or mercenary. Born in India, the brothers and their sisters Gladys and Eileen were left in the care of relatives in Scotland while their parents, stalwarts of the British Raj, pursued their life in India, the only home their mother Alice, née Hunter, really ever knew, having born on a troopship bound for Madras. From the age of seven, Caryl saw his parents only infrequently, emerging in adult life as a solitary individual, seeking the companionship of kindred spirits. But he was grateful to his father for one thing: the name, with its Welsh antecedents evoking links with an historic, rebellious past. Born into the ruling class and raised in the glow of Empire, for Caryl the name was always an icon never to be tampered with. Remarkably, when his exploits attracted the attention of the world, few ever got it wrong, possibly because of the unsettling habit he had of jabbing a loaded six-gun or Winchester in the general direction of anyone who did.

The family's ties with its ancestral estates at Gogerddan, near Aberystwyth, had long been severed by one of those twists of marriage that separate the very wealthy from the moderately rich. But when Caryl and his brother Henry were baptised at the Madras Presidency, their father reminded them of their heritage and perhaps put down a marker for the future, by christening each with the Welsh epithet 'ap Rhys', translating as 'son of,' the dynastic device Celts use to identify an ancestral blood bond. In their case, direct descent was from Gwaethfod, Lord of Cardigan, a Prince of Wales two decades before the Battle of Hastings, a noble family through whom Caryl could claim kinship with the Welsh revolutionary, Owain Glyndŵr.[3] At the time of Glyndŵr's rebellion against Henry IV in 1401, the majority of Welsh gentry hurried to produce pedigrees proving descent from Welsh chieftains, and, better still, links to the Royal Houses of Wales. Since eligible sons and daughters usually married within their circle, the wealthiest and most influential of gentry families were always likely to be related to each other to some extent.

Gwaethfod's descendants, the Pryses (*sic*) of Gogerddan, dominated their corner of Wales for a thousand years, the ancestral estates of Caryl's forebears covering 30,000 acres of lush pastures, forests of native oak, hills of gold, silver and lead. There were rich pickings, too, from the wild Celtic Sea. The neighbouring town of Aberystwyth, derided by Daniel Defoe during a visit in the early 18th century as 'a populous, very dirty, black, smoky place', the streets filled with dunghills and piles of rotting fish, was home for scores of fishermen, each obliged to deliver to the Pryses, as agents for the King, a *meise* of herrings, 630 fish, at the start of every season. For centuries this was no great hardship, the waters of Cardigan Bay providing a rich harvest of herrings, cod, whiting, pollack and man-size monkfish. Oysters were plentiful, so were whales, sharks and porpoises. On one night alone, the fleet landed 1,386,000 herrings, mostly for salting into barrels for shipment to the Mediterranean.

The Pryses controlled the Court Leet, to the extent of creating bogus Burgesses to secure the return as Mayor of persons favoured by Gogerddan. The election of the Mayor of Aberystwyth in 1767 continued over two days, costing John Pughe Pryse £102-13s-3d for 407 gallons of ale at ¼d a pint, 168 quarts at 4d a pint, meals for 343 men at 8d each, and two nights grazing for 35 horses. Aberystwyth was part of a family fiefdom that believed it had the absolute right to rule, even to the extent of fixing Parliamentary elections, which usually became trials of strength between rival landowners. County families expended much energy and money on political activities because success not merely lent colour and excitement to their otherwise quiet and often dreary round of estate duties, but also gave the family additional power and prestige in the locality. Westminster and successive governments showed little interest in the corrupt actions of these remote Welsh families, until the Pryses of Goderddan took a step too far by presuming it could command the same fealty as the monarch by requiring the Burgesses of Aberystwyth, at one and the same time, to swear allegiance to the King and to "the House of Gogerddan." For failing to attend the House of Commons to account for his actions, Lewis Pryse was expelled for contempt in 1717. Such duplicity was not unusual. At the time of Glyndŵr's uprising in the early 15th century the Pryses had succeeded, simultaneously, to back their revolutionary ancestor and the King, switching sides at the most opportune moment. Support for what was eventually another lost cause, Oliver Cromwell, also failed to dent the family fortunes.

The golden age of Gogerddan had arrived in 1690 with the discovery of silver and lead in the mountains between the rivers Rheidol and Dyfi. After defeating the Crown in a legal battle over mineral rights, the then head of the family, Sir Carbery Pryse, raced from London to Aberystwyth to deliver the good news, completing his historic ride in only 48 hours. Bonfires blazing from the hillsides lit a fiery path to the front door of Gogerddan, in his pocket even better news – an assayer's report calculating Sir Carbery's annual profit from the new Esgair Hir mine at £70,500 a year in 1693, more than £3 million at today's values.

When two hundred years later Caryl ap Rhys Pryce first saw the light of day in Andhra Prad Province, India, he was adrift from his Welsh ancestors, snapped off by that great tide of marital colonisation that had left him only with a name to evoke the spirit of Owain Glyndŵr, apart from his rebellious streak, which manifested itself early in life. Joining his brother Henry at Trinity College, Glenalmond, in the Michaelmas term of 1887 after two years at St Salvator's School in St Andrews – a prep crammer for the sons of expatriate parents like the Pryces – Caryl was soon expressing himself more enthusiastically on the sports fields, than in the classics for which this 'Winchester of the North' was distinguished.[4]

17

Glenalmond College, Perth, shortly after it was built in 1850.

Hidden away in The Cairnies, a stretch of wild and open Perthshire countryside north of the Forth, Glenalmond had been founded by the Scottish Episcopal Church forty-six years earlier as an institution combining 'general education with domestic discipline and systematic religious education'. Quite deliberately, the founding fathers, among them William Ewart Gladstone, four times British Prime Minister, chose a location far removed from the influence of any large town and while still holding to its ecclesiastical traditions, the school was by the end of the 19th century chiefly regarded as an alternative for those who could not afford Winchester, Eton and Rugby, and one ideally suited to preparing the sons of the upper middle-class for careers in the Indian Civil Service and the Army. Several of Glenalmond's former pupils had died in the Indian Mutiny and for Colonel Douglas Pryce, expecting both sons to follow in his footsteps, the school could not have been a better choice.

Glenalmond's austere regime produced a healthy, resilient, uncomplaining young inmate, equipped for the privations he was to face during an eventful life. Porridge and bread for breakfast with one pat of butter and jam; then a brisk run around the grounds, no matter what the weather; a snatched hunk of bread for lunch before compulsory football or cricket; and for dinner, meat and pudding washed down by either water or beer (depending on age), served by lads from the village dressed for the occasion in blue jackets with shiny buttons. Winters in The Cairnies were so bitterly cold, the only warmth from open fires, it was not unusual for the boys to drag fallen branches into school to fuel a glorious roasting. As for bath time, this was once a week, and with only four tubs, the young Pryce could expect to share his water with some other boy. For those unfortunate to draw the 'second bath,' it was never more than tepid.

The staff and trustees of Glenalmond were committed to replicating the English public school system in every detail. At school, Pryce wore an Eton collar and jacket, flannels and a black clerical coat with a silk hat on formal occasions. After morning school, the boys changed from their 'uniform' into tweed suits. Football was played in knickerbokers. Parents rarely contacted their sons during term. Letters were discouraged, while tuck boxes stuffed with goodies from home were confiscated as unhealthy distractions.

Caryl and his brother Henry as Tweedledom and Tweedledee in a production of 'Alice in Wonderland' at Glenalmond College.

19

For its stewardship of his sons, Colonel Pryce paid Glenalmond 90 guineas a year, plus the cost of one vital optional extra – membership of the college Rifle Corps, schooling its cadets in the military mind and accompanying code of discipline, in every way an apprenticeship for Sandhurst Military College. Participating fully in the pomp and ceremony of Glenalmond, the Rifle Corps, with the Pryce brothers in its ranks, provided the military escort for Gladstone's coach when their venerable founder returned to celebrate the school's golden jubilee. Afterwards the cadets, most of them crack shots, fired a *feu-de-joie* in honour of their founder.[5]

An institution inspiring individualism and feeding the spirit of adventure, Glenalmond was encouraged by the prevailing mood, rooted as it was in the absolute certainty that the English and only the English were born to rule. Pryce came from a generation that took as its moral tenet and prophecy John Ruskin's address:

> We are still un-degenerate in race; a race mingled with the best northern blood . . . Will you youths of England make your country again a Royal Throne of Kings, a sceptered isle . . .? This is what England must either do or perish; she must found colonies as fast and as far as she is able, formed of her most energetic and worthiest men; seizing every piece of fruitful waste ground she can set her foot on, and there teaching these her colonists that their chief virtue is to bear fidelity to their country and that their first aim is to advance the prowess of England by land and by sea; and though they live on a distant plot of land, they are no more to consider themselves disenfranchised from their native land than the sailors of her fleets do because they float on distant seas.

While Glenalmond was committed to improving the social calibre of entrants, there was an occasion when a shortage of funds required it to admit a certain 'rough element,' which threatened to lower its social tone. The Headmaster's response was to appoint a member of staff to tutor the boys in how to speak proper English, 'eradicating all dialectal peculiarities in vocabulary and idiom.' By all accounts, Pryce's cut glass English accent survived throughout his adult life, a verbal eccentricity that by marking him out as a gentlemen of superior breeding would have sat uncomfortably with those he encountered on disembarking from the *SS Victoria* at Seattle. It was here he stumbled upon a comradeship the likes of which he would never have experienced previously.

There was an army on the move along the Pacific West Coast of America in January 1911, an army of migratory workers, surviving on poor-house wages, living in unsanitary, over-crowded camps with only straw to sleep on, and tin plates to eat their grub off. Those who shared mattresses and blankets became so infested with lice and bed bugs, that they soon opted to carry their own blankets, or bindles, wrapped around a rope and slung like bandoliers across the chest. A familiar sight in California, these 'bindle stiffs' as the migrants were known, drifted between the shantytowns strewn along the rail tracks, a half-a-million men stealing a ride on a freight train somewhere across the United States every day. Jobs never lasted long. Thousands were laid off at a moment's notice. With unemployment at 35 per cent, the West Coast was alive with migrants, mostly white, with no families to speak of, the only rule never to pry into another man's affairs.

Moving and working in miserable conditions, these electorally and economically disenfranchised workers stood ready to fight capitalism. Their only allegiance was to the Industrial Workers of the World, an anarcho-syndicalist organisation formed in 1905 to create one Big Union, pledged to bring a new social order to America by defeating the capitalist system through General Strikes, sabotage and other forms of direct action. From among the migrant workers, the IWW recruited a million members, otherwise known as the Wobblies, the foot soldiers of the revolution, each carrying a little red membership card. From all walks of life, they were almost always penniless. There were 'snipes' and 'jerries,' the men who laid railroad sections; 'splinter bellies' were untrained carpenters; dish washers were 'pearl divers', ditch diggers 'sewer hogs', while 'timber wolves' felled trees.

Assailed by a Wobbly army bent on destroying the social order, the capitalist Press joined forces with big business to stop the 'bums' at all costs. But the hobos revelled in their notoriety, taunting their detractors with their anthem, 'Hallelujah, I'm a Bum,' adding a new defiant verse after every victory over capitalism. America's industrial landscape in the early 19th century was marred by violence, most of it blamed upon the Wobblies, a nickname reputedly coined by a waiter in a Chinese restaurant who meant to ask a group he was serving 'Are you IWW,' but instead mouthed something that sounded like, 'All loo eye wobble wobble?' However it originated, the name stuck. So did the newspaper jibe that IWW stood for 'I don't Wanna Work'.

The IWW came close to inciting a working-class revolution long before the Bolsheviks in Petrograd in 1917. In the process, it pushed America to the brink, revealing extremism in thought and deed of a kind rarely seen in the United States. While the rank-and-file slugged it out with police and company guards on the picket lines, the more visionary Wobbly leaders like the founder, one-eyed 'Big Bill' Haywood, were looking beyond the class war to a Utopia in which the wage system was abolished, where government was eliminated, the state replaced by one Big Union. The founders of the IWW believed in the historic mission of the working-class to eradicate capitalism, and made no secret of their objectives, proclaiming loudly at every opportunity that 'the working-class and employing class have nothing in common.' Their manifesto trumpeted:

> There can be no peace so long as hunger and want are found among millions of working people and the few who make up the employing class have all the good things in life. As a revolutionary organisation, the IWW aims to use any and all tactics that will get the results with the least expenditure of time and energy. The tactics used are determined solely by the power of the organisation to make good in their use. The question of right and wrong does not concern us.

This was pretty strong medicine, a political formula that appealed at one and the same time to drifters and wasters, loafers and workers, idealists and the exploited, anarchists, socialists, and deserters from the harsh regime of the U.S. Army. Tens of thousands flocked to the IWW banner, providing muscle at flash points between unionism and capitalism, riding freight trains, camping in hobo jungles, heating cans of mulligan stew over cook fires, and singing defiant Wobbly songs.[6]

Apart from the fact that by the time he reached Los Angeles he, too, was penniless, Pryce had very little in common with this army of anarcho-syndicalists. Not for a moment in his life had he experienced poverty or unemployment. After leaving Glenalmond, he had found a secure, though boring, position in the British Linen Company Bank in Glasgow, his only relief from the tedium, Saturday afternoon appearances for Glasgow Academicals soccer side, and training sessions with the 1st Lanark Rifle Volunteers, a unit receiving drill and weapons instruction from regular army officers. What privation Pryce suffered was self-imposed when, imbued with the spirit of adventure and dazzled by the prospects of personal fortune on the frontiers of the Empire, he had left Britain to join Cecil Rhodes in Africa as a trooper in the British South Africa Police.

Caryl filled with the spirit of adventure, taken shortly before he sailed for Africa.

It would be stretching credulity to imagine that a man who in later life was a political agent for the Conservative and Unionist Party, and whose brother Sir Henry crowned an illustrious military career as Aide de Camp to King Edward VIII, should join the American working-class in its titanic struggle with capitalism. But Pryce appears to have done just that, and not as an anonymous foot soldier, but as a class-war leader in an audacious attempt to size Mexico's Baja Peninsula, or Lower California as it is known, an area a third of the size of its northern neighbour, California proper, there to build a Utopia, a new Jerusalem for the Industrial Workers of the World and their anarchist allies, the *Partido Liberal Mexicana* (Mexican Liberal Party) of Ricardo Flores Magon.

Publicly a Liberal reformer, yet secretly an anarchist, Ricardo Magon, a price of $20,000 placed on his head by the Mexican

Government, lived in exile with a handful of conspirators at 519½ East Fourth Street, Los Angeles. Magon cared little for the noble, tolerant sentiments usually associated with western liberalism, his speeches and writings drenched in bloody invective, his political philosophy more in tune with the ideology of Michael Bakunin, the Russian 'father' of revolutionary anarchism. The short, tubby, middle-aged Mexican, revered today by Mexicans in much the same way as James Connolly is regarded in Ireland, had, in 1911, forged a shaky alliance with the Industrial Workers of the World to wage war against the aging Mexican President Porfirio Diaz whose tyrannical regime was besieged by revolutionaries. While Diaz was most certainly doomed, it was another Mexican exile, wealthy landowner Francisco Madero, who was generally regarded as the man most likely to replace Diaz in Mexico City with the assistance of an army led by the former bandit, Pancho Villa in the northern state of Chihuaha, and Emiliano Zapata, the peasant leader of Morelos in the south. Accusing Madero of betraying tens of thousands of poor *peons,* Magon opened a second revolution- ary front, raising his banner proclaiming 'Land and Liberty' in the Baja Peninsula, a largely barren, mountainous, finger of desert land, longer than Italy, jutting eight hundred miles out into the Pacific. With the assistance of Wobbly fighters from the Industrial Workers of the World, this was to be the Magonista bridgehead into their anarchist Utopia – and Caryl ap Rhys Pryce would become the *gringo* chosen to lead the revolutionary assault.[7]

NOTES

1. Pryce Papers. Undated letter from Caryl ap Rhys Pryce to Hattie Biggs.
2. Pryce Papers. Undated letter from Caryl ap Rhys Pryce to Hattie Biggs.
3. Pryce Papers. Birth certificate from Madras.
4. Ibid. Pryce family tree.
5. Correspondence between author and Felicity Given, Archivist, Glenalmond College, Perth, 1998.
6. G. St Quintin, *The history of Glenalmond: the story of a hundred years,* (Edinburgh, 1956, Constable).
7. Patrick Renshaw, *The Wobblies: the story of syndicalism in the United States* (New York, 1967, Doubleday and Co, Inc.); Joyce L. Kornbluh, *Rebel Voices, an I.W.W. Anthology* (Ann Arbor, University of Michigan Press).
8. Ward S. Albro, *Always a rebel: Flores Nagon and the Mexican Revolution* (Fort Worth, Texas, 1992, Texas Christian University Press).

Chapter 1

A Generation of Braggarts

> There is rock to the left and rock to the right,
>   and low lean thorn between,
> And ye may hear a breech-bolt snick where never
>   a man is seen.
>
> Rudyard Kipling

For Caryl ap Rhys Pryce the road to Mexico began with the attempt by the Jameson Raiders in December 1895, to start a civil war in the Afrikaner republic of the Transvaal. Dr Leander Starr Jameson was Cecil Rhodes' Administrator in Rhodesia, comprising Matabeland and Mashonaland, the wilderness between the Zambesi and Limpopo, which Rhodes' British South Africa Company was busy seizing from the Africans by right of conquest. When Pryce left Glenalmond in 1893, civilisation had barely laid a finger on this fabled Kingdom of Ophir, the reputed site of the fabulously rich King Solomon's Mines. For Rhodes, the favourite son of Imperial Britain, Rhodesia and neighbouring Transvaal were vital pieces in his grand design for an Empire extending from the Cape to Cairo. Identifying with much that was common coin in England of the 1890s, he had fired the imagination of a generation with a potent mix straight from the pages of *Boys Own Paper* and Rudyard Kipling.

Rhodesia was not unlike England on a warm summer's day, a rich and fertile land, in April the flaming red and gold of the *msasa* trees reminding white settlers of the autumnal beech of the mother country. Above 5,000 feet, it was open and flat, very cold in winter but nonetheless a delight for Europeans. The terrain became more difficult as the altitude dropped, passing through huge stands of native timber before merging into waist-high bush dotted with *kopjes*. Beneath these crowns of granite rocks three to

25

four hundred feet high, were huge caverns, one containing a seemingly bottomless lake, another large enough to hide five thousand Mashona warriors. But along the valley bottoms the heat for much of the day was oppressive and unhealthy, the *tsetse* fly driving horses frantic as their riders struggled to traverse muddy tracks frequently swept away by torrents rushing from the heights. Here, the early settlers, hunters and prospectors died not from the stabbing *assegai*, but from malaria and blackwater fever. Nevertheless, Ruskin, Rhodes, Kipling, and Rhodesia proved irresistible to the young Pryce when he tired, finally, of his job at the bank in Glasgow.

But Africa was not his first choice. After family and friends had failed to pull the appropriate strings to obtain a training commission for him at Sandhurst Military Academy, his preferred destination was Burma, ignoring the objections of his parents.[1] And the twenty-year-old might well have been persuaded to remain in Britain, had it not been for the failed Jameson Raid on 29 December 1895, which robbed the British South Africa Police of the majority of its troopers, leaving Rhodesia's white settlers dangerously exposed to native unrest. It was directly on account of this that an advertisement for new police recruits appeared some months later in English newspapers, aimed at adventurous, young men aged between 20 and 35, able to 'produce certificates of good character and to pass a medical examination, and be tested for riding and shooting before being enrolled.' A trooper would get 5s a day, those recruited from England to pay their own passage – then about £20 – as far as Cape Town.[2]

The Jameson Raid was a botched coup. The plan, with the Empire builder's covert backing, was to overthrow Afrikaner President Kruger by supporting a rising among the 60,000 *Uitlanders*, or foreigners, believed to be on the point of rebellion over the discrimination they were suffering at the hands of the Afrikaner minority in the Transvaal, mostly Boer farmers. These *Voortrekkers* (pioneers) had trekked out of the British Cape Colony to found their homeland north of the Vaal River. There had already been one Boer War over the status of the territory in 1880, this ending with the Boers granted self-rule in the Transvaal, under British oversight. The discovery of gold there had, however, triggered a stampede of non-Boer European settlers into the Transvaal, the

Uitlanders very soon contributing a large part of the wealth of a country in which they had little or no representation. It seemed only a matter of time before the growing friction between the two sides boiled over into open warfare, the *Uitlanders* preparing for this by organising themselves behind a Reform Committee, pledged to take some kind of direct action if the Boers continued to refuse them equal rights. All this suited Rhodes' plans for a British Empire from the Cape to Cairo, because the Transvaal stood in the way of that dream. But as Prime Minister of Cape Colony, he could not be directly implicated in any coup, and so delegated the leadership of this to his right-hand man, Jameson who with six hundred men, crossed the border into the Transvaal, the signal for an armed rising by the *Uitlanders*. Not only did this fail to materialise, but the Boers, having been warned of the raid when Jameson neglected to cut the overhead telegraph wires, ambushed the raiders on the road to Johannesburg. After a six-hour battle against a superior force, Jameson surrendered, and with several hundred others, mostly police troopers from Rhodesia's British South Africa Police, was carted off to Pretoria and prison. Repatriated to Britain, Jameson and his officers were subsequently jailed for their part in the invasion of the Transvaal. In the meantime, the Boers had rounded up the Reform Committee's reluctant revolutionaries, convicting some of High Treason, although most were later freed on payment of a £25,000 fine.[3]

The failure of the Jameson Raid removed 90 per cent of the police from Rhodesia, including most of the officers, all locked up in the Transvaal. Instead of 150 men to police Mashonaland, and 250 for the virtually untamed territory of Matabeleland – small enough numbers at any time – the British South Africa Police was left with 80 to cover a country larger than California. The Matabele were the first to seize upon this weakness, hacking to death 130 men, women and children in the first week of their rebellion against white settlers who had stolen their cattle and their land. A rinderpest epidemic had made matters worse by decimating what was left of the native cattle herds. Then came a disastrous drought in the summer of 1895-96, followed by swarms of locusts, sent by the white man, or so the Matabele believed, to destroy their crops. Very soon more whites were being slaughtered than at any other time in the history of African colonisation. Armed only with spears, and rusty muskets acquired from generations of trading with the Arabs and Portuguese, their muzzles stuffed with nails, glass stoppers from discarded soda bottles and bits of commandeered telegraph wire, the weapons inflicted terrible injuries at close range. Rhodes, who by then had resigned as Prime Minister of Cape Colony in the aftermath of the Jameson Raid, was seized with a blood lust. Most of those massacred had been settled by *his* Charter Company in *his* wilderness! He knew many personally, and was determined to revenge them in a world where the white man's law was paramount, justifying the killing of any number of blacks as retribution for the loss of a single white. The rebellious natives would be subdued with a savagery at least equal to that which they had perpetrated against white settlers. Rhodes's instruction to his police troopers was to spare no one, even if they pleaded for mercy. 'You should kill all you can,' he said.[4]

The Mashona, unlike the Matabele, were not a fighting people. Having passively submitted to the white man's rule, they were not expected to take advantage if, as it happened, their territory was further depleted of police cover when more troopers were transferred to deal with the Matabele uprising.[5] Two months later, however, on 15 June 1896 violence erupted in Mashonaland, ultimately claiming the lives of 119 Europeans, the first of these, two prospectors who were seized, bound hand and foot and thrown into the Umfuli River. Very quickly, defensive laagers were erected around the scattered towns of Salisbury (now Harare), Victoria, Melsetter and Umtali, there being little prospect of outside help on account of the now desperate shortage of police manpower. This was the increasingly dangerous situation facing Police Inspector Randolph Nesbitt – under whom Pryce was to serve – when he received an SOS from the manager of the Alice Mine in the Mazoe Valley, about thirty miles from Salisbury. The mine manager, a Mr Salthouse, his neighbours and their wives, fearing an attack by the Mashonas, had set off in a covered wagon for Salisbury, only to be forced to return to the mine after three of them were killed by natives. While the survivors built a makeshift laager on top of the nearest *kopje*, two of the party, telegraph operators named Blakiston and Routledge, set off on the same horse to raise the alarm from the telegraph office, little more than a pole and grass hut with a thatched roof standing among trees. Surprisingly, it had not been burned down by the rebels, but as the pair returned from sending their SOS, Blakiston was shot dead as he rode the horse, and Routledge, who was running beside him, was chased into the bush and killed, all within sight of the laager at Alice Mine. Without question, if the pair had not sacrificed themselves to send the message, the entire party trapped at the mine would have perished.

After a patrol from Salisbury to reconnoitre the situation also found itself trapped at the mine, Inspector Nesbitt was dispatched with twelve men on a rescue mission. Fighting their way through the Mazoe Gorge in total darkness, attacked from all sides by Mashonas hidden in the dense bush, the relief party reached the besieged mine at dawn on 20 June, by then surrounded by fifteen hundred Mashona warriors armed with Lee-Metford, Martini and Winchester rifles. The escape, which Nesbitt led, was to win him the Victoria Cross, and remains one of the most heroic episodes in colonial history.

After bullet-proofing a coach with iron sheets, and posting four men to cover the rear and another four as an advance guard, the party set off for Salisbury. For most of the way, they were under almost continuous fire from the Mashonas. Horses were shot from beneath the outriders, and by the time the party reached the out-skirts of Salisbury, there were only three horses left to drag the battle-scarred wagon into town. The survivors were either trudg-ing alongside the wagon, or lay wounded inside, cared for by the three women, two of whom had seen their husbands killed, but calmly continued to hand ammunition to the men as they made their escape.[6]

With many of the outlying districts like the Mazoe Valley by now abandoned to the rebels, Rhodes had a very urgent need for reinforcements from England. Arriving in Salisbury with thirty others on 1 May 1897, Pryce was one of these, attesting as Trooper 401 of the Mashonaland Division of the BSAP, and assigned to D Company commanded by Inspector Nesbitt VC.[7] As might be expected from the urgency of the situation, many of those recruited not only lacked any knowledge of Africa or police work, but also failed to match the advertised requirements, one of their officers (unnamed) describing the newcomers as, 'Such a mixed lot I never saw in my life, all sorts and conditions from the aristocratic down to the street Arab, peers and waifs of humanity mingling together like the ingredients of a hotch-potch.' Some like Pryce were crack shots, and others expert horsemen. But none was prepared for the fever that followed them every foot of the way, turning healthy men into physical wrecks. Within a short time, seven of Pryce's comrades were dead from malaria despite the quinine administered by an orderly passing down the line, dipping the point of his knife into the powder and tipping it on to the back of each trooper's tongue. A pound of bully beef was the daily ration to be shared between four men, and when the weevil-infested biscuits gave out, there was a helping of Boer-meal with its equally lively population. The best grub the troopers had came from the stew pot dangling from the back of the commissary wagon, always on the boil, into which they tossed any game they shot. 'The best food I've ever tasted,' Pryce recalled many years later.[8]

Pryce very quickly learned that after his rifle his most important piece of equipment was his black waterproof cape, protection from regular African downpours, its deep pockets serving as dry storage for most of the ingredients of his meal. When it was raining, the sugar ration went straight into his mouth, the tea into another pocket of the cape to be brewed at leisure. During the rainy season, the chances of starting a fire were as remote as the White Cliffs of Dover. About the only relief from this continuous grind was the 'eye-opener,' a shot of whisky and milk at dawn, reputedly the sauce that fertilised the luxuriant 'Imperial' moustaches sported by Pryce, and most other members of the BSAP.

Although by the time Pryce enlisted, the Mashonas were on the retreat, what remained to be done to suppress the rebellion would provide his apprenticeship as an African fighter. The BSAP, supported by a contingent of Natal Police, were on the trail of the most important rebel leader still at large, Matshayongombi, whose stronghold was a large kraal located amongst a group of *kopjes,* a series of low hills, which, while not precipitous, formed a complex labyrinth of paths and small plateaus. At its centre was the chief's stronghold, surrounded by a ring of forty-foot boulders. When Nesbitt's D Company, under the command of Colonel F. de Moleyns, breached this on 24 July 1897, Matshayongombi and his people escaped into a network of large, deep caves formed by a jumble of massive sheets of rock lying against or upon each other, the product of some ancient geological upheaval. But even here they were not immune from attack. After placing pickets around the entire complex, so that none of the rebels could escape, the police troopers wriggled on their stomachs up to the mouths of narrow crevices in the rocks, dropping pipes stuffed with dynamite on to those hidden below. Great clouds of smoke belched from the cave entrances after each explosion. Matshayongombi himself eventually emerged from the smoke, only to be shot down mercilessly. During the following four days, 278 survivors surrendered, mostly women and children. Hundreds more were entombed.[9]

This was the decisive engagement in the suppression of the Mashonaland Rebellion (now referred to as an Uprising), for which Pryce was decorated with the Mashonaland Medal.[10] Whether it was the sort of operation he expected to be involved with, will never be known. Was this twenty-year-old aware when he enrolled in the British South Africa Police, that he was joining the private army of Cecil Rhodes; that it would mean waging a ruthless war against native Africans fighting only to recover the land and cattle stolen from them by the British South Africa Company, and by the settlers it imported to colonise Rhodesia? If the name itself – Rhodesia (now Zimbabwe) – was a measure of one man's egotism, it was no less seductive to a generation inspired by Rhodes's grandiose ambitions. Nevertheless, the vigour with which the Mashona Rebellion was suppressed was considered by many at the time to be excessive, even by African standards. The public outcry was such that, Lieutenant Colin Harding, one of those involved, felt obliged to defend the order to dynamite the Mashonas as a legitimate act of war:

> What compelled us to use dynamite was the fact that the Mashonas, when attacked, retreated at once into these caves, refusing to come out and surrender, even when their lives were guaranteed, and shot down our men at all times, without the slightest risk to themselves. Repeatedly, I have sat for a considerable time outside the caves, urging men, women and children to come out to safety. I have helped

many a man from a cave, which was to be blown up and
not until I was convinced that only men remained, was
dynamite inserted into the strongholds. The great risk to
the people who used dynamite was that unless it was
placed right inside, its value was negligible. To do this, one
had to go right up to the mouth of the cave, when you
would be a sure mark for any hidden armed native whom
you could not see or locate.[11]

The police lost 33 troopers during the action against the
Matabele and Mashona – some killed while attempting to get
close enough to the cave entrances to toss in their sticks of dynamite.[12]

While the death of Matshayongombi was the watershed in the
military campaign, most knew Mashona resistance to white man's
rule would not be broken until two religious leaders, one a woman,
Nehanda, in central and northern Mashonaland, the other a man,
Kagubi, in the western part of the territory, were captured, better
still, killed. The Mashona believed in ancestor worship, Nehanda
being the reincarnation of a guardian ancestor spirit pledged to
expel the British from their lands. Ascribed with magical powers,
she coordinated Mashona resistance along with Kagubi, and from
August until October 1897, Pryce and his BSAP patrol were
preoccupied with the hunt for the pair.[13] When they were eventually captured, Nehanda was charged with the murder of a native
white commissioner, and Kagubi with killing an African policeman, Kagubi only escaping a death sentence by converting to
Christianity. Nehanda, however, remained defiant, denouncing the
British until the moment she was hanged, her dying words, 'My
bones will rise again.' Although her body was buried secretly, to
prevent it being exhumed by her supporters, the spirit of Nehanda
found a new medium seventy years later in an elderly woman,
who was consulted about military decisions by ZANLA (Zimbabwe
African National Liberation Army), in its struggle with Ian Smith's
white-dominated government after its Unilateral Declaration of
Independence in Rhodesia in 1965.[14]

When the Mashonaland rebellion ended, the war the British
South Africa Company had never expected had lasted more than
fifteen months, almost bankrupting the company. Brought under

Nehanda (front), the female spiritual leader of the Mashonas, hunted down and hanged by the British South Africa Company Police. Seventy years later, the Zimbabwe African National Liberation Army claimed that Nehanda's spirit had entered the body of an elderly woman whom its leaders consulted about military strategy during the struggle that followed the unilateral declaration of independence by the Rhodesian Premier Ian Smith.

closer administrative control by the Home Government, the company became less repressive, and while the abuses directly responsible for the uprising (or *chimurenga*, 'war of liberation') – forced labour, suppression of religious practices, confiscation of land and cattle – did not entirely disappear, they were less apparent. This left the police to resume normal duties, collecting taxes and dealing with local tribal disturbances, a routine which coincided with a outbreak of drunkenness and spate of desertions among the troopers, some of whom were disciplined for being drunk on patrol. The death toll from malaria and blackwater fever was also increasing, and of the 33 members of the BSAP who died in 1897-1898, only nine were killed in action against the Mashona.[15]

The mopping-up operation continued for several months, and Trooper Pryce was one of a detachment of twenty men sent to the outstation at Marandellas to collect weapons and disperse natives.

Pryce's Natal Police Force with their Maxim machine guns in 1897.
(Courtesy University Library, Cambridge).

Anticipating perhaps an easier posting, Pryce had obtained a licence from the Mining Commissioner to peg ten claims in the district, presumably intending to make use of any spare time, and the assaying equipment he had brought with him from England, to search for the gold of King Solomon's Mines. But, like many other prospectors before him, he never found his gold mine, probably because Zimbabwe has since been shown to be relatively poor in precious metals.[16] On three separate occasions, he also obtained licences from the authorities to import ammunition for Mauser rifles, totalling more than five hundred rounds. By March the following year, Pryce took his discharge from the BSAP at the end of twelve months service, almost immediately enlisting in the Natal Mounted Police at Pietermaritzburg on 1 May 1898, after once again demonstrating his horsemanship and proving he was a crack shot.[17] The corps then advanced him a loan to buy his own horse and equipment, the amount debited against each month's pay. If the horse survived, the trooper could sell it back to the corps on completing his term of service. Few ever did because of the appalling injuries the animals often suffered on patrol, and the terrible wounds inflicted by Boer bullets when war eventually came. In anticipation of this, each trooper contributed 3s a month from his pay, of 6s a day, into a Remount Fund for providing a new mount if a horse was killed or so badly injured it had to be destroyed.[18]

For the moment, Natal remained relatively peaceful, the police serving summonses, executing arrest warrants, administering the annual census, and collecting hut and dog taxes from the natives, often involving expeditions up-country to remote *kraals* in the high mountain passes. But the war clouds were gathering over South Africa, the Transvaal Boers demanding that Britain withdrew its troops from its borders, while continuing to refuse political rights to the predominantly English population of the mining areas. More importantly, the gold discovered on the Witwatersrand ridge in southern Transvaal in 1886 threatened Britain's economic dominance in Africa. Johannesburg, located near the centre of the Rand, was already seen as the emerging powerhouse of the South African economy, so that when the war came it was as much about the scramble for Africa's riches as anything else.

Mobilised on 11 October 1899, the Natal Police with their knowledge of the country, were employed immediately as scouts and dispatch riders, called upon day and night to cross a *veldt* teeming with the enemy. Provided with all the remounts they needed, the police were in the saddle almost continually, unless caught by the Boers when they were shot, the corpse left across the trail for the vultures to feast upon – a graphic warning for anyone following behind. Even this was not close enough to the action for Pryce who purchased his discharge from the police for £10 so he 'could get to the front,' but not before he was decorated for his part in the Relief of Ladysmith on 28 February 1900.[19]

The Battle of Elandslaagte, on a low, rocky, hogsback ridge 800 feet above the railway line a few miles from Ladysmith, was the first major engagement of the Boer War. Two thousand Boers, led by the frock-coated Julius Kock who fought with a bible in one hand and pistol in the other, held the ridge with the assistance of two Maxim-Nordenfeld artillery pieces captured from the Jameson raiders. On 20 October 1899, Major-General Sir John French, accompanied by five squadrons of Imperial Light Horse, left Ladysmith to reconnoitre the Boer position. The Imperial Light Horse, with their familiar wide-brimmed bush hats turned up on one side, had been formed by Major Aubrey Woolls-Sampson as the British answer to the lightning raids of the Boer Commando. The first regiment to take the field at the outbreak of war, it had recruited from the ranks of the *Uitlanders,* the non-Boer European settlers forced to flee the Transvaal after the abortive Jameson Raid. They thirsted for revenge, especially Woolls-Sampson, an extraordinary man best remembered for the intensity with which he hated Boers. Some years later, when Pryce was leading the Magonista revolutionaries against the forces of President Diaz in Mexico, he boasted to a newspaperman of 'riding with Woolls-Sampson.'[20] Those who did would have recalled a man of spare frame but great physical endurance. Paradoxically, despite his hatred for the enemy, Woolls-Sampson counted many Boers among his friends. His was a Holy War, his passion, to see the Boer beaten by the British. Born in Cape Colony, he had already lost one war to the Boers in 1881, during which he was wounded. Thereafter, his impatience for revenge would always cloud his judgement, challenging a belief in his own invulnerability that flirted with the lives of the men he commanded.

This recklessness showed itself at the Battle of Elandslaagte. After French's reconnaissance force discovered a much larger Boer Commando than it had anticipated, entrenched on the plateau on top of the ridge, it retreated to await reinforcements. Battle was joined the next day, with the Imperial Light Horse in the vanguard. Forced by the rocky terrain and blistering enemy fire to dismount, Woolls-Sampson strode on, defying bullets and fate, and cursing his men for failing to take cover from the fusillade poured down upon them by the Boers commanding the heights. As the British took the plateau, the frock-coated Boer leader General Kock fell, mortally wounded, but still clutching his Bible. So did Woolls-Sampson, his thigh shattered by a bullet, and left for dead. It was not until the smoke of battle cleared from the hillside several hours later that he was discovered by a stretcher party. Strapping a rifle barrel to his leg as a rough splint, they carried him into Ladysmith – soon to be besieged by the Boers – where it was found the rifle was cocked, a cartridge in the breech, and muzzle pointing directly into Woollos-Sampson's armpit! Intense, brooding, in many ways a flawed character, always restless for the chase – Woolls-Sampson was all of this, but no one could ever doubt his sincerity or bravery. Resolute and fearless, difficulties that would have discouraged most men were pure oxygen to Woolls-Sampson, his very life-blood.[21] But even the Imperial Light Horse grew exhausted by a commander with fire in his belly and nerves of iron, capable of spilling his dinner on the *veldt* and saddling up the regiment if a *kaffir* whispered the word 'Boer' in his ear, on the off-chance of a scrap rather than the dead certainty of a hot-meal. Around him, he gathered a small group of trusted admirers, like Pryce, each of whom learned from him how to survive on the smell of an oil rag, and the whiff of cordite.

The Boer War could have been over after the Battle of Elandslaagte if the Commander of the British forces at Ladysmith, General Sir George White, had pursued the fleeing Afrikaners all the way to Pretoria. Instead of this, White ordered his troops to fall back on Ladysmith, then little more than a village at the end of the railway line, lying in a hollow dominated by a ring of hills, which the Boers promptly re-occupied with their heavy artillery. The ensuing siege propelled Ladysmith into newspaper headlines for 120 days. Gripped by the unfolding drama of the trapped garrison, the world watched helplessly as the troops survived on stewed bones, afterwards horse flesh, and by the time the siege was lifted by General Buller, just one biscuit a day.

The Relief of Ladysmith stirred people more than anything that generation had previously witnessed. For almost four months, reports of the garrison's privations, accompanied by an overwhelming sense of helplessness, had lain like a dark shadow across the spirit of Empire, the siege becoming by the day too painful even to talk about. When it was lifted, delight was universal, among the rich and the poor, among clubmen and cabmen, while the relief from what had seemed certain humiliation, was immeasurable. To commemorate the Relief of Ladysmith, all those involved were awarded a clasp to their Queen's South Africa medal. Pryce was one of those so decorated.

A large number of his comrades from the Natal Mounted Police had been bottled up in Ladysmith, together with their commander, Colonell Dartnell, at that time attached to General White's staff. Most of those left, about forty, formed General Buller's bodyguard racing to be the first relieving force into the besieged township, as the Boers abandoned their positions in the surrounding hills. But Buller was beaten into Ladysmith by a good two hours by a detachment from the Imperial Light Horse, a company of Natal Carabineers, and fifteen Natal Police. Without hesitation, the Imperial Light Horse troopers headed straight for the dugout where their commander, Colonel Aubrey Woolls-Sampson had spent the siege, the leg he almost lost at Elandslaagte hanging limp and lifeless across the side of his chair, as he counted the shells from the Boer 'Long Toms' raining down upon the trapped garrison. Woolls-Sampson should have died in Ladysmith. Virtually a cripple, he remained a splendid figure, often gripped by pain, but a warrior whose every defiant gesture commanded the respect of all those he encountered, urging them to greater vigour in defence of the town. As it happened, more were to die from fever and dysentery than Boer shelling, the hospital at Ladysmith treating 10,688 casualties during the siege, 600 of these fatal.

Woolls-Sampson had refused to allow doctors to amputate his shattered leg, the indefatigable soldier emerging from his dugout to greet his troopers, waving the bottle of champagne he had secreted early in the siege against the day when victory would be celebrated. It is not known whether Pryce entered Ladysmith as part of Buller's bodyguard, or as one of the small contingent of Natal Police who led the final charge. But what is certain is that he decided that if he was to get even nearer the front, then it would be with Woolls-Sampson, enlisting as Trooper 1037 in the Imperial Light Horse a year later on the 13 September 1900.[22]

By the time Pryce reported for training at Potchefstroom, Woolls-Sampson had sufficiently recovered to resume command, dragging his poor leg along the ground as he inspected his troopers, most of whom, while admiring his courage, were fearful for their own chances under a man who did not set a pin's value on his own life. The new recruits at Potchefstroom learned quickly how to fight a guerrilla war, because the man they were up against would be General de la Rey, one of the most capable and determined of the Boer leaders who, with 2000 Burgers supported by artillery, was known to be in the immediate neighbourhood. The vigilance, horsemanship and marksmanship Pryce had acquired, first in the British South Africa Police during the Mashonaland Rebellion, honing these skills to perfection in the Natal Mounted Police, equipped him to serve in a regiment where his life depended on the speed with which he could mount and dismount, shoot straight and quickly, while making the utmost use of any ground cover. If the situation called for retreat, then this would be at full gallop; if they were required to stand and fight, it would be to the last man.[23]

To volunteer for the ILH, a man needed to be a very special person, either a British refugee from the Transvaal with a burning sense of injustice and bitter hatred of the Boers, or someone with an unquenchable thirst for adventure, as was probably the case with Pryce. A graphic account of what he might have experienced is provided by some hitherto unpublished letters written by a contemporary, Trooper Cyril Hawkins, to his sister and mother in the months following the Relief of Ladysmith. Hawkins appears to have hated almost every moment he spent with the regiment, and was particularly critical of its commanding officer, Woolls-Sampson, who he accuses of ordering his troopers around 'like Kaffirs:'

> Everybody in camp (is) suffering from severe headaches and several have fever and dysentery; a few have gone

under . . . All the Ladysmith troops I hear are to go down to highlands for a good feed . . . poor chaps, they must want it badly after being so short of rations and having to eat horses and mules . . . I tell you, I will be pleased when this war is over. I am thoroughly tired of it all.

On another occasion, writing to his mother, Hawkins expresses relief that some relative or friend had been persuaded not to join the ILH, thereby avoiding 'hard biscuits and wet through for twenty four hours at a stretch.' From the nature of his remarks, Hawkins would probably have been considered a 'five bobber,' the name coined for troopers who griped constantly; interested only in the day's pay they would probably never live to collect. 'I thank God the day I leave this regiment, we are always on the move, not a minute's peace to ourselves,' Hawkins complained to his mother. By the middle of 1900, the British had won the last of the set battles in the Boer War. The Boer capitals of Bloemfontein and Pretoria had fallen, and President Kruger had fled the country. Trooper Hawkins was evidently expecting his discharge any moment, only to be ordered to rejoin his regiment after recovering from a flesh wound. 'Sampson won't hear of disbanding the Corps,' he whined to his mother. 'He intends seeing the end now that he has started. Everybody is thoroughly disgusted with him.' By August 1900, the month before Pryce enlisted in the ILH, Hawkins was probably speaking for the majority of Troopers when he wrote, The ILH are sick of it and long for the day when we are disbanded . . . Sampson is going to see it through to the end, so they say. We would have been disbanded if it wasn't for him.'[24]

But it was not all over. Although apparently well beaten – most Boer fighters having either surrendered or returned to their farms – those generals still at large, like de la Rey, prepared to launch a new phase in the war: a guerrilla campaign to counter their enemy's numerical superiority. At the same time, Woolls-Sampson was about to lead his Imperial Light Horse to disaster, in the early morning mist shrouding a rocky *kopje* at Cypherfontein. They had been trekking in the Magaliesburg district, looking for de la Rey's commando, the column halting high in the hills overlooking some rolling country. In the distance, through a pass between the hills, the ILH watched a continuous file of horsemen moving slowly, before disappearing behind a grassy knoll. General Babington, the overall commander, instructed Colonel Woolls-Sampson to attack the Boer position 'at the gallop,' choosing to ignore his Colonel's protestations that it was too strongly held. Woolls-Sampson took his orders literally, instructing his two companies to mount, and in extended order, at a few yards interval, gallop hard on the heels of the scouts sent to reconnoitre the situation. The Boer position was two miles away, across a small valley, but the mist meant it was impossible to spot the enemy until the scouts mounted the top of the ridge, followed closely at a gallop by Woolls-Sampson and his ILH. The colonel ignored the advice of fellow officers to slow his advance while more scouts were sent into the field, and reinforcements arrived. Driving his horse forward even harder, Woolls-Sampson retorted, 'The regiment is your escort.'

At that moment, the Boers emerged from the cover of the long grass, by now the hill bristling with the enemy. Men and horses went down like grass before a mower, the bullets flying as thick and fast as machine gun fire. Those who survived the first volley, dismounted, their horses plunging wildly, riders scrambling to take cover and return fire from behind the bodies of their dead and dying animals. Others, kneeling to take aim on the open hillside, had their heads blown off. In all, nineteen troopers were killed, another 32 wounded. Realising after ten minutes their position was hopeless, Woolls-Sampson shouted, 'Retire! Retire,' his staff sergeant galloping along the line, waving his hat at the survivors in the direction of their retreat down the hill towards the relative safety of the pom-pom guns. Those who could escape did so on foot, their clothes and equipment shot to pieces by a withering barrage of Boer gunfire.[25]

If Pryce, as he claimed later, 'rode with Woolls-Sampson,' then this would have been his last opportunity, because afterwards the colonel was stripped of his command for the impetuosity that led him to rush the ridge before fully reconnoitring the position. Held partly responsible for the ensuing carnage, he was transferred to the Intelligence Service for the duration of the war, his unique knowledge of the country, of the enemy, and extraordinary sense of where to find the Boers, a deciding influence on the eventual outcome of the campaign. For this he was knighted.

A month after Woolls-Sampson was removed from the ILH, Pryce was also discharged, having completed six months service.[26] But the guerrilla war was to drag on for another year, the British Army forced to adopt unconventional tactics to defeat the tenacious Boer commandoes. Blockhouses were built to flush the enemy into the open; farms were burned; food destroyed, and more than 20,000 women and children packed off to concentration camps, a tactic Hitler would perfect forty years later. Left without food, clothing, ammunition or hope, the last Boer commando surrendered in May 1902 and the war ended with the Treaty of Vereeniging.

Within two days of his discharge from the Imperial Light Horse, Pryce had enlisted in the South African Constabulary, now reorganised by General R. S. S. Baden-Powell, the hero of Mafeking, to police the Transvaal and Orange Free State in preparation for future British colonisation of the defeated Boer republics. Trooper Pryce was a mounted policeman again, rising quickly through the ranks to Second Lieutenant in January 1903. Although the guerrilla war in the Transvaal continued for some months, Pryce served most of his time across the border in the relatively peaceful Orange Free State, either as an assistant, then later, District Commandant in the districts of Bethlehem, Springfontein, Flicksburg, and Jacobsdal. In the latter district, his principal duty was to patrol the border. Each district was the size of a British county, and as Commandant, Pryce was judge and jury, not only enforcing the law, and instigating prosecutions, but also administering justice as acting magistrate.[27]

Whether he had grown tired of police routine, or was disappointed when the South African Constabularly refused him a service pension, after leave in England in 1905, Pryce applied for a position as a Chief Constable in an English county, a post for which he considered himself eminently qualified. Nothing came of it, and within a few months of returning to South Africa he was given command of a mobile police squadron with orders to enforce the 'Chinese Cordon.' Because of a desperate shortage of labour, more than 50,000 Chinese had been imported on three year contracts to work the gold mines in the east Rand. After striking in April 1905, many headed for the coast and home to China, robbing white settlers as they went, in some instances, murdering any who resisted. Pryce and his squadron were sent to track down the thieves and murderers, and protect the white population from further outbreaks of violence. It took almost a year to restore order, by which time Pryce had been given command of another mobile squadron. This time, his orders were to prevent the escape across the Swaziland border of survivors from a Zulu rebellion led by a minor chieftain, Bambata, 500 of whose followers had been trapped and killed by detachments from the British Army.[28]

This would be his last policing assignment in Africa. Pryce had spent ten years as native fighter, Boer War soldier, and mounted policeman, risking his life on numerous occasions. By now, the tenderfoot from the British Linen Bank in Glasgow was a 30-year-old battle-hardened warrior, with all the accompanying skills: a leader of men in a country of hard-riding, hard-living frontiersmen who were slaves only to Mammon and Bacchus. When Pryce arrived from England he was the fresh-faced product of Empire, lusting after adventure, taking for his inspiration fearless soldiers, like the unpredictable Woolls-Sampson. Africa had trained him for one thing only: a soldier's life, there being no discernible difference between that and the para-military police with whom he had served, first, in cruelly suppressing the Mashonaland Rebellion, and afterwards chasing fugitive Blacks and Coolies across Natal, the Transvaal and Orange Free State. That Pryce was never seriously considered as a candidate for the Chief Constable's position back in England is probably explained by his curriculum vitae that read like a list of battle honours, rather than the more staid and urbane qualifications required by a peaceful rural county in England. But as with all professional soldiers searching for a profitable niche in a changing society, he was well equipped for a career as a mercenary, a brigand maybe, even a revolutionary although in this last respect there is no evidence that Africa stirred his social conscience. With nothing to return to in Britain, Pryce, quite naturally, cast around for another frontier for which his service in Africa was his apprenticeship.

NOTES

1. Pryce Papers, Weybridge. Letter from relative, 12 November 1894, regarding efforts to obtain Queen's Cadetship for Pryce at Sandhurst; also letters from Pryce to grandmother, Dora Isabella Beatson, 26 July, 2 September and 19 October, 1896, regarding his plans to go to either Africa or Burma; also parents opposition.
2. P. Gibbs, P. and H. Phillips, *The History of the British South Africa Police, 1889-19* (Salisbury, 1980), p. 82.
3. ibid., p. 71.
4. V. Stent, *A personal history of some incidents in the life of Cecil Rhodes* (Cape Town 1924), pp. 27-62
5. Gibbs, Phillips, p. 72.
6. ibid., pp. 79-80.
7. National Archives of Zimbabwe, Harare, S183/2.
8. Recollections of John ap Rhys Pryce, Weybridge, Surrey, great nephew of Caryl ap Rhys Pryce.
9. Gibbs, Phillips, pp. 91-92.
10. Pryce Family Papers, Caryl ap Rhys Pryce 'Record of Service.' It should be noted, however, that there is no mention of Pryce receiving the Mashonaland Medal in the medal application and receipt forms in the National Archives of Zimbabwe, Harare, although some of these records have been lost.
11. C. Harding, *Frontier patrols: a history of the British South Africa Police and other Rhodesian Forces* (1937).
12. Gibbs, Phillips, pp. 92-93.
13. NAZ, Harare, 'British South Africa Company: Reports on the Administration of Rhodesia, 1897-1898'.
14. D. Martin, and P. Johnson, *The Struggle for Zimbabwe: The Chimurenga War* (1981, Zimbabwe Publishing House).
15. NAZ, Harare, S 183/2; for details of deaths amongst BSAP troopers, 'BSA Company: Reports on the Administration of Rhodesia, 1897-1898.' NAZ.
16. NAZ, Harare, M 19/13/4; Pryce Papers, letters to grandmother (1893-96).
17. NAZ, Harare, S 183/3.
18. Pryce Papers, unidentified/undated newspaper cutting from South Africa.
19. Pryce Papers, letter of application for post of Chief Constable, January 1905.
20. Peter Kyne, 'The gringo revolutionary,' *Sunset Magazine,* September 1911.
21. G. Gibson, *History of the Imperial Light Horse,* pp. 259-260.
22. C. Simpson, 'Natal Volunteers, Officials and Police in the Boer War 1899-1902' (unpublished manuscript, 2004).
23. G. F. Gibson, *The History of the Imperial Light Horse* (1937), pp. 241-242.
24. Col. Gibson, The Hawkins Letters. Imperial Light Horse Regimental Association, Kelvin, Johannesburg.
25. Gibson, *The History of the Imperial Light Horse* (1937), pp. 241-248.
26. Pryce Papers, Weybridge. Application for post of Chief Constable.
27. ibid.
28. ibid.

Chapter 2

The Red Army

Workers of the world, awaken!
Break your chains, demand your rights.
All the wealth you make is taken
By exploiting parasites.

Joe Hill, *IWW Song Book*

The new frontier on which Pryce had set his sights was the Canadian Yukon Territory. Gold had been discovered there in 1896, around the time he went to Africa. While most of it was played out within five years, prospectors were still streaming in from all parts of the world. Pryce might even have joined them briefly, one of his future comrades-in-arms claiming to have met the former African soldier-policeman in the Klondike.[1] For British Columbia and Alaska the legacy of the gold rush was an invigorated economy offering opportunities for everyone to strike it rich. That did not seem to extend to Pryce, his sister Gladys, and her Canadian husband Ken Hodge, partners in a ship towing business in which Pryce's father, the colonel now retired to Southsea in England, had invested heavily. By 1911, three years after Pryce had arrived in Vancouver, its prospects were so poor that Gladys and her husband bought some land at Cowichan Bay on Vancouver Island where they planned to set up a chicken farm.[2] As for Pryce, he had only the army to fall back upon, enlisting in a militia unit, the 6th Duke of Connaught's Own Rifles, immediately on landing in Vancouver, his enthusiasm for soldierly contact apparently undimmed.[3] Then there was Miss Hattie (or Alice) Biggs, a clerk in the local branch of the Yorkshire Insurance Company.[4] If anyone was likely to cure Pryce of his wanderlust, then it was Hattie, by his own admission an 'intensely practical and sensible' lady whose relationship with the Welshman was to survive even his restless temperament and escapades. The latest of these followed not long after he walked out on her that winter's night in 1911, his evening stroll through downtown Vancouver ending some days later in Los Angeles.[5]

It is not difficult to imagine his thoughts on seeing the Seattle ferry berthed at the Canadian Pacific Wharf. His towing business was going down the drain, Hattie was trying to pin him down, and at 35, there were those who thought him down and out: the 'black sheep' of the family, and a failed one at that! Pryce had precious little to show – not even a pension – for the ten years he had fought defending the Empire in Africa. His elder brother Henry, on the other hand, was carving an impressive career for himself in the Indian Army from which he would progress into the military hierarchy on his return to Britain. All this, accompanied by an irresistible tug in the back from an inherent sense of adventure, were to propel Pryce in a direction that, in normal circumstances, this former son of the Raj would not have contemplated for a second, not even in his wildest dreams. Pryce, the ex-policeman, with the cut-glass accent and demeanour of a British aristocrat, was about to embark upon a new career – as an anarchist revolutionary – and it was this that propelled him southwards, far beyond Los Angeles where his money ran out, to Mexico, a country then tottering on the verge of revolution after thirty years of rule by the ruthless dictator Porfirio Diaz. When asked much later to explain his motives for joining the revolt against Diaz, Pryce blamed his uncharacteristic lapse into revolutionary anarchy on reading *Barbarous Mexico,* by the American investigative journalist, John Kenneth Turner.[6] Turner's book first appeared as a series of newspaper articles exposing the exploitation and enslavement of peasant farmers in Diaz's Mexico. The misery suffered by these 'poor peons' was to be the improbable, but only, explanation offered by Pryce for his spur-of-the-moment decision to abandon everything and everyone in Vancouver for an affair that almost cost him his life. Privately, he admitted he did not quite know why he jumped aboard the Seattle ferry, other than it was 'on the spur of the moment.'[7]

Arriving in Los Angeles, penniless, and not very different from the thousands of drifters flooding the Pacific West Coast, Pryce soon found himself part of a very different kind of army – the

'Red Army,' comprised mainly of migrant workers who followed the harvests. Most were members of 'Big Bill' Haywood's Industrial Workers of the World, the Wobblies, and were seen by vested interests as part of a great socialist conspiracy to destabilise America. These seasonal workers worshipped "Big Bill," his face the scarred battlefield of picket line violence; his promise, to deliver better pay and conditions for a vast reservoir of unskilled, un-represented workers at the bottom of a heap that was preyed upon by labour gang bosses, who took a cut from every cent they earned.[8] When not living in filthy shantytowns beside the railroad, the Wobblies road led eventually to a *Red Tavern* or *Red Flag*, most Pacific Coast towns having its political hot spot for revolutionary debate fuelled by home-brewed grog. Usually large, single-storey, buildings of stout wooden beams and planks, furnished with rough-hewn tables and stools, a black pot-bellied stove providing warmth and the occasional smoky belch, taverns were traditionally centres for stirring political debate, and rendezvous for patriots of all persuasions. Since the War of Independence, they had often played a prominent part in affairs of state, Thomas Jefferson writing the Declaration of Independence in the *India Queen Tavern* in Philadelphia.

By January 1911 the debate in the taverns had centred around two events – the first, a victory for the Wobbly revolutionaries, the second, what was seen as a serious setback. Fresno in California's San Joaquin Valley was a prosperous fruit-growing region whose farmers were unable to recruit pickers because of IWW agitation against low wages. The mayor responded by banning public meetings, sending his baton-waving police to break up every IWW picket line. But as fast as IWW activists were thrown into jail, others were arriving from all parts of the west coast to join the free speech fight at Fresno. Before long, Fresno's jail was overflowing with militants lecturing their guards on the class struggle, and singing their famous Wobbly songs. Fearing a mutiny, and unable to cope with the escalating cost of feeding and guarding the inmates, the mayor repealed his ban and released the prisoners.[9] Wrapping their blankets bandoleer-style across their shoulders, the Wobblies marched off, victorious, and heading for the next flashpoint in the class war, in the meantime adding a new couplet to their anthem as they went:

Springtime has come and I'm just out of jail,
Without any money, without any bail.

Despite its socialist ambitions, and its manifest contempt for the established order, the IWW had won for itself a surprising amount of public sympathy, because not everyone in early 20th century California was descended from those who had 'gone West' and made their fortune. This land of opportunity was also one of unbridled capitalism. Violently opposed to unionism, employers demanded ten and twelve hours a day for slave wages, the ensuing confrontation between capital and labour directly responsible, or so the Wobblies claimed, for '660,000 workers killed, maimed or injured.'[10] In addition to this, the economic shock waves from the San Francisco earthquake five years previously had been almost as cataclysmic as the event itself. The American working-class had a mountain to climb, many families, meanwhile, surviving on the breadline.

What public support the IWW had managed to muster was to leak away, rapidly, after a pair of disgruntled print workers, protesting at opposition to a closed shop in the *Los Angeles Times* print works, bombed its offices in October 1910. Twenty-eight people died in the outrage at the *Times,* the owner and editor, General Harrison Gray Otis, already a sworn enemy of unions and radicals, declaring all-out war on the 'Reds.' Baying for revenge, rival newspapers and politicians rushed to his support, demanding that every Wobbly should be strung up from the nearest lamppost or shot on sight, even though as it transpired those responsible for the bombing were not Wobblies but members of the more respected American Federation of Labor. From the moment the bomb exploded, however, the public would equate working-class militancy with extremism.[11] Even though the IWW was not directly involved, it made the perfect scapegoat, and a target for increased attention from 'bulls' (police) and their 'finks' (informers). He would not have realised it, but Pryce found himself rubbing shoulders with the Wobbly army at a defining moment in the history of the IWW. A syndicalist movement that had been locked in a generally unsuccessful pay-and-conditions battle with often wealthy and unscrupulous employers was now leaning towards revolutionary socialism to achieve its elusive

Utopia. For this it needed allies, and casting around the IWW found one – the Mexican anarchist, Ricardo Flores Magon.

When Pryce reached Los Angeles in January 1911, Ricardo Magon, leader of the Mexican Liberal Party, was living in exile at 519½ East Fourth Street, where, with a group of fellow conspirators, he was planning a revolution in Mexico. It would have as its slogan 'Land and Liberty,' its objectives very different from Francisco Madera's revolution which had broken out the previous November when his supporters crossed the border at Piedras Negras from Texas into Coahuila Province, only to be driven back after the anticipated support failed to materialise. This incursion was a signal for uprisings throughout Mexico. Soon, Madero was joined by the former outlaw Pancho Villa, the peasant leader Emiliano Zapata, and 17,000 armed revolutionaries, in a concerted attempt to overthrow the dictatorship of Diaz, which had concentrated wealth in the hands of a few, while creating huge social injustice. This was particularly true of the countryside, because of Diaz's policy of seizing peasant land for sale to his political accomplices and foreigners for a few *centavos* an acre. The Americans and British had been particular beneficiaries, the Los Angeles newspaper tycoon General Otis owning an area the size of a small Principality, and the London-based Mexican Land and Colonisation Company, 15,000,000 acres, a territory three times the size of Wales.

The sequestration of their land had driven peasants into the arms of rich landowners, the *haciendados,* on whom they now depended for the very threads of survival in an ever-hostile world. With this policy, Diaz had reshaped the Republic into one where 72 million hectares, a third of the country, belonged to a handful of Mexican and foreign owners. In the whole of Mexico there were only 834 *haciendados,* their power, prestige and size such that Mexico had become a country composed almost entirely of isolated fiefdoms.[12] The properties of the Terraza family in Coahuila state were as large as Costa Rica. The Central Railway, one of the great achievements of Diaz' modernisation programme, passed through Escandon family estates for a distance of 90 miles. One state, Morelos, where Zapata's peasant revolution started in March 1910, belonged to just 32 families.

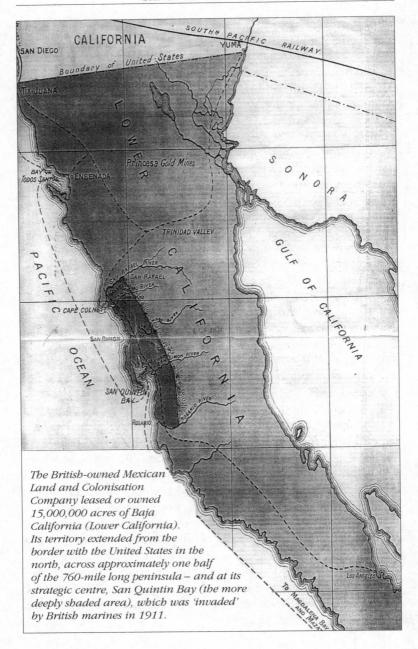

The British-owned Mexican
Land and Colonisation
Company leased or owned
15,000,000 acres of Baja
California (Lower California).
Its territory extended from the
border with the United States in the
north, across approximately one half
of the 760-mile long peninsula – and at its
strategic centre, San Quintin Bay (the more
deeply shaded area), which was 'invaded'
by British marines in 1911.

*Magonistas and Maderistas: Ricardo Flores Magon and his brother,
Enrique, leaders of the Magonista Junta based in downtown Los Angeles,
and (below) Pancho Villa, one of Madero's victorious generals.*

The institution of the hacienda lay like a dead hand upon the land, absorbing the life-blood of the people while their masters wasted their inheritance in idle pursuits in distant cities and lands. Paris was a particular favourite with wealthy expatriate Mexicans, their estate managers with instructions to transfer profits to some foreign bank account. Often Spaniards, interested only in lining their own pockets, these managers transferred their responsibilities down the line by sub-leasing the land, leaving peasant sharecroppers with the eventual responsibility for producing a profit for the estate. An impossible task, it reduced them to penury and destitution, trapped in a cycle of debt only relieved by the benevolence of the *haciendado*. If a wage was ever paid – 25 *centavos* a day had been the rate for more than a century – it was in coin, only exchangeable at the hacienda store where most peons quickly ran up huge debts. Like a cancer, debt penetrated every crevice, the peons borrowing for marriage, birth and death. A priest charged nine weeks wages for a wedding. If the peon couldn't pay, he went to his *patron*, cowed, clutching his sombrero, pleading with the father of his people to lead him further into debt.

At the centre of the estate was the *hacienda,* a big house built like a fort with narrow windows and slits in the walls for defence against marauding bands or passing revolutions, guarded by armed men day and night, and surrounded by a high wall with strong gates. Around this fortified stone castle, huddled the peons in their miserable huts of baked clay. It was a cash-less society. Everything, whether grown, made or consumed was generated by the *hacienda,* quite independent of the rest of the world. The *hacienda* provided its own wood for construction, water for irrigation and pasture for livestock. The mill ground the flour, it distilled the *mescal* so important in the lives of the peons. Primitive tools were made, saddles fashioned from hides, blankets and ropes woven from the fibre of local plants. Little came from outside and little was paid for in cash. Villagers supplied their labour in return, not for money, but for a piece of land to till, one day's work a week for each hectare. In effect, they were reduced to being sharecroppers on the very land they once owned.[13]

By the 20th century, however, many of the *haciendados* were living beyond their means. Idling their lives in Mexico City or

Paris, they failed to notice that the wealth successive generations had taken for granted was running out. Once again the Mexican countryside echoed with the cries of *'Tierra y Libertad'* (Land and Liberty), and everywhere there were rebels with itchy fingers, convinced that after thirty years of iron rule the days of Diaz were numbered. He was an old man; so were his Regional Governors who orchestrated his reign of terror. It could only be a matter of months before Diaz was forced to resign. Already he had offered to do so, but then reneged, further fanning the flames of revolution. The battle for the hearts and minds of the *peons* was starting.

Ricardo Magon had waited a lifetime for this moment. When the opportunity arrived, however, he had not long been released from the Arizona State Penitentiary at Florence for violating America's neutrality laws. There was also Madero, the new pretender to the throne, leader of the "Anti-reeleccionista" Party, committed to restoring political liberty to Mexico by deposing Diaz. But Magon saw the removal of Diaz as meaningless unless accompanied by economic freedom. While Madero posed as a reformer, his promises to redistribute land to the peasants were exposed as bogus, leading to disillusionment among radical supporters suspicious of a man whose immense wealth came from huge family estates extending along the Mexico-Texas border. As it became increasingly evident Madero had no intention of honouring his pledge to introduce agrarian reform, Magon, who by then had distanced himself from mainstream Mexican liberalism, denounced the Maderistas with the same vituperation as he had Diaz and his clique. But when the revolution started in November 1910, it was Madero who was first in the field, leaving Magon and his Mexican Liberal Party looking like a spent force on the margins of the struggle.

After spending half his adult life behind bars, Ricardo Magon refused to stand aside while the opportunity for which he had waited was seized by an adversary. Living as a political exile, and watched day and night by agents of the U.S. and Mexico governments, the business of plotting a second revolutionary front from his base in downtown Los Angeles was no easy matter. If there had to be change in Mexico, then the United States, for whom Diaz had represented thirty years of stable, modernising government, preferred the more moderate political views of Madero to the anarcho-communist ambitions of Magon and his fellow con-spirators – brother Enrique, Antonio Villarreal, Librado Rivere, Juan and Manual Sarabia, Lazaro Gutierrez de Lara, Praxedis Guerrero, and Antonio de Pio Araujo. Constantly hounded by government agents, and fearful of being extradited to face a certain firing squad, the group became secretive and withdrawn as it plotted a revolution in the only region where it still had support – Baja California.

Better known to its American neighbours along its northern border as Lower California, Baja California was torn free from mainland Mexico five million years ago when a cataclysmic earth-quake ripped it asunder, allowing the Pacific to flood the chasm to form the Sea of Cortes (or Gulf of California) and isolate the 800-mile peninsula. A largely barren finger of land longer than Italy, and with a wall of arid *sierras* rising to 10,000 ft as its spine, Baja California would be shaped by isolation, its natural and human evolution as distinct from mainland Mexico, where Madero was waging revolution, as brothers raised on opposite sides of a mountain range. It was a land where the sun almost always shone, temperatures soaring to 140°F, the scraggy carcasses of the few goats that dared confront the dreadful heat, testimony to its harshness. High in the sometimes snow-capped *sierras* tempera-tures plunged below zero in winter. Wherever water sprung from a crack in the arid wasteland, an oasis bloomed, a sweet respite for the few roving bands of *Tohono O'Oodham* Indians, seeking out the valley bottoms watered by flash floods for a patch to grow a little corn and a few *tepary* beans. For them, red meat was a delicacy, so prized they customarily tied a string around each morsel, chewed and swallowed, then pulled it back for the next man to share. In summer they gorged themselves on cactus fruit, dried their faeces in the sun, picked out the seeds, which they ground up and ate again. The descendants of these nomads still gathered mesquite pods and cactus pads, baked the agave plant and brewed *tequila* from its roots. The 'poor peons,' in whose name Magon would make his revolution, were the Indians who had stayed to scratch a living from a land no one seemed to want, apart from those foreign ranchers and investors persuaded to invest in President Diaz's desert wastes. By the early 20th century many *peons* had become *mestizos,* peasants of mixed Spanish-

Indian blood, sharing the same wretched life as they eked a living from the desert margins.

Emerging from the state penitentiary in April 1910, Magon and his small band of followers were frustrated revolutionaries with no financial support, and only one weapon, the Liberal Party newspaper *La Regeneración*. Though by now committed to violent anarchism, there was little hint of this in the columns of *La Regeneración*. For the moment, at least, the *compadres* had decided to present themselves as democratic socialists, painting a picture of a Mexico beyond the wildest dreams of the 'poor peons': the restitution of land rights; a guaranteed minimum wage; the confiscation of Diaz's illegally acquired riches; a guarantee of basic civil liberties; Mexican citizenship as a prerequisite for property ownership; and the abolition of child labour. The Magonistas certainly believed in all of this, but also much more than the *peons* could ever understand. Writing shortly before release from his last prison sentence, Flores Magon, described his revolutionary philosophy as a 'mere question of tactics':

> If from the start we had called ourselves anarchists, only a few would have listened to us. Without calling ourselves anarchists we have inflamed minds . . . against the possessing class . . . No Liberal Party in the world has the anti-capitalist tendencies of we who are about to begin a revolution in Mexico . . . We would not have been able to achieve this had we called ourselves anarchists instead of socialists. Thus everything is a question of tactics.[14]

Until September 1911 when Magon openly adopted an anarchist programme, the Magonistas appeared to identify with much that was common coin among the leaders of the American socialist movement, most important of these, the American Federation of Labor and Industrial Workers of the World. All appealed to the same culturally alienated groups; all subscribed to the idea they were engaged in nothing less than a class war in which direct action might be necessary to achieve their goals. The IWW's grand scheme for One Big Union was intended to abolish wage slavery, creating in its place a Utopia where the workers would control the means of production. Not surprisingly, Magon and his Liberal Party turned to the Wobblies – the socialist army on the march – for support in launching his revolution in Baja California. At the very moment the Liberals were preparing to raise the flag in Mexico, promising to kick-out Standard Oil and other foreign-owned companies, and return the land to the peasants, the IWW leader 'Big Bill' Haywood was preaching a similar message across Europe, the high point of his tour a visit to South Wales during the bitter Cambrian Coal Combine struggle of 1910-11.

On 27 February 1911 Magon addressed himself directly to potential Wobbly recruits with a seven-column headline across the front page of *La Regeneración* labelling Francisco Madero a 'Traitor to the Cause of Liberty':

> Our salvation lies not alone in the fall of Diaz, but in the transformation of the ruling political and social system; and that transformation cannot be effected by the mere over-throw of one tyrant that another may be put in his place, but by the denial of the pretended right of capital to appro-priate to itself a portion of the toiler's product.[15]

His message was transmitted to IWW supporters by their newspaper *The Industrial Worker*, together with a direct appeal to the membership to join their comrades battling for workers rights south of the border. But Magon believed he was addressing an even wider audience – nothing less than international socialism and the global proletariat – and that his Mexican Revolution was destined to have worldwide repercussions.[16] Vested interests dared not ignore this, especially after the Magonistas struck an alliance with the one million card-carrying Wobblies, in the van-guard of the socialist revolutionary upheaval shaking West Coast America at the start of the 20th century. The Republican and Democratic parties had been expecting a serious political threat from the left since 1904 when Socialist Party leader Eugene Debs polled a highly significant 400,000 votes in the Presidential election. Everywhere, opponents saw 'reds under the bed' in a country inflicted with an increasing radicalism, from which might spring a third party to challenge the political establishment.

In defence of the socialist coalition, the novelist Jack London delivered a characteristic rebuke to the *Los Angeles Times* denun-ciation of them as a 'chicken thief band . . . of Mexican criminals and mongrel Americans'. Addressing his call-to-arms to the 'Brave

Comrades of the Mexican Revolution,' London proclaimed before a Liberal Junta public meeting on 5 February 1911 at the Labour Temple in Los Angeles:

> We socialists, anarchists, hobos, chicken thieves, outlaws and undesirable citizens of the U.S. are with you heart and soul. You will notice that we are not respectable. Neither are you. No revolutionary can possibly be respectable in these days of the reign of property. All the names you have been called, we have been called. And when graft and greed get up and begin to call names, honest men, brave men, patriotic men and martyrs can expect nothing else than to be called chicken thieves and outlaws. So be it. But I for one wish there were more chicken thieves and outlaws of the sort that formed the gallant band that took Mexicali. I subscribe myself a chicken thief and revolutionist.[17]

At the same time, however, suspicions were growing amongst the socialist leadership over the real intentions of the Magonistas. It was becoming apparent Magon had an even more extreme agenda than they had first believed, while he in turn feared a U.S. military intervention in Mexico unless his North American socialist allies agitated in favour of the revolutionaries. When President Taft moved 20,000 troops to the border with Mexico, on 'manoeuvres,' Magon wrote to Samuel Gompers, President of the American Federation of Labor, asking him to lodge a protest with the U.S. Government. Gompers hesitated, deciding instead to ask the Magonistas for a clear statement of their revolutionary intentions:

> I think the American people should be told by the authorised spokesman of the revolutionary movement of Mexico, what it aims to accomplish as a constructive power if entrusted with the powers of government in Mexico. If the present regime is to be supplanted by another, the present revolutionary party, without fundamentally changing the conditions, which shall make for the improvement of the workers' opportunities, and a greater regard for their rights and their interests, then the American labour movement can look upon such a change with entire indifference.[18]

The reply from Magon, while still giving no hint of his anarchist ambitions, must have sounded to Gompers more like a threat than an attempt to cement common cause with American socialists. After declaring that his Liberal Party was struggling for 'possession of the land, reduction of hours of labour and increased wages,' Magon warned Gompers that if American labour stood idly by and permitted the Mexican people to be 'crushed by militarism, at the behest of the money power, they will drag with them to the lowest depths, their immediate neighbours – the American workingmen.'[19]

Impatient to be seen in contention for the hearts and minds of the Mexican people, the Magonistas had a small force of *insurrectos* in action by the end of 1910. This was led by Praxedis Guerrero, a 28-year-old member of the Liberal Junta who, unlike Magon, who remained safe in 519½ East Fourth Street for the duration of the revolution, was not prepared to let others do the fighting. Guerrero had crossed the border from El Paso with twenty-two men, hoping to establish a base from which to attack Chihuahua Province. Seizing a train, they blew up bridges as they went, until overwhelmed by a superior force of *federales*, and Guerrero killed.[20] After this disappointment, support inside Mexico for the Magonistas melted away, the passion for reform not helped when Magon refused to leave his sanctuary in down town Los Angeles. When the flag *'Tierra y Libertad'* (Land and Liberty) was raised again by the Magonistas in Baja California, none of the Liberal Junta would fire a shot in anger. That would be left to others – Wobbly idealists recruited in the belief they were in the vanguard of socialist revolution, U.S. army deserters, border bandits, escaped convicts, mercenaries, and most of all, Caryl ap Rhys Pryce.

Apart from his innate sense of adventure, it remains a mystery why Pryce, after ten years in Africa defending the British Empire as a policeman and soldier, should, suddenly, have sought to destroy the status quo, to which he had pledged his life, to be carried like a mantra, from the cradle to the grave. The only word of explanation offered by an individual who, a few years previously, had applied to become a Chief Constable – one of the highest law enforcement officers in the land – was his concern to help the 'poor peons.' Nothing that followed his intervention in the Mexican Revolution of the Magonistas, however, suggests a man burning with social righteousness. If at all possible, he avoided even the mention of his 'revolutionising,' almost as though it were a closed chapter in his life, best forgotten. Listed among the *Who's Who* of the great and the good in Britain after he was awarded the Distinguished Service Order by King George V for capturing a German machine gun nest during World War I, Pryce omitted all mention of his 'revolutionising' from his biographical entry in this prestigious publication.[21] Was he ashamed of his lapse, or was there some other reason for trying to expunge this episode from the official record?

The word on the street and around the Wobbly shantytowns when Pryce arrived in Los Angeles was that there was a revolution down in Mexico and its leader, Ricardo Flores Magon, was recruiting fighters. In fact, there were *two* revolutions, the other led by Madero about to resume after its earlier setback. Whether or not he was confused, Pryce enlisted with the Magonistas who were offering a dollar a day, with a $100 dollar bounty and 160 acres of free land in Baja California if he were on the winning side. If Mexicans responded to the call, much the better, but as it transpired, Flores Magon was to recruit mainly white soldiers-of-fortune to achieve this first small advance down the road towards his anarchist Utopia.

The Mexicans had a long history of using foreign mercenaries to fight their wars. Four foreign-born generals served with the Mexican army in its Texas campaigns, and there were sixteen by the time of the war between the United States and Mexico in 1846-1848 during which so many deserted the U.S. Army that one of their number, John Riley, formed the San Patricios. The Saint Patrick's Battalion, also called the Legion of Strangers, or Irish Volunteers, had only a superficial Irish-Catholic link although fighting under an emerald flag emblazoned with the Irish harp and shamrock, did provide distinctive symbolism and cohesion for a group comprised mostly of deserters.[22]

Rarely did deserters have fraternal feelings for the Mexicans alongside whom they fought, or sympathy for their cause. They enlisted purely for the money, and the promise of land grants. During the war with the United States, agents were employed – one an Englishman Nicholas Sinnot – to distribute leaflets in the north offering 200 acres for a private, up to 8000 acres for a colonel.

To combat this, the U.S. Congress enacted legislation a year later, authorising payment of a bonus of 160 acres for any veteran honourably discharged after twelve months service. Sixty years later Magon was offering an almost identical deal to Pryce and company. Deserting to the Mexican army was for some also a way to gain rapid promotion, a U.S. army private on seven dollars a month suddenly earning fifty-seven dollars as a lieutenant in Mexico.

Besides the money and the land, there were other reasons for deserting. The U.S. Army was a harsh, uncompromising regime, maintained by cruel punishments for the most minor offences. Although outlawed by the beginning of the 20th century, the 'hole' and 'spread-eagle' across the barrel of a gun to roast for hours in the sun were still commonplace. Fear of punishment for persistent drunkenness caused many to desert, while discrimination against foreign-born soldiers and constant taunting of 'Micks' and 'potato heads' drove others into the arms of Mexican recruiting agents.

If Magon had imagined his appeal for volunteers to 'go to the battlefield, enter the portals of history to make history . . . for your own class,' would have recruited a dedicated band of class war warriors, he was mistaken. Instead, he got a very mixed bag.[23] He also needed to be extremely careful how he went about it, because if he was seen to be recruiting an army in the United States to fight a war in Mexico, he would land back behind bars for violating America's neutrality laws. Accordingly, those interested in his offer were advised to report to Holtville where an agent would escort recruits across the border into Mexico. The border territory was by now awash with agents of all nationalities, but especially from a United States determined to ensure the repercussions of the Mexican Revolution did not threaten its Monroe Doctrine, the assertion that Central America was an integral part of the United States' sphere of influence. While Britain seemed to have pretty much given up its claims in the region by the beginning of the 20th century, it and other countries, notably Japan, Germany and France were far from being idle bystanders. For some, the twin revolutions of Magon and Madero provided another opportunity to ignore the 'Keep Out' signs. All three European countries had nationals with major property interests in Mexico acquired under the Diaz regime and protected by his dreaded *rurales,* once the highest paid police force in the world. Revolution had, however, swept away this protection, and European investments, mostly property and mining, were as much at risk as those of neighbouring Americans from the struggle between Diaz and the revolutionary forces of Magon and Madero.

Britain had dispatched its Pacific West Coast Squadron, the coal-fired sloops, *HMS Algerine* and *HMS Shearwater,* each with a contingent of marines, to guard British interests in Baja California. These were considerable, the Mexican Land and Colonisation Company, a London-based consortium, owning or leasing 15,000,000 acres of Lower California, accounting for half the land area of the entire peninsula where, shortly, a British national, Caryl ap Rhys Pryce, would be engaged in a revolution, which if successful would mean the seizure of these assets by anarchists. And Caryl was not the only Pryce family member likely to become engaged in the imminent conflict – a brother-in-law, Lieutenant Graham, was serving aboard the *Algerine* as it patrolled the Pacific coast of the Baja Peninsula!

Dwarfing anything owned by the Americans in the Baja, the English consortium's property interests were equivalent in size to the states of Vermont, Massachusetts, Rhode Island and Connecticut combined. Appropriately, the area was coloured pink on company maps at its London Office, while the list of shareholders read like an extract from Burke's Peerage of English nobility, sprinkled with a dozen noble lords, a handful of Knights of the Garter, and dignitaries drawn from the higher orders of the Church of England, representative of a class that prospered from exerting influence in the right places while investing in the relentless expansion of the British Empire. Barons Hillingdon and Wolverton were partners in the family bank of Glyn, Mills, Currie and Co., Lord Hood was descended from Admiral Hood who defeated the French during the American Revolution, and Sir James Kitson was the Chief Paymaster to the British Army.

Assembled by Sir Edward Jenkinson, veteran of the Indian Mutiny, and at one time Assistant Under-Secretary for Police and Crime (Ireland), the consortium set out to buy Lower California and colonise it in much the same way as the British Government had settled its far-flung dominions. The difference on this occasion was that the territory had not been acquired by exploration, conquest or gift but by private purchase from a failed American company. The U.S. was not happy with the deal, Washington viewing it as a backdoor challenge to American hegemony in the region. By-passing political objections, Sir Edward obtained from President Diaz a Charter to exploit the area, coincidentally in the very same year, 1889, Cecil Rhodes was granted a Royal Charter for his British South Africa Company to colonise and exploit the resources of Matabeleland and Mashonaland, later Rhodesia.

The consortium had purchased all the land between North Latitude 32 degrees 42 minutes, marking the border with the United States, down to North latitude 28 degrees, including the islands of Cedros, Socorro, Coronados, Clarion and Venado. The Charter from Diaz granted concessions to build and run railroads, and operate steamship lines linking with San Diego, and to Guatemala whose neighbour British Honduras (now Belize) was Britain's only Crown Colony in Central America. The consortium mined gold, phosphate, sulphur, as well as large guano deposits off the coast, operated the only telegraph line between Lower California and the United States – and ran the best hotel in the capital, Ensenada, headquarters for its local office.[24]

To the south of the Mexican Land and Colonisation Company's largely desert kingdom was another smaller principality, a mere four million acres, hugging the coastline and including the strategically important Magdalena Bay, possibly the finest natural harbour in the world. Owned by a Boston/New York consortium, the bay was used by the U.S. Navy in 1911 for firing exercises. It was also of considerable interest to the Japanese whose Pacific fishing trawlers discovered Magdalena's tranquil waters while hunting the large schools of grey whales that enter the Bay every spring to calf before continuing their annual migration from Alaska to the Southern Ocean.

Ever since defeating China in 1895, the Japanese had ignored the implied sanctions of the Monroe Doctrine, boasting they were strong enough to compete with America in its own backyard. These ambitions were fanned by Germany and Kaiser Wilhelm's obsession with his 'manifest destiny' to challenge Britain's naval supremacy. He figured Germany would profit from provoking a conflict between the U.S. and Japan in Mexico while he tackled Britain in Europe.

To this end, German intelligence spread the story that there were 10,000 well-armed and trained Japanese troops stationed in Mexico, in civilian clothes, plotting to wrest control of the Panama Canal away from the United States, the intention of this being to provoke the Americans into action. But the report was ignored by the U.S. as unfounded. Nevertheless, this incident was a measure of the lengths to which Germany, and Japan, were prepared to go to establish a Pacific coast naval base – and Magdalena Bay would have been ideal. Before long American newspaper correspondents were spotting Japanese nationals all over Lower California, the Hearst newspapers the first to give 'Yellow Peril' its common currency. There were even reports of a secret Treaty between Mexico and Japan for a coaling station in Magdalena Bay.

Even more important to the future of Baja California than this miasma of political intrigue, was the subject of colonisation, vital to the stability of the foreign interests. The first attempt at this was at San Quintin, a small Indian fishing village 180 miles south of the border with the United States. On a headland protruding into the shallow waters of another fine natural harbour, a new town was planned by the Mexican Land and Colonisation Company as a terminal for a network of railroads criss-crossing the Baja peninsula, and for the steamship line linking with San Diego and the Mexican mainland. San Quintin was intended to be an agricultural community, dependent on dry farming in an area where barely six inches of rain fell each year. Beyond the small settlement there was nothing but desolation, arid and overgrown with cacti, for much of the early morning shrouded in great banks of fog rolling off the Pacific. When it lifted, the days were stifling, so hot at night it burned through a man's blanket. Save for the *mesquite* that lined the shallow *arroyos*, the face of the country was veiled entirely in cacti. But the first settlers were optimists, convinced that with water the soil would prove highly productive. Sadly, they had arrived in the middle of a sixteen-year drought, the colonists reduced to eating the pulp of *viznaga* cactus when their pathetic crops failed. Within ten years the pioneer colony was defeated by the searing heat and drought, farms and twenty miles of railroad abandoned to the wilderness, all that remained, the bones of those early colonists lying in the English cemetery beside the bay.

Even though few of its grandiose schemes materialised, the Mexican Land and Colonisation Company did not give up until 1920 when it was finally dissolved, and its assets surrendered to Mexico.[25] In 1911 its investment in Baja California was still generating a useful return mainly from mining activities. The company had been reassured by Madero that he had no socialist designs upon its assets; that he sought only to replace Diaz by a more democratic government. The Magonistas, soon to be camped on the northern edge of the company's property, would become a far more serious threat to investors. Pearson (later Lord Cowdray) had huge oil interests in mainland Mexico, vital to Britain in the event of a war with Germany in Europe. If the Magonistas were successful and confiscated America's Standard Oil Company as they threatened, Pearson's were certain to follow. The pressure on the British Foreign Office to intervene grew by the day. Aware of this, President Taft became more and more suspicious of British motives, especially at a time the two countries were negotiating an Arbitration Treaty designed to defuse potentially dangerous disputes such as this.

Into this political quagmire marched Caryl ap Rhys Pryce, Stanley Williams and 'Melbourne' Hopkins. For a dollar day and a land grant, Flores Magon had acquired Pryce, a man whose leadership credentials were exceptional, Williams (sometimes known as William Stanley), a deserter from the American Army, and Hopkins, an Australian Boer War veteran. Pryce was drinking *mescal* rather than Cape Smoke brandy, but the company must have seemed familiar.

NOTES

1. *Los Angeles Times,* 30 September 1911.
2. Pryce Papers. Letter from Caryl ap Rhys Pryce to his father, Col. Douglas Davidson Pryce, from Los Angeles, 3 February 1912.
3. Pryce Papers. Copy of Record of Service. Records of Pryce's service in Canada prior to 7 November 1914, have been destroyed in accordance with PAC 69/014 (DNDP 11): Mr John H. Paveling (Director, National Personnel Records Centre, Public Archives Canada, Ottawa) to Brigadier (ret) M. H. ap Rhys Pryce, 15 March 1983.
4. Pryce Papers. Letter from Hattie Biggs on Yorkshire Insurance Company notepaper to Gladys Hodge, 28 August 1911.

5. Pryce Papers. Letter from Caryl ap Rhys Pryce to his parents, Col. and Mrs Douglas Davidson Pryce, from Los Angeles, 25 August 1911.
6. J. K. Turner, *Barbarous Mexico* (1910).
7. Pryce Papers. Letter from Caryl ap Rhys Pryce to Hattie Biggs (undated). The letter was written shortly after his arrest and incarceration in 1911.
8. Grace Heilman Stimson, *Rise of the Labour Movement in Los Angeles* (University of California Press, 1955), pp. 35-38, 308, 323-24, 336-430.
9. Patrick Renshaw, *The Wobblies: the story of syndicalism in the United States* (New York, 1967), pp. 121-122.
10. *Industrial Worker,* 11 September 1911.
11. Colin M. MacLachlan, *Anarchy and the Mexican Revolution: the political trials of Flores Magon in the United States* (1991, University of California Press), pp. 41-45.
12. Mexico National Archives, Mexico City, Census Returns 1910.
13. L. B. Simpson, *The Encomienda in New Spain* (1950), for conditions of peonage.
14. Ward S. Albro, *Always a Rebel: Ricardo Flores Magon and the Mexican Revolution* (Fort Worth, Texas, 1992, Christian University Press), p. 102.
15. *Regeneración,* 27 February 1911.
16. ibid., 25 February, 25 March, 1911.
17. *Los Angeles Times,* 6 February 1911.
18. Gompers to Flores Magon, 18 March 1911, TLpS, reel 154, vol. 166, pp. 773-74, SG Letterbooks, DLC.
19. Flores Magon to Gompers, 29 March 1911, Executive Council Records, Vote Books, reel 11, frames 608-9, *AFL Records*; quotation at frame 609.
20. Martinez Nunez, *La vida heroica,* pp. 221-239.
21. Pryce Papers. Letter from Caryl ap Rhys Pryce to Hattie Biggs (undated). The letter was written shortly after his arrest and incarceration in 1911.
22. Dennis J. Wynn, *The San Patricio Soldiers: Mexico's Foreign Legion* (El Paso, 1984, Texas Western Press).
23. *Regeneración,* 3 September, 1910.
24. Public Record Office, BT31/31161/28841, 'An Agreement, between The International Company of Mexico, called the American Company of the one part and the Mexican Land and Colonisation Company called the English Company of the other part, 1889.'
25. PRO, Mexican Land and Colonisation Company, 28841, Ref. No. BT31/31161.

Chapter 3

The Foreign Legion

The People's flag is deepest red,
It shrouded oft our martyred dead;
And ere their limbs grew stiff and cold,
Their life-blood dyed its every fold.

                                                                Jim Connell

Was Pryce confused about which revolutionary force he was
joining – Magonistas or Maderistas – or wholly indifferent to the
situation when he crossed into Mexico with his new Wobbly
friends, Stanley Williams and Melbourne Hopkins? What is certain
is that they were about to engage in an act of war which, if successful, would culminate in the raising of the Red Flag over Baja
California by Ricardo Flores Magon and his anarcho-socialist
allies.[1] The new front in the Magonista revolution was to be at
Mexicali, a dirty little town, just a hop, skip and jump across the
irrigation canal that fed California's Imperial Valley with water
from the Colorado, the 'liquid gold' transforming desert into rich
farmland. But Mexicali was in Mexico and not part of this new
oasis. Here, the heat hung choking in the air while thirst, delirium,
death hovered on the wind. Although flooded a month earlier
when the Colorado burst its banks, the only evidence of this was
the occasional patch of fresh green grass sprouting amongst the
cactus. Once more, the insatiable desert was showing its teeth,
the sparse vegetation stiff with grey alkali dust, rocky ridges poking
through the surface like so many skeletons.

    Mindful of the risks of infringing American neutrality by recruit-
ing foreign mercenaries on U.S. soil, all volunteers were instructed
to make their own way to Holtville, where they would be met and
escorted across the border before being provided with weapons
and horses. Holtville was only 125 miles from the Pacific coast,

but with the San Diego-Arizona Eastern Railroad still five years away from completion, it remained one of the more isolated townships in southern California. Dubbed 'The Impossible Railroad', the twin obstacles to construction of the Eastern were the route, because it was partly through Mexico, and the Carrizo Gorge, a precipitous canyon thirty miles long, rising to almost 4000ft, and only eventually conquered by blasting 15 tunnels through solid rock.[2] The pass had defeated previous attempts at railroad construction, but the latest project had the backing of the U.S. Government, and the millionaire sugar baron, John D. Spreckels.[3] Both realized the strategic importance of the new railroad, Spreckels, as a beneficiary of the thousands of acres of Mexican ranch land acquired from President Diaz for a pittance, and the Government on account of its not inconsiderable investment in the region. While track was being laid, U.S. Army engineers were building a network of levees to tame the mighty Colorado River delta. Once flooding was prevented, Holtville and its neighbours in Imperial Valley would take advantage of their year-round sunshine to become California's most important agricultural area.[4] With Madero's revolution already underway across the border from Texas, the U.S. Government was understandably nervous about another breaking out on California's doorstep, in an area where it was investing millions of dollars in public works. A few sticks of dynamite in the new embankment protecting Imperial Valley farmers from flooding was all that was needed to wreck the burgeoning Valley economy.

There was, however, another rail route into Holtville, a circuitous one via the Southern Pacific to Yuma, which is probably how Pryce and his companions arrived, choosing to 'ride the rails' hobo style, the more expensive Butterworth Overland Stage beyond their financial reach.[5] By the time the three men reached Holtville they would have appeared more like hobos than revolutionaries. Just eighteen had so far responded to Flores Magon's call to arms, four of these foreigners and Wobblies.[6] Waiting to lead them across the border was their first *generalissimo*, a Mexican, Jose Maria Leyva, and his second-in-command, Simon Berthold. Both were socialist activists; neither had military experience. Leyva, who had spent most of his life in Los Angeles working as a hod carrier, introduced himself to his small band of insurgents as 'El

General en Jefe de las Tropas Insurgentes,' a grand title for the leader of a group that excited more amusement than fear as it paraded on the eve of its first battle. Born in Mexico to German parents, abandoned at birth and raised by a Mexican woman, Berthold might best be described as the insurgents' political commissar. Well-known for his extremist activities in a number of West Coast cities, he worked as a truck driver when not drilling subversives on a back lot in Los Angeles. A high-profile activist, he was at one point suspected of complicity in the bombing of the Otis-owned *Los Angeles Times* office the previous autumn.[7]

The force that marched on Mexicali was intended to ignite a revolutionary fire in Baja California that would sweep across the Sea of Cortez into mainland Mexico. But this ragged band of *insurrectos* wore no uniforms, the only thing distinguishing them as an army, the anarchist emblem, tiny red bows, pinned to their sleeves, a very early sign of the real intentions of the Liberal Junta. Some sported red button badges inscribed, 'Los Angeles to be taken in 1912.' Of the eighteen men, only eight were mounted, some riding bareback, with only halters to guide their horses. The four foreigners in the company were described as having the appearance of typical raw-boned ranch hands.' But all were armed with rifles and side arms, and there was an abundant supply of ammunition.[8]

On the day of the invasion, 27 January 1911, Mexicali had a population of a thousand, served by thirty-seven saloons, most of which doubled as brothels. Under cover of darkness, Leyva and Berthold led their group across the border a few miles west of the town, rendezvousing with a band of Indians at Laguna Salada, a large, shallow salt lake, once an inlet from the Sea of Cortez until it was closed by the build-up of silt from the Colorado. After distributing weapons to the Indians, the rebels set out across the sand dunes to Mexicali twenty miles away, entering the town at dawn on Sunday, 29 January.

There was no resistance. Most of the inhabitants of this wild border town were sleeping off the night before. Leyva headed straight for the jail. When the jailer refused to release the inmates, someone poked a rifle through the bars and shot him. The prisoners were then freed but only on condition they joined the revolution. Meanwhile, Berthold had proceeded to the Mexican barracks alongside the international line, capturing the tiny garrison without a struggle.[9] The Custom House was next to fall, the sub-prefect Gustavo Terrazas taken hostage – and immediately offered back to his family on payment of a $500 ransom. Heartbroken when none of his relatives volunteered to stump up even *dos reales* for his freedom, the despondent Terrazas was pushed across the border to raise the ransom from friends in America while another relative was held in his place.[10]

After the first shot was fired, the rebels wasted no time in cashing in their principles, demonstrating that dollars and gold were more important than anarchism and the sacred cause of liberty championed by the Liberal Junta resident in downtown LA. Mexicali was turned upside down by Leyva and Berthold in their frantic search for booty but the biggest prize of all – $350,000 in gold, supposedly lodged in a bank by the Mexican Government as a payment to the Lower California Land and Water Company – had vanished. The gold shipment had been cancelled at the eleventh hour when officials got wind of the invasion. Instead, the transfer was made in bonds, worthless pieces of paper to the penniless recruits of the Magonista army.[11]

No sooner had they taken Mexicali than it rained, torrential rain, at times rain that fell from the clearest of blue skies, the strangest phenomenon. Flood waters from the Colorado began roaring down the town's usually bone-dry New River, carving out a fresh channel, fringed on either side by twenty-foot high cliffs of soft red sandstone, indented by tiny creeks where the torrent ate into the flood plain. Across the border U.S. farmers and ranchers watched, fearful not of the rebels but of the rising flood- waters. Then the worst happened, not from the rain but when unseasonally-high temperatures in the upper reaches of the Colorado north of Denver released a mountain of melt water, the force of it sweeping away levees and devastating thousands of acres of Imperial Valley. As construction crews raced to close breaches in the embankments, Valley settlers reached for their rifles, announcing they would countenance no interference by *insurrectos* in the river defence works.

But nothing could dampen the spirits of the victorious rebels, small in numbers but large in noise, dancing in the tree-lined plaza, fortified against the downpour by bottles of looted whiskey.

Joining in the celebrations was a drunken Englishman who had slept through the Battle for Mexicali.[12] Proclaiming himself 'King of Mexicali' and waving a pair of pistols, he herded the last group of terrified Mexican residents across the border at Calexico, only to find himself stranded on the U.S. side and thrown into jail by Sheriff Meadows, of Imperial County. Angrily, the man wired the British Ambassador in Washington: 'British subject in Mexicali abused and robbed. Send us assistance. Veteran Boer War, Bill Taylor.'[13]

Anticipating further trouble, Sheriff Meadows quickly deputised a posse. Only a few hundred yards over the border, the rooftops of Calexico provided an ideal vantage point from which his men could watch the revolution unfolding below them in the streets of Mexicali. In the meantime, he sent his cousin 'Arizona Charlie,' reputedly the fastest gun in the southwest and former sheriff of Maricopa County, Arizona, to parley with the *insurrectos*, so successfully, it appears, he was almost persuaded to join the revolution! Arizona Charlie's place in the history of the southwest would be assured – not by his intervention in the revolution – but because he predicted the precise moment of his death. Born in a Colorado snowstorm, he would die in one, he said. And so he did, when for the first time in living memory it snowed at Gila Bend, the driest, most sizzling corner of the United States.[14]

Not every visitor to the rebel camp was as friendly and charitable as 'Arizona Charlie'. The special correspondent at Calexico for the Otis-owned *Los Angeles Times* described the rebels as, 'a chicken thief band . . . hobos and drifters from the outcast stations of the United States . . . most of the revolutionists either Mexican criminals or mongrel Americans who have good reason for not risking their presence again on American soil.'

By any measure of warfare, the capture of Mexicali was a miserable little affair. But it had its effect, the first wave of new recruits arriving within days of the triumph, the strangest assortment of hobos, desperadoes, Army deserters, soldiers-of-fortune, and socialist idealists ever to inflict themselves upon a southwest that had suffered its share of ne'er-do-wells. Not all of them made it safely across the border. Joseph Webber, a bearded, middle-aged, heavy-accented German out of San Francisco, was arrested by a patrolling U.S. sentry as he knelt among the sagebrush close to the international line. Beside him, packed in a brown suitcase, were dynamite, a clock, dry batteries, and small coils of copper wire, all apparatus he insisted for 'treating rheumatism'.

Ordered by Corporal Frank O'Dell of the Eighth Infantry to throw up his arms, Webber reached for his revolver, second thoughts proving the wiser when a shot from the corporal's rifle whistled above his head. Hauled off to the patrol camp a few miles away, Webber was recognised by Corporal O'Dell's comrades as the very same man who a day earlier had harangued them with his anarchist speeches. Now, he preferred to describe himself as a German scientist indulging in his favourite hobby – electrical fixtures, albeit in the middle of a desert not far from a revolution.

'I used to wire houses and instal electrical alarms and bells,' Webber told his interrogators.

'What do you do with these fine field glasses?' he was next asked.

'I was working on a big ranch and needed the glasses to find the cattle,' he replied promptly.

'And what are you doing with dynamite?'

'Oh, I use a little in my experiments,' he said, offering an excuse for every piece of peculiar equipment. As for the dry batteries, they were for treating cataracts on his eyes!

But Webber could not resist haranguing his interrogators, insisting he did not pay taxes to 'keep ruffian soldiers in business'.

Although declaring himself hostile to the Magonistas, and denying any intention of crossing the line to join the insurgents, Webber was undoubtedly a German anarchist – 'I am a socialist but independent of every organisation in the world. Governments are wrong as they are and the time is coming when we will have things fixed to suit ourselves.' With this parting shot, he was handed over by the army to Sheriff Meadows for trial on charges of concealing weapons and high explosives.[15]

Back in Los Angeles, Magon and the Liberal Junta milked the capture of Mexicali for every last drop of propaganda, swaggering across the pages of West Coast newspapers with their grandiose claims. While not even registering as a skirmish on the Richter scale of military conflict, it had established the Magonistas as an independent revolutionary group in control of part of Baja California. Isolated from mainland Mexico and close to the U.S. border,

Mexicali was easy to defend against a counter attack by President Diaz's *federales*. Its closeness to the international line was a bonus, since the *federales* would never be allowed by the Americans to cross it for the purposes of mounting an attack from the U.S. side. As for the revolution, the cost could be partly financed from revenues collected at the Mexicali Customs post.

Until Mexicali, Francisco Madero and his allies had monopolised the scene, the headlines all about the exploits of Pancho Villa and Emiliano Zapata. Suddenly, there was a new force to be reckoned with, one that appeared to have much in common with the Industrial Workers of the World, and the American Federation of Labour. For Washington, these were worrying times, the industrial landscape scarred by a conflict that could so easily explode into revolution. One contributor to *The Industrial Worker* probably spoke for the majority of the IWW's one million members when he wrote, 'The growing anxiety at Washington and the persistency with which the United States authorities are injecting themselves into the conflict also point a lesson that the dullest should be able to understand – in a word, that revolution threatens most seriously the vested interests of monopoly, native and foreign, is beyond question.'[16] Magon's confidence after the small victory at Mexicali soared, encouraging him to pull further away from mainstream socialist opinion, towards anarchism.

But the insurgents were shortly to face their first real test in battle. Resisting pressure from the Imperial Valley settlers, and the demands of Otis and Spreckles, to intervene in the border troubles, Washington asked the Mexican Government to send a force to protect the Colorado River defence works from possible attack by insurgents. The 'Fighting Eighth', one of Mexico's crack regiments, commanded by Colonel Miguel Mayol, was, consequently, dispatched by sea from the mainland to Ensenada. Before it could disembark, however, the state Governor, Colonel Celso Vega, accompanied by 100 *federales*, left Ensenada on a ten-day forced march across the mountains with the inention of re-capturing Mexicali from the Magonistas.[17]

While the winter rains had stopped, temperatures in the mountains had plunged to below freezing. Vega's soldiers, clad only in their flimsy white cotton pyjama uniforms and leather sandals, were barely able to grip their Mauser rifles in the bitter cold. To reach Mexicali in such a short time, the *federales* had abandoned much of their equipment, each man carrying his meagre rations of green coffee, coarse flour, cornmeal and bone-hard chunks of salted beef, wrapped in red and blue handkerchiefs, the bundles tied to their belts. Ill-prepared for battle, each was ready to meet his maker, every soldier's name stitched neatly beneath the sweat-band of his white and blue cap. The *federales* arrived at the swollen New River before dawn. Blundering about in the darkness, they were quite unaware the river had cut a new course. Before even a shot was fired, some of the advancing Mexicans had stepped off the rim of the steep-sided channel into the foaming floodwater. On the bank opposite the *insurrectos,* plastered with camouflage mud, crouched in the caves and ditches gouged from the banks by the torrent. Both sides waited for sunrise. So did scores of Americans watching from the rooftops of neighbouring Calexico in anticipation of a grandstand view of the first major engagement in the Magonista campaign.

Fortunately for the Mexicans their bungled attempt at recapturing Mexicali was matched by the Magonistas lack of firepower. Only half the *insurrectos* had rifles, the remainder told to hoist their caps on sticks above their dugouts to invite enemy fire, or momentarily to expose themselves so as to draw the fire of the Mexican sharpshooters before ducking out of sight. The situation was partially redeemed by Berthold riding fearlessly along the bank of the river urging his troops to greater bravery.

The exchange of fire was more furious than dangerous, sufficient however to persuade five Mexicans to break ranks, driving their horses at a gallop for the border where they threw their weapons at the feet of an American cavalry patrol, declaring they were through with fighting. Not long afterwards Governor Vega was hit in the neck and side, at which point he ordered the retreat, the *federales* carrying their wounded leader from the battlefield on a make-shift litter, stopping only long enough to commandeer a wagon from a local rancher before hurrying back across the mountains to Ensenada. Three *federales* and two *insurrectos* were killed in the two-hour battle, the retreating Mexicans abandoning their dead to the buzzards. From the *insurrecto* bank of the New River, a coloured sentry took pot shots with his Springfield at a maggoty dog sniffing at the bodies. General Leyva was jubilant.

Stretching out his arms and pointing to the equipment jettisoned by the fleeing *federales,* he declared, '*We could have held Mexicali against a thousand men.*'[18]

Like a recharged bottle of soda pop, the comic opera revolution sizzled and subsided until Leyva and Berthold faced a more serious challenge to their leadership – from Stanley Williams, Caryl ap Rhys Pryce, and Melbourne Hopkins. From his very first day in Mexicali it was evident Williams, alias William Stanley, had little time for Mexicans, no matter what side they happened to be fighting on. Relations between Mexicans and Americans in the *insurrecto* camp grew daily more strained and when the balance of recruits swung in favour of the *gringos,* Pryce and Hopkins backed Williams in calling a snap election that deposed Leyva and Berthold.[19] Adjourning to the bullring for evening mess, the victorious conspirators stacked their weapons against a wall. As they celebrated their coup, Berthold and his supporters stole off with the cache of rifles, so that when he ordered his bugler to sound the call to arms, the *gringos* spilling out of the bullring found they were staring down the business end of Mexican rifles. At their head was Berthold announcing menacingly, 'Any man who says he is a friend of Williams will be shot.' No one moved. The ringleader Williams was clapped in irons for two days, and afterwards pushed across the border on pain of death if he dared return. Fuming and plotting, he retreated to the Wobbly recruiting-centre at Holtville to await developments.[20]

The Mexicans may have stifled the attempted coup but dissension continued. A further week of acrimony culminated in a shooting fracas in which two Mexicans were wounded. By then there was only a handful of *insurrectos* left behind to man the rifle pits, the majority having decided to try their luck with Madero and Pancho Villa down the road at Ciudad Juarez. Another ballot was demanded. Once again the result was a vote of no confidence in the leadership of Leyva and Berthold. But it meant little. By then only 30 or so rebels were still armed – all of them Mexicans. [21]

Back in Los Angeles at Junta headquarters, Magon stared failure in the face. His revolution was in imminent danger of collapse unless somehow he could resolve the dispute on the front line. The socialist writer John Kenneth Turner, author of *Barbarous Mexico,* whose account of the suffering of the 'poor peons' Pryce claimed was the reason he went 'revolutionising,' was sent to Mexicali to mediate. The camp was plunged into even greater turmoil, when on his arrival Turner announced to correspondents from a dozen newspapers that the Junta was itself dissatisfied with the leadership of Leyva and Berthold, believing both to be outlaws. By disregarding the result of the ballot they had violated the cardinal principle for which the men were fighting, said Turner.[22]

With rebellion in the ranks and disowned by the Junta, Berthold exploded in violent rage, hurling volleys of abuse at everyone in range, including the U.S. troops watching from just across the border. Marching up and down and pointing angrily in their direction as if they were responsible for all his troubles, Berthold shouted:

> We will fire on them if they dare cross the boundary and then we will die as martyrs to the sacred cause of liberty. The Washington Government is as tyrannical as that of Diaz. We are fighting capitalism everywhere and it will cost the lives of at least a few servants of American despots the moment they step off their own territory.[23]

The quarrel between Turner and the two Magonista generals, punctuated by loud shouts, curses and violent gestures, was close to blows. Visibly upset by the whole affair, his mission a failure, Turner informed the waiting Press, 'The movement is doomed if this is not settled at once.' After hours of argument, Turner failed to oust Leyva and Berthold. They had the rifles and were staying. At last he persuaded the pair, grudgingly, to allow Williams to rejoin the revolution as *generalissimo* of the *gringos*. And so, the 'Second Battalion of the Liberal Army', otherwise the 'Foreign Legion', was formed.[24]

On his victorious return to Mexicali the following day, Williams, a U.S. army deserter and veteran of the war in the Phillipines, announced he had been given an independent commission and that there would henceforth be three generals in the field. No one was named supreme commander although it was generally accepted from that moment that whoever commanded the 'Foreign Legion' was *de facto* commander-in-chief of the Magonista Army in Baja California in deference to the wishes of Turner and the Liberal Junta.

Williams wasted no time stamping his new authority on the rebel army. Declaring he wanted action quickly, he, Pryce and Hopkins, together with forty other *gringos,* hijacked a train to raid Algodones about thirty miles down the line towards Arizona. Bridges were blown, telegraph lines cut, and the terrified inhabitants sent fleeing across the border.[25] Before leaving the town, General Williams posted a proclamation declaring the Magonistas would shoot every captured official and army officer, in retaliation for President Diaz's threat to execute all *insurrecto* prisoners of war. After accumulating large quantities of provisions, cattle, horses, mules and wagons, from their raids, the *gringos* returned to Mexicali at a thunderous gallop, accompanied by great excitement and shooting, all to impress the handful of Mexican revolutionaries who still stood behind Leyva and Berthold.[26]

By now, the ranchers of Imperial Valley were clamouring for the Federal Government to intervene. Besides the threat of flooding from the Colorado, their livestock was disappearing at an alarming rate. Not even vigilante patrols could stop the rustling by the Magonistas, one night 600 mules disappearing from the Cudahy Ranch, after the manager Thomas P. Daly and three ranch-hands patrolling the border in a shiny new automobile were chased fifteen miles through the mesquite by *insurrectos.* Flying over rocks and ditches at full speed, the air above its head thick with bullets, the auto plunged through the boundary fence, dumping the quartet in a patch of vicious *cholla* cactus at the feet of a U.S. Infantry Patrol. What made matters worse was the Magonistas appetite for the fat thoroughbred Herefords on the Cudahy Ranch – owned by the Chicago meat packing family – while ignoring common steers.[27]

Railroad construction camps scattered along the line of the San Diego-Arizona Eastern Railroad were another favourite source for provisioning the Magonistas. Raids became so frequent that whenever railroad workers spotted a dust cloud approaching on the horizon, they knew the *insurrectos* would soon be arriving to commandeer their provisions. The *insurrectos* insisted they never stole, issuing receipts for every heifer and bag of beans, these to be redeemed if the revolution was successful.[28]

Because of the border troubles, pressure from Imperial Valley settlers and from powerful absentee landowners, Washington sent

General Tasker H. Bliss, commanding the Department of California, to investigate the threat to U.S. property. Although accompanied on his visit to the border by the powerful newspaper publisher, H. G. Otis, owner of 800,000 acres in the immediate vicinity, Bliss refused to be intimidated, reporting to the War Department that not only was there no risk to American interests but most ordinary folk sympathised with the rebels. From his report it was evident Bliss had very little time for wealthy Americans who having crossed the border to buy vast tracts at a few cents an acre, were using the revolution as a means of legitimising their often defective title to Mexican land.

In his *Los Angeles Times* Otis countered with a flurry of reports from his reporters at the front line, one of these, John M. Steele, writing from Calexico that there was:

> Much anxiety here concerning the future movements of the *insurrectos,* not because of any considerable interest in the conflict between the rebels and the Mexican Government but by reason of the immense damage imminent to the holdings of nearly every farmer and ranchman in Imperial Valley north of the boundary line in the event that dynamiting attacks be made upon the dams and levees of the Colorado irrigation System. At any one of several points in Mexico, damage could be done that would return the upper Imperial Valley back to the desert from which it has just been redeemed. There is a lack of confidence in the ability of the Mexican forces to prevent disaster to the irrigation system should the *insurrectos* reverse their present avowed policy and seek to deprive the country north of the boundary line of its water supply.

By 6 March the pressure was getting too much for President Taft. The Washington Press corps knew something was up when on a warm spring morning, General Leonard Wood, Chief-of-Staff, U.S. Army, was spotted climbing out of a rear window at the White House in a bid to evade reporters. Within two hours the War Department announced the largest mobilisation of troops and naval vessels ever undertaken by the United States in peacetime.

Twenty thousand soldiers, a fifth of the U.S. Army, together with most of the Pacific Fleet, and 2000 marines recalled from their base at Guantanamo in Cuba, were converging on the border with Mexico. The official explanation for this massive movement of men and equipment was "manoeuvres." After thirty years of dealing effectively with insurgents, Diaz was about to be toppled but by whom? The U.S. was worried about the possible new political complexion of its neighbour.[29]

Two days after the mobilisation, President Taft was travelling south for the up-coming Lent vacation at Atlanta. The question he had wrestled with all that winter, whether to run for a second term, was now put aside for more important matters. The Mexican Revolutions of Madero and Magon had already seriously disrupted trade and put at risk U.S. investments in Mexico valued at $1 billion. If the breach in the Colorado River could not be plugged before the spring floodwaters arrived, the river would bleed across the desert, threatening millions of acres either side of the border. The potential civilising influence of the Imperial Valley irrigation works was widely considered as significant for southwest California as the waters of the Nile were for Egypt. The prediction was that controlled irrigation would immediately add 500,000 to the region's population, water and almost continuous sunshine transforming it into the garden of America. In the last decade a start had been made on this but the completion of the irrigation works was now jeopardised by an unmarked border stretching 1,700 miles from Texas to the Pacific, one now infested with insurgents.

As the presidential train passed through Charlottesville, Virginia, on route to Atlanta, Taft gave an unscheduled briefing to an Associated Press reporter accompanying the train. The border blockade, he said, was being enforced to bring the revolution in Mexico to a speedy conclusion by cutting off the supply of smuggled arms and men across it. Since neither the Maderistas nor Magonistas had accomplished anything so far, the conflict needed to be brought to a speedy conclusion. By stationing the U.S. Army along the border, the United States was also sending a signal to foreign governments, whose agents were active in the area, that they should not intervene if Mexico was to collapse into anarchy. In such an event, the U.S. stood ready to act.

Then Taft admitted that America's main concern was not with the revolutionaries of Francisco Madero, the main players in the bid to unseat Diaz, but with the Magonistas and their plans for a socio-anarchist republic in Lower California. From its interview with the President, the Associated Press reported:

> The situation in Lower California is said to have caused more concern to the United States than at any other point. It was reported the revolutionists were exceptionally strong there and threatened to set up a government of their own. The line between the United States and Lower California is but an imaginary one, and a revolutionary government there would be a source of constant worry.[30]

Taft, who stood on the far right of the Republican Party, was no friend of the labour movement. While not objecting to the workers' right to unionise, he was sickened by the picket line riots, the Wobbly Free Speech campaigns, and the general paroxysm of violent confrontation between labour and business convulsing America's larger towns and cities. The last thing he wanted was a workers' Utopia on America's doorstep.

Very soon San Diego was an armed camp, a naval force two miles long assembled in the bay, all shore leave cancelled, and the fleet under orders to keep up steam. The *San Diego Sun* was carried away by the military build-up, trumpeting, 'Texas was conquered by Americans . . . If Lower California should wake up one morning to find the Stars and Stripes floating over it, San Diego would suddenly become more than ever a City of Destiny.'

All this was just too much for Kaiser Wilhelm. Another team of German agents was dispatched to San Diego to determine how serious the situation was in Lower California. With U.S. troops by now stationed along the unmarked border, the Mexican Foreign Minister thought it advisable to deny newspaper reports of a secret treaty of co-operation with Japan. They were both good friends, he admitted, but there were no plans for a treaty against the interests of the United States, or any kind of 'alliance for war purposes.' Nevertheless, the U.S. Ambassador in Mexico City had reportedly delivered to Taft a copy of the very treaty under whose terms Texas would be returned to Mexico in the event of a successful war against the United States.[31]

The movement of U.S. troops did discourage the more daring raids into California by the Magonistas. But with many ranches straddling the line there were still rich pickings on the Mexico side for Williams and his Foreign Legion, the 1,700-mile long border unmarked except for the occasional landmark, a hill, canyon, or dried-up *arroyo,* recognisable only to the locals. By March 1911 Williams and his second-in-command Pryce had accumulated sufficient provisions, cattle, mules and wagons to supply the 300 Magonistas camped at Mexicali. But still short of rifles and ammunition, they sold some of their rustled livestock back to the ranchers to raise the cash for weapons. Another problem was the ambulatory nature of many of the recruits. No sooner were some handed a horse, saddle and rifle, and they vanished in a cloud of dust for pastures new. Not a single cent, not a rifle, nor box of ammunition had arrived from Magon and the Liberal Junta. The only communication the rebel generals received was a reminder that revenue from the Customs House at Mexicali should be sent regularly to Los Angeles to finance the propaganda campaign. All the *insurrectos,* both *gringo* and Mexican, felt increasingly estranged from the leadership hiding in its redoubt in downtown LA, suspecting Magon and the comrades of using the revenues from the Customs House to pay for an extravagant life style, instead of purchasing the weapons that were so urgently needed. Consequently, it was not long before the flow of cash northwards reduced to a trickle, most of it remaining in the army's war chest.

In the absence of clear, positive leadership from the Junta, Mexicans and Americans quarrelled constantly, although it was generally agreed their next move should be against the frontier town of Tijuana, some 90 miles to the west, and after that on to Ensenada on the Pacific coast. With the U.S. border at their backs, and Madero and Pancho Villa holding the territory east of the Colorado delta, there was nowhere else they could go! South of this line, the country was arid and mountainous, all but abandoned to the Indians and the more adventurous prospectors familiar with the *caminos,* cut by the Jesuit brothers through the wilderness, during their evangelising expeditions centuries earlier. A decision by the Magonistas became all the more pressing when they learned Colonel Miguel Mayol had finally disembarked his

500 seasoned *federales* of the 'Fighting Eighth' at Ensenada and, in response to the wishes of the U.S. Government, was marching directly to protect the Colorado river works from rebel interference.[32] His route was sure to bring him close to Mexicali, where by far the strongest of the Magonista force was the Second Battalion, eighty per cent of who were by now either of American or European origin. They were also better fed than the poor Mexicans of Leyva's First Battalion who were growing daily more mutinous.

The hostility between the two battalions was now such that 'burying their differences' had come to mean exactly that. Not for the first time a dispute between Mexican and *gringo insurgents* was settled by a gun fight, at the end of which Leyva's First Battalion was minus another man.[33] Hoping to reduce friction, the opposing generals agreed to billet their troops at opposite ends of the town.

In a desperate attempt to reassert his authority, Leyva, rather than wait for the army to move on Tijuana, dispatched a group of insurgents, led by Louis Rodriguez, an escaped murderer from Ensenada jail, to capture the small border town of Tecate. Once established at Tecate only thirty miles from Tijuana, Leyva calculated his First Battalion would be one jump ahead of the *gringos* and that very soon he could assume control of all Magonista forces in Baja California.

Rodriguez took Tecate without a shot being fired. The raiding party faced far greater danger in crossing the *sierras* through Picacho Pass en route to Tecate, a mountain passage so narrow in places a pair of mules were barely able to pass. Rodriguez had his men scramble up the mountains with their bare hands in blistering temperatures, guns and ammunition strapped to their backs, and all other equipment and food abandoned. By the time they reached the high *chaparral* five thousand feet above the desert floor they were exhausted, canteens bone dry, and in no condition for a battle.[34]

In Tecate, their first objective was the liquor store, where they found the courage to swagger along along the international line that bisected the town, hurling insults at the U.S. border patrols. With high ground at his back, Rodriguez thought his position impregnable, the occupation becoming more like a fiesta as scores of new recruits poured across the line to celebrate the rebels' latest 'victory'. But the Mayor, Jose Morales, had fled before the town was taken, and riding across the mountains raised the alarm with an advance party from the 'Fighting Eighth,' which he persuaded to divert to Tecate. Led by Captain Justrino Mendieta, a veteran of the Yaqui Indian Wars, they fell upon the drunken rebels asleep beside their campfires. The surprise attack was witnessed by John F. Haley, a reporter from the *San Diego Union*. Standing in the doorway of Thing Brothers Store in American Tecate, just a few yards from the line, the telephone receiver in his hand held towards the crackle of gunfire to dramatize his account for those back at the *Union* office, Haley reported:

> Taken unawares, the rebels seized their guns and returned the fire poured in upon them but without effect. Outnumbered and demoralised, they made a break for the hills. Rodriguez attempted to reorganise his force but his command was beyond control. Fighting to the last ditch the rebel commander retreated to the hills to the south followed by a detachment of federales. As he climbed a butte south of the town he levelled his gun, firing his last bullets at Justice Morales, an old enemy. One shot grazed the back of Morales left hand, and the next instant the rebel leader fell from the fire of Morales' followers.
>
> The battle continued for nearly two hours. For a time the rebels entrenched in several houses stood off the fire of the federales. However, the fire of the Government troops became so hot, the bullets from the Mausers piercing the adobes and light timber shacks like paper, that the rebels sought safety in a dash for the hills. It was in this dash most of them were killed. Five fell within the precincts of the town. Those who were able to reach their horses picketed in the corral succeeded in getting away. The slower ones were picked off by the sharpshooters of the famous Mexican Eighth Battalion. Chief among the latter were a number of Indians recruited from among the Indian labourers of the El Cajon Valley. These savages, not knowing the first rudiments of warfare, were so confused they were shot down like sheep.[35]

When the survivors struggled back to Mexicali with the story of the massacre, Leyva was devastated. Without waiting to consult Williams and Pryce, he raced off to Tecate to avenge the death of Rodriguez, taking with him half the remaining Mexicans. The rest were to head south with Berthold to El Alamo, a gold mining camp, deep in the Sierra San Pedro Martir, the highest and remotest part of the mountain range that forms the backbone of Baja California. The plan was for Berthold to move north from El Alamo to rendezvous with Leyva for the attack on Ensenada. Just what part the more disciplined, better-equipped Foreign Legion would play in all of this was never considered. The Liberal Army had split into two independent factions. If ever it was to be united again it was clear this would only be possible under a *gringo generalissimo*.[36]

Most of Leyva's men were almost too ill to fight by the time they reached Tecate. Crawling up to the ridge of a hill just below the town, they could see the white-uniformed *federales* playing games in front of the adobe houses. Then one of Leyva's men dropped his rifle. It exploded and all hell broke loose.

The *San Diego Union's* reporter John Haley still on the steps of Things Store, reported, 'Flames belched from the muzzles of *federale* and *insurrecto* rifles tonight, the hills of Tecate resounding with the din of warfare. The whiz of bullets was heard overhead – but deafening all of these noisy pandemonium were the challenging battle cries of the opposing forces.'

When the firing stopped, the deathly silence of the desert settled across the valley, broken only by the occasional tap-tap-tap of a metal cartridge on the stocks of rifles as the rebels signalled to each other in the darkness, a trick they had incidentally learned from *gringo* comrades who had picked it up during the Boer War. Shortly after dawn, just over the border in American Tecate where the U.S. Army had been observing events, a Stoddard-Dayton automobile roared to a halt in a cloud of dust with free copies for the troops of the *San Diego Union's* account of the previous night's battle.

Concerned that the conflict might spill over into the U.S., Lieutenant John Fiest, in command of the army patrol, called the Mexican Captain Mendieta to a parley at the border. In a bizarre confrontation, the two stood on the summit of the mountain, the toes of their boots brushing what was assumed to be the international line. With Mayor Morales as interpreter, and a company of *federales* standing-by with arms shouldered, the Mexican commander gave an undertaking not to violate U.S. neutrality by carrying the battle across the border.[37]

Twice during the following day Leyva tried unsuccessfully to dislodge Mendieta from his rocky fortress. That night, after setting fire to the scrub below the besieged garrison, the rebels retreated all the way back to Mexicali. Disgraced by the retreat, Leyva was driven out of camp, deposed by a villainous Mexican, Francisco Salinas, a man wanted on both sides of the border for murder.

NOTES

1. *Industrial Worker,* 30 March, 25 May, 8 June 1911; *Los Angeles Times,* 16 February 1911.
2. Bill Jennings, 'The Impossible Railroad', *Desert,* June 1977, Arizona State University; 'San Diego and Arizona Railway,' *San Diego Short Line Information,* Arizona State University.
3. ibid.
4. *San Diego Union,* 4 March, 15 March 1911.
5. Orion Zink, 'Warren's not Warner's: a postscript to the stage to El Centro,' *Journal of San Diego History,* Summer 1974, Arizona Historical foundation, Tempe, Arizona; 'Overland to Texas,' Ephemera File, Arizona Collection, Arizona State University.
6. *Los Angeles Times,* 30 January, 31 January 1911.
7. ibid.
8. ibid., 31 January 1911.
9. ibid., 30 January 1911.
10. ibid., 31 January 1911.
11. ibid., 30 January 1911.
12. ibid., 1 February 1911.
13. ibid.
14. ibid., 30 January, 1 February 1911;and for more biographical detail of Meadows, see *Prescott Courier Centennial Edition,* 15 May 1964, C 7-8, Arizona Collection, Arizona State University, Tempe.
15. *San Diego Union,* 13 March 1911.
16. *The Industrial Worker,* 'Mexican Liberals denounce Madero,' 16 March 1911.
17. *San Diego Union,* 4 March, 15 March 1911.
18. *Los Angeles Times,* 13 February 1911.
19. ibid., 8 March 1911; *San Diego Union,* 7, 8 March 1911.
20. *Los Angeles Times,* 8 March 1911.
21. *San Diego Union,* 9 March 1911.

22. *Los Angeles Times, San Diego Union,* 9 March 1911.
23. ibid.
24. *Los Angeles Times,* 21 March 1911.
25. *San Diego Union,* 12 March 1911.
26. *Los Angeles Times,* 13, 14 March 1911.
27. *San Diego Union,* 8 April 1911.
28. ibid.
29. *San Diego Union,* 7, 8 March 1911.
30. ibid., 9 March 1911.
31. *San Diego Union,* 11, 12 March 1911.
32. *Los Angeles Times,* 13 February 1911.
33. ibid., 19 March 1911.
34. *San Diego Union,* 12, 14 March 1911.
35. ibid., 18 March 1911.
36. *San Diego Union,* 24 March 1911.
37. ibid., 21, 22, 23 March 1911.

Chapter 4

The Battle of John Little's Ranch

Calexico was the last stop on the Southern Pacific spur from Yuma. When Peter Kyne, correspondent for *Sunset Magazine,* disembarked, he hailed the conductor who was searching the horizon for a fare. With a revolution just across the border, and the railroad expected to become a prime target, passengers were hard to find, apart from visiting newspaper correspondents.

Kyne asked about the chances of a room with a bath in Calexico. The conductor eyed him, pityingly. 'I kind of thought you were a war correspondent,' he chuckled. 'Take my advice and don't ask for a bath. If you do, they'll shoot you.' Kyne slid his bag towards the only other sign of life, a cinnamon-tinted urchin, dug *dos reales* from his pocket, and together they headed for the Calexico Hotel. 'Come down to write up the trouble,' inquired the proprietor. Kyne's mental thermometer fell. As a war correspondent in Cuba in 1898, he hated to hear a revolution referred to as 'trouble?' as if it were no more than a bar room brawl.[1]

That night, he slept fitfully, the suffocating heat of the Sonoran desert invading every corner of his grimy, stale-smelling room. The following morning, after a breakfast of black coffee, Kyne fished out a map and took stock. His assignment was to locate the mysterious Welshman, Caryl ap Rhys Pryce, who had assumed command of the Second Battalion of the Liberal Army in Lower California, better known as the 'Foreign Legion,' the majority of whom were thought to be renegade Americans and European-born Boer War veterans.[2] Other correspondents awaiting developments from the relative security of Calexico had warned him that Mexicali, where the two Magonista battalions were garrisoned, was far more dangerous than the usual 'naughty little towns' strung along the Mexican border. To reach the Foreign Legion safely, Kyne must make a detour around the Mexican battalion now commanded by the cutthroat half-breed General Salinas. Ignoring the warnings of his colleagues, he hired a horse and buggy and clattered off along a rocky trail, in the general direction of the gun-metal blue ramparts of the Cocopah Mountains shimmering on the horizon, their sides as smooth as a baby's bottom, wiped clean of the last grain of soil by centuries of drought, wind and erosion. On either side of the trail, the desert threatened, the dried carcasses of steers rattling in the breeze against the boundary fences where they had perished in the winter floods.

Pryce had taken command of the Second Battalion after it was caught in a cornfield by Colonel Miguel Mayol's 'Fighting Eighth.' Landing at Ensenada, Mayol and his troops were heading for the Colorado River, under strict orders from Diaz not to delay by engaging with any Magonistas they might encounter en route.[3] Concerned at the Mexican Government's failure to police the construction works at Andrade, President Taft was threatening to send U.S. cavalry across the border to round up the renegade Americans riding with the Magonistas.[4] Because of this, Mayol planned a detour around Mexicali to avoid confrontation with the rebel forces – until Williams and Pryce decided otherwise.

In the certain knowledge that they could expect a counter attack after the wounded Vega had retreated, the two battalions of Liberal insurgents, camped at opposite ends of the town, sat behind their barbed-wire defences awaiting developments. Salinas and his Mexicans were perfectly content to wait; not so Williams and Pryce, some of whose men had been kicking their heels in Mexicali for two months while others, losing interest, had beat it across the border with horses and equipment. The Foreign Legion was in very real danger of bleeding to death if it did not make a move. Since they were by then well-armed and provisioned, although still short of horses, Williams and Pryce that attack was the best policy, Mayol merely the first step towards Tijuana ninety miles away.

On 8 April their scouts reported that Mayol and his 600 Mexican regulars, supported by artillery, had reached a flat-topped *mesa* five miles south of Mexicali. Unaware that they intended by-passing the town, Williams and Pryce rode out to meet them at the head of an 80-strong force of insurgents, only thirty of these mounted, the rest trailing behind on foot beside a wagon with a canvas top, red crosses stitched on either side. This was the battalion 'ambulance,' driven by 'Doc' Larkins, a 24-year-old who claimed to have received his medical training in Canada. Several supply wagons, and a herd of prize Herefords followed at the rear, from which it was evident to anyone watching that the Foreign Legion had no plans to return to Mexicali. It was Tijuana or bust after defeating Mayol![5]

Crossing the sixty-foot wash of the New River, bone-dry again following the winter flood, the *insurrectos* turned south, advancing slowly after reconnoitring the desert ahead. But two hours later on John Little's Ranch they were caught in an open cornfield by Mexican machine gun and artillery fire. Shells screamed overhead, kicking up great clouds of dust and sand, the Magonistas diving for cover in the craters gouged in the desert floor. Pinned down by two chattering Hotchkisses, with Williams dying at his side, part of his head blown off, and the ambulance wagon abandoned by 'Doc' Larkins after it was hit, Pryce sent 'Dynamite' Bill, the oldest man in the Second Battalion to attack the machine guns with his homemade bombs. Bill had always been concerned about the absence of rebel artillery, so he had cut a long rusty section of two-inch iron water pipe into nine-inch lengths, filled these with dynamite and stopped up each end with a wooden plug, leaving a small hole at one end through which he could insert a piece of fuse wire. The fuses were tucked in the crown of the black round hat Bill always wore.

Crawling to the edge of the Encina Canal, he lit the fuses from the end of his cigar, lobbing his bombs at the enemy. As each sailed across the canal, Bill was heard to shout, 'Go away, bad men.' Convinced the *insurrectos* had artillery, the Mexicans did pull back for a time. But soon the Hotchkisses were back in action, the *insurrectos* even more exposed to the deadly chatter of the machine guns as the tall grain was flattened. It was only after one of Bill's homemade bombs knocked out a machine gun that they were able to escape the ambush, the survivors struggling back to Mexicali, protesting that the *federales* took no prisoners, bayoneting the wounded where they fell in the cornfield. Carried to a field hospital set up by U.S. Army surgeons in Calexico to receive the wounded from both sides, Williams survived for about two hours. Before he died, he was identified as a deserter from the Ninth U.S. Infantry.[6]

News of the Foreign Legion's defeat was taken to the Mexican General Salinas by a mounted rebel, his one arm shot clean through and flapping uselessly at his side. Falling exhausted from his saddle in front of Salinas' headquarters he burst into tears. 'We have been slaughtered,' he cried. 'My pal was killed beside me.' Asked who that was, he replied, 'General Stanley' – the name by which Williams was affectionately known to his troops. Salinas was indifferent to Williams' fate. 'I told him he was a fool when he said he was going out to fight. If he had remained here the *federales* would have been forced to attack us in a position of our own choosing.'[7]

That anyone escaped the massacre in the barley field was because Mayol chose not to press home his rout of the rebel army. The scrap with the Magonistas may have been a diversion en route to the Colorado River water works at Andrade, but it had cost the lives of 40 insurgents and twelve Mexicans. The following morning, Pryce led his men, this time unmolested, on to the battlefield, to recover the bodies, loading them aboard the supply wagons abandoned by the insurgents as they fled. The mules had been shot in their harness, but the provisions aboard the wagons were untouched, the Mexicans suspecting they were booby-trapped. Later that day, Williams and the rebel dead were buried in a mass grave in the small cemetery behind the bullring in Mexicali.

Colonel Mayol decided to rest his regulars for a day at the Encina Canal before resuming the march to the Colorado. Provided they did not advance within a mile of his camp, the *insurrectos* were permitted to move about freely. Then from behind their barbed-wire fortifications they observed a quite remarkable scene on the afternoon after the battle when the entire Mexican army, together with camp followers – scores of women and children – stripped naked and bathed together in the Encina Canal. Like an infection, the urge to wash away the dust, dirt and fear of battle spread to the *gringos* who had themselves accumulated a small band of camp followers. Together they too plunged into the water, the two armies soon fraternising in what was the main source of drinking water for the settlers of Imperial Valley. When surprise was expressed that Mayol had so many camp followers he said, 'The women are good marchers. We came all the way from Ensenada in thirteen days.'[8]

That same night, the surviving *gringo* insurgents gathered in the bullring to take a vote, unanimously electing the Welshman Caryl ap Rhys Pryce the new *generalissimo* of the Second Battalion of the Liberal Army in Lower California. 'Melbourne' Hopkins would be his second-in-command.[9]

After the massacre in the cornfield at John Little's Ranch, Pryce prepared to lead his ragged band of desperadoes, deserters, political idealists and escaped convicts (the Magonistas now had several including Mojave Red, a giant with a reputation for beating people to death) across one of most inhospitable tracks of country in the whole of Mexico, to Tijuana, and another battle. Perhaps Pryce was flattered that his undoubted military expertise and leadership qualities were recognised by a rascally rabble, none of who would have given him the time of day if they met in any other circumstances. Most felt they owed their lives to Pryce; that without his leadership they would be lying with their comrades in the small cemetery at the back of the bullring. To them, he was a mercenary, pure and simple, the only man capable of leading them to the elusive pot of gold, if it existed. It did not concern them that unlike some of those they fought alongside, Pryce was not constantly ranting on about the socialist Utopia that awaited a Magonista victory, although there would be moments when even he would unearth the most cherished thoughts of Ricardo Flores Magon for public consumption.[10]

The idealists were still drifting into camp, but for the majority the focus had moved beyond the paltry 160 acres of desert that Magon had promised each volunteer. By now their sights were set on the millions of acres that American and European investors had bought from Diaz for a few dollars. When Diaz was gone it would be 'to the victors the spoils.' Who was to say in the political and social upheaval that inevitably followed revolution, whether Otis, Spreckles, and Randolph Hearst, another newspaper tycoon with huge interests in Mexico, had any legal title to their 'principalities'? No wonder foreign investors wanted their governments to end the uprising in Baja California quickly.

By the time Pryce took command, the promises and political objectives of the Liberal Junta in Los Angeles were already beginning to wear thin. None of those who now carried the Magonista flag in Lower California had ever met any member of a Junta that chose to run its revolution at arm's length. Up to that point, no one from Los Angeles had even visited the front line, their only communication being telegrams instructing the Magonistas where to send the money collected from persons crossing the border at the Mexicali Customs Post. When much later an emissary did arrive from the Junta, he was more concerned with auditing the insurgents' war chest, than offering tactical advice, fleeing at the first sign of trouble.

The only reward the rebels could see for their efforts was land, and as their leader, General Pryce was probably expecting to take the largest slice. President Diaz and his ruling clique always insisted that because the majority were Americans, the Magonistas were a front for a filibuster, a huge land-grab supported by powerful U.S. interests, the ultimate goal being the annexation by the United States of the Baja Peninsular of Lower California. There were many precedents for this, the most celebrated the filibuster led by William Walker, the so-called 'grey-eyed man of destiny.' Sixty years earlier with a force of 46 bigoted, white supremacists from Kentucky and Tennessee, Walker, then only 26, had sailed to La Paz, capital of the southern half of the Baja Peninsula to establish a 'slave state' well out of reach of the emancipators in Washington. Lower California had always been thought of as Uncle Sam's lost province, many in the United States turning a blind eye to attempts at annexation. At the time, Walker's filibuster was seen by southern senators as an opportunity to add new slave votes to their lobby in the United States Senate. As soon as he landed at La Paz, Walker established the Louisiana Code, a simple method of introducing slavery to Baja California. A flag was raised and he proclaimed himself President, an event the native Indians viewed with little interest.

Walker's next stop had been Ensenada, the northern capital. Reinforced by several hundred more pro-slavers, all strapping six-footers from the South's wealthiest plantation families, he seized several towns along the coast, issued more proclamations, in the process impressing the Mexicans by his bravery, always leading his men in a fight. When finally they rebelled against his iron discipline, Walker shot those who tried to desert and flogged the rest. But the colony was collapsing, and after leaving a small garrison at Ensenada, he headed eastwards with the bulk of his force across the mighty sierra of San Pedro Martir and down to the Colorado Delta, losing most of his provisions, cattle and horses in the swollen river. Close to starvation, and fighting Indians every step of the way, the filibusterers finally reached the U.S. border at Mexicali, surrendering to an army patrol. For his action against a friendly nation, Walker was tried in a San Francisco court – and acquitted. The garrison at Ensenada held out as long as its ammunition lasted – then died from the dagger and garrotte.[11] Walker was later killed when he attempted a similar stunt in Nicaragua.

To Diaz and his supporters, Pryce and his Foreign Legion were no different, filibusterers, trying to seize Baja California. Even the Mexicans among the insurgents would have been conscious of the ambitions of their foreign *compadres*. Texas, New Mexico, Arizona and southern California had already been lost to Uncle Sam, while much of the land, on which the Magonistas now unfurled their revolutionary banner, had already been misappropriated by foreigners. On account of this, the friction between the Mexican and *gringo* insurgents was probably congenital, almost certainly irreconcilable.

Cast adrift by their political masters in Los Angeles, and left to fend for themselves in an inhospitable wilderness, the opportunity to acquire land gave the Magonistas their only real sense of purpose. And now with Pryce as leader they may have seen themselves following in the footsteps of 'Filibuster' Walker across the high sierras to Tijuana, and then on to the capital at Ensenada. While Pryce might never have subscribed to the anarchist aspirations of Ricardo Flores Magon, a filibuster was something this son of the British Raj could understand after ten years defending British interests in Africa. Unless Pryce had a more profound, yet undisclosed, reason for continuing to 'revolutionise,' there appears to be no other explanation why he chose not only to remain, but to re-arm, re-provision, and to continue the campaign as leader of the Second Battalion.[12]

Peter Kyne from *Sunset Magazine* caught up with Pryce not long after the rout at John Little's Ranch. A few miles west of Calexico, Kyne turned his buggy south towards the border only to find his crossing blocked by a U.S. Infantry corporal and his patrol. Anticipating this, the reporter had brought along two dollars worth of 'makin's' and some 'chewin', aware from his time in

Cuba that no soldier on active service could survive without tobacco. As the corporal puffed away contentedly, Kyne discovered the corporal had covered himself in glory on a certain day in a certain cornfield in Cavite province, Cuba. The greater surprise was that he, Kyne, was hiding behind a cornstalk in the very same field! After this, the two were brothers for life, the corporal turning a blind eye while Kyne jumped the irrigation ditch. So it was that Kyne became the first correspondent to speak at any length with the Welsh commander of the Magonistas Second Battalion.[13]

Sunset Magazine was popular among older readers, many of whom still believed Wyatt Earp was camped down by the creek, while Geronimo and his Chiricahua Apaches were still raiding wagon trains. Filled with dramatic pictures and short stories glorifying the Old West, its reports were invariably awash with sentimental romanticism. Kyne's report of his meeting with Pryce was not very different but its perceptiveness cannot be discounted on account of its colourfulness. In many ways the lively exchanges between Kyne and the *insurrectos* paint a more accurate picture of the men who were the Magonistas than any pieced together afterwards from sifting through the ashes of the revolution. Later newspaper interviews were the product of snatched conversations with Pryce as the revolution unfolded, then moved towards its finale. Strangely, the only other detailed account of an encounter with a man who came close to changing American/Mexican history – the official report of his subsequent trial – has vanished, there remaining remarkably little in the U.S. National Archives to show that the Magonista insurgency ever took place at all! It is possible the official court record, if it were found, might reveal much about Pryce's intentions. For his part, the Welshman offered few words of explanation. In almost the last paragraph of his account of his meeting with Pryce in Mexicali – and again in San Francisco when the Magonista leader was a fugitive – Kyne hinted he was holding something back: that there was much more to the affair than what he had reported to the mawkish readers of *Sunset Magazine*. If this were true, then Kyne took the secret to the grave, his private papers revealing only how he milked his experiences as material for novels and film scripts in which Pryce may well have been cast in a leading role.

Kyne's first introduction to the Second Division of the Liberal Army came at the *insurrecto* outpost no more than fifty feet from the line. All white, if they had not been burned brown by the desert sun, the seven rebel border guards had an average age of twenty-three, the youngest a nineteen-year-old who laid claim to having served one and a half years in the military academy at San Mateo. An engaging bunch of rascals, the group squatted amongst the baked-clay ruins of an *adobe*, Springfields cradled in their laps or stashed against a crumbling chimney breast.

Their advice to Kyne before he pressed on to rebel headquarters was to conceal the Kodak that hung around his neck. This proved one of his more sensible decisions when suddenly he found that instead of the detour he had planned, he was bang in the middle of the First Division of the Liberal Army, commanded by General Francisco Vasquez Salinas. Kyne deduced the General was the one with rings dangling from his ears, a red, white and green silk handkerchief wrapped around his wicked head, the whole lot half-buried beneath a large straw *sombrero*. The scarf struck him as particularly odd since the colours represented those of President Diaz' Mexico. The Mexican general's gravelly invitation to *vamose* was reinforced by a rusting Long Tom 45-70 Springfield pointed at the abalone-blister scarf pin shielding Kyne's wishbone, his trigger-finger hovering between 'a nasty accident and an execution.' Needing no second invitation, he hopped aboard his buggy and drove at a fast trot through the wrecked town to that part Pryce and his Foreign Legion had made their own.

The line between the two rebel divisions was guarded by a gigantic black man sitting on an empty tomato crate, beneath a shade tree, and nursing a Marlin .32. As the reporter approached, he uncoiled himself and with a crack like a pistol slapped his weapon into port arms. Too big to be cavalry, Kyne guessed he was an infantry deserter, hailing the man with a friendly, 'Hello you buffalo soldier. When did you escape the 24th?'

> Black Guard: 'Teddy Roosevelt done hove me outer de service after that mix-up in Brownsville, Texas,' replied the Negro, bringing his Marlin to order arms. '. . . ahm, dead sorry old-timer but 'less you-all has come ter take on with us, you-all caint go no further.'

94

Kyne: 'Then call the corporal of the guard, if there's such a functionary. I want to have an interview with General Pryce.'

The giant, towering two feet above Kyne, roared like a cannon, 'Corporal o'de guard!' The corporal emerged from one of the few undamaged buildings, a clay-baked adobe with two tiny windows, and after asking the reporter his business, disappeared inside. He emerged a few moments later with a man who identified himself as Captain F. J. Leclare, of Wenatchee, Washington, ex-private First Washington Volunteers, ex-private U.S. Cavalry, ex-sergeant 22nd U.S. Infantry, and whose father was a 'Johnny Reb.' After a hard look at Kyne, he smiled and said General Pryce would see him.

The general, 'a mild-mannered man of 34' with a blond moustache beneath a prominent nose, stood up as Kyne entered and offered him a man's handshake. After Kyne explained his assignment, Pryce invited him to meet the 'boys'. First on parade was 'Melbourne' Hopkins, his second-in-command who had seen service – 'Nytive disturbances in New Guinea,' he called it. Then there was 'Bulldog' Smith, second lieutenant and one of the many 'Smiths' in this scallywag army. 'Slim' Dunn was the third lieutenant, all friendly souls, anxious to show Kyne they were not wicked drifters and thieves but the Christian champions of the poor peons. It was soon evident the Welshman was not amused by the wild allegations about his intentions made by unprincipled American reporters on behalf of their land-owning publishers. Despite these irritations, Pryce remained 'a thorough-going gentleman,' confident and self-assured. He treated everyone with equal politeness, and seemed perfectly at ease in company others of his caste would have found most disagreeable.

The general interrupted his admonition of the Press to introduce a new arrival, top sergeant Paul Schmidt, otherwise P. Smith or P. Silent, late of A Troop, 13th United States Cavalry, a bearded one-time German drill sergeant with a 'a wide mouth like a salmon smiling incessantly, when he wasn't rolling his r's.' When Kyne thought the introductions all over, 'Shorty' O'Donnell shuffled on to centre stage, a position he rarely relinquished. Although a mere private in the Magonista army, he acted like a brigadier, always ready with advice for Pryce, in fact, for anyone within earshot.

'Shorty' had 'large brown eyes, honest like a horse, spoke knowledgeably on every subject, delivering his opinion in a mix of Texan, English and Spanish.' He had never known his father who had died with Custer at Little Big Horn. Shorty rode Texan-style with a double cinch and a hemp rope on his saddle horn. A long-barrelled Colt.45 swung well forward from his shooting hip; two cartridge belts strung Mexican-fashion across his chest.

It was soon unbearably hot and stuffy in the tiny orderly room and at Pryce's suggestion they adjourned to the porch outside the *cuartel* for a friendly chat and distribution of tobacco, the Second Division, almost to a man, crowding around:

> Kyne: General, the impression prevails in the land that you and your troops are freebooters and anarchists, whose sole purpose is plunder; that you're fighting the Federal forces because you think you can whip them and later whip the insurrectos, after which you will cut Lower California away from Mexico and establish a new nation governed on socialist lines.

> Pryce: Not so, I assure you.

> Kyne: Then what are you fighting for?

> Pryce: We are all down here fighting out of sentiment to help these Mexican peons to get their rights. Under the constitution of 1836 – or was it 1858 . . .

> 'Shorty' O'Donnell, interrupting: What's the odds?

> Pryce, continued: Well, that was an excellent constitution, only the Diaz regime didn't carry it out, and now . . .

> Captain Leclare, interjecting: We're fighting por tierra y libertad. That means land and liberty.

> 'Shorty' O'Donnell softly, winking his bright brown left eye, signalling that he could tell the inside story of the Second Battalion: 'Mostly land.'

Kyne: I heard you stole six hundred mules from the Cudahy ranch, and chased Mr Daly, the manager, twenty miles through the mesquite, firing at him in an effort to steal his automobile.

Pryce, sighing: That is not true. We did commandeer about forty mules, and this morning we gave seventeen of them back. Here's a receipt for them, signed by Mr Daly himself. We had five or six mules killed in the scrap last Saturday, and some of the others got away from us, and I guess we have about a dozen left. We took what we needed and when we want more we will go back and get them. These big ranchers are a queer lot – quite queer. If a mountain lion or a bear kills a few heifers and colts, they never know it unless they come across the carcasses; they never think of charging it up to profit and loss because they don't really know how many head of cattle they own. Yet there's the Cudahy Ranch and the California-Mexican Land and Cattle Company actually circulating falsehoods about a few head of mules and cows commandeered in the cause of an oppressed people. Of course these ranchers are Diaz sym-pathisers. Why shouldn't they be? Didn't they get millions of acres of land down here for two bits an acre and don't they work the ranches with peons that they pay thirty cents a day Mex? Suppose we do take a few mules and cows and raid a warehouse? Do they expect us to fight on a slack stomach? This is a war of the common people, and these big rancheros will have to pay the fiddler. Isn't there abstract justice in that?[14]

The Second Battalion's medical orderly was next to introduce himself. 'Doc' Larkins was still smouldering after Mayol's regulars had fired on his ambulance wagon at the Battle of John Little's Ranch the previous Saturday. He swore to Kyne he had carried nothing more dangerous than a pocketknife during the battle. Asked where he had acquired his covered wagon, Larkins replied: 'The Cudahy ranch kindly donated that wagon. But I'll have to move the seat forward next time we go into action or else the legs of the wounded will dangle too far over the tailboard.'

By this time, Kyne was accepted, the rebels assuring him he would always be welcome. As he prepared to leave, an orderly arrived from General Salinas with a message instructing Pryce to exclude visitors from his camp. Clearly, this was directed at Kyne who instinctively rose, until Pryce, holding out a restraining hand, said, 'Sit down, old chap. Pray do,' 'Shorty' O'Connell chipping in, 'T'll with that order. That boy Salinas has all he can do to boss his own outfit. Stay and have dinner with us, roast Hereford heifer, brown gravy, brown potatoes, stewed prunes, boiled rice, onion and lettuce salad, coffee and tortillas.'

After dinner, Kyne drove his buggy down to the California and Mexican Cattle Company Ranch, which straddling the border covered seventy-five square miles of range. The manager, Walter K. Bowker, had seen his cattle raided dozens of times by 'Pryce's bunch who have a lot of my horses and saddles and mules, and I wish they'd give them back.'

Kyne: Why don't you cross the line to Pryce's camp and tell them you want your mules? They're good fellows down there. They won't execute you.

Bowker: I guess I'm safer on this side of the line. They have the mules and they won't give them up and I can't make them, and what's the use? I wouldn't care a rap if it was a real war; but it isn't, and it makes you mad when a man walks up and tells you to get off your horse and walk home, while he takes your best saddler out to be shot in a dirty little fight that doesn't amount to a shucks anyhow. Down at our next ranch we don't have a saddle left and it's commencing to be an annoyance. I could stand anything if they'd only leave our thoroughbred Hereford stock alone. Doggone it – common cow isn't good enough for that gang. No, they must ride into a registered herd, shoot a heifer, and load her in a wagon, while a ten-dollar range cow is exempt. It makes me sore.

Kyne: You can expect nothing less. General Pryce and his division are opposed to special privilege, and are waging war against the aristocracy. They would reduce all cows to a democracy; hence their preference for registered beef.

98

> Bowker (laughing): Going to be here a few days? If you are and you see something you want, ask for it. Everybody does that down here. Need a horse and a saddle? Tell the foreman and he'll give you the pick of the corral.

Before he left, Kyne promised to intercede with Pryce about the manager's blue-blooded Herefords. Returning to the Magonista camp, he was greeted by Second Lieutenant 'Bulldog' Smith, sporting an ivory-handle revolver he had taken from the body of a lieutenant in the Mexican *rurales* (police) after they had hijacked the train to Algodones. Told that General Pryce had a headache and was sleeping, Kyne said to Smith, 'The manager of the C and M ranch presents his compliments to the commanding officer. He knows you boys must eat, but requests you have the goodness to leave his registered Hereford stock along and confine yourself to common cow. He says he has eaten both kinds and has never been able to tell the difference,' to which Smith replied, 'the best in the world is none too good for this outfit.'

Laughing at his little joke, Smith, a good-looking boy of 24, strode out into the hot sun for a spot of baseball practice with a black deserter from the 9th Cavalry. Soon they were joined by others, and as Kyne watched them fielding grounders and flies, he was startled by a grave, refined British voice at his elbow. 'We're all fans here,' said General Pryce, standing in the doorway to the *cuartel*, stroking his blond moustache, watching proudly as his 'boys' romped in the dust.

> Pryce: A bully fine lot. I thought I'd lose half of them after the first fight, but it only seems to have wet their whistle. Still, they haven't looked on their own dead, and that makes a difference. I'll lose lots of them if I don't give them more action. The young bloodhounds! They must have it.

> Kyne nodded: They'll respect even a federale after they've got into the blast of a machine gun some day, and a dozen of them get themselves killed. If they'll stick for the insurrecto cause or the sheer love of fighting after that, you'll have a great troop and I'll meet you down in Ensenada. You can invite me up the capital for dinner.

Pryce: Quite so, quite so. I was in the Imperial Light Horse under Woolls-Sampson, and I know. I have the two medals and the four bars. My boys have much to learn but they won't run until I tell them.

Kyne then delivered his message from the manager of the C and M Ranch about his Hereford stock.

Pryce: My compliments to the manager, the pleasure of whose acquaintance I don't happen to have, and tell him that if he'll have his boys drive up some of the common stock where we can get them without too much trouble, we'll be very glad to leave his Herefords alone. By the way, we're awfully hard up for some thread, some shoemaker's needles, a bradawl and some beeswax. About fifty cents worth, I would so – if you don't mind. Thank you very much.

Pryce returned to his *cuartel*, reappearing minutes later with his six-shooter and hat.

Pryce: I say, old fellow. I suppose you'll want an interview with General Salinas. I'm going up to his quarters and if you care to come along I'll be very glad to introduce you and do what I can, you know.

Together, the pair strolled through Mexicali to the Mexican camp, where the general left Kyne's side to enter an *adobe* warehouse. After successfully pleading the reporter's case, Pryce came to the door with Salinas beside him, a stocky character of about fifty-five, a large roan moustache, and eyes red and bloodshot after a night on mescal. The Mexican glared at Kyne's Kodak as he raised it for a picture. Producing a pack of Mexican cigarettes, Salinas gave one to Pryce, deliberately ignoring Kyne who got the message and turned to leave. According to Kyne, Pryce was so embarrassed by the snub to his guest that he 'rested his blue eyes affectionately on the Salinas Adams-apple, and but for his British reticence would probably have observed: "Why, you outrageous Indian idol you, I soldiered where you couldn't be a dog robber, and if it wasn't for the little spiggoty men around you with Spring-fields, I'd take your cartridge belt away from you and spank you with it."

After this, Pryce took Kyne to the back of the bullring and the graves of General Stanley Williams and the others who died at the Battle of John Little's Ranch.

> Pryce: He was quite a man. They turned a couple of old Hotchkiss on us and Stanley was hit in the back of the head. Williams was semi-conscious for two hours after he was hit. At four o'clock he opened his eyes – we were lying in the barley field – and Shorty gave him a drink. "Are you still fighting", he asked. Shorty told him we hadn't started yet, and he murmured "Good boys! Good boys!" That was the last he said. He was quite a man.[15]

NOTES

1. *Sunset Magazine*, September 1911.
2. *San Diego Union*, 12 April 1911.
3. *San Diego Union*, 11 April 1911.
4. Ibid., 8 April 1911.
5. Ibid., 18 April 1911.
6. Ibid.
7. *San Diego Union*, 10 April 1911.
8. Ibid.
9. Ibid., 11 April 1911.
10. Ibid., 19 April 1911.
11. Lowell Blaisdell, 'Was it revolution or filibustering?' *Pacific Historical Review* (1962), pp. 147-164.
12. Pryce Papers. Copy of undated letter from Pryce to Hattie Biggs written at time of his incarceration in Los Angeles.
13. *Sunset Magazine*, September 1911.
14. Ibid; also *San Diego Union*, 19 April 1911.
15. *Sunset Magazine*, September 1911.

Chapter 5

Buenos Dias, Tijuana!

I write you to instruct your people not to come on our battlefield. Every time we have a battle your people run excursion trains to the border. This causes embarrassment and interferes with the discipline of our troops as your girls make catcalls to my men. Your people are buying the loot of Tijuana from Madero's rebels (*sic*) and they are saying it is priced too high. There are many other things we could complain of but if these rules are observed we can fight out this war in peace.[1]

President Diaz to President Taft

General Pryce's 'young bloodhounds' were tired of licking their wounds in Mexicali. After being routed by Mayol's regulars they were thirsting for revenge, beating out the message by rattling their tin plates on the wooden trestles at mess time in the bullring. The General stroked his blond moustache, muttered, 'Patience lads, patience,' and sent them out to rustle more cattle and commandeer more groceries. After three weeks, the commissary was well provisioned, and the armoury re-stocked, a consignment of battered Springfields arriving from San Diego, bought not by the Junta but by the writer, John Kenneth Turner, who had spotted them in Hamburger's Hardware Store, on special offer at $1-98 each as cosy-corner ornaments. Only later did the *insurrectos* discover that very little of their ammunition fitted the antique Springfields. Encouraged however by the delivery of the rifles, Pryce announced they would break camp the following morning and head for Tijuana. In doing so, Pryce violated one of the few direct orders he was ever to receive from the Liberal Junta, which had instructed him to march east to attack Mayol's *federales* guarding the dykes under construction along the Colorado. Any officer ignoring the orders of his commander-in-chief could, in normal circumstances, expect to be dismissed the service, and Pryce the professional soldier would have known this. But these were far from the normal circumstances of war, and Pryce's insubordination was quietly forgotten.[2]

The largest centre of population in Lower California with 2000 inhabitants, Tijuana, fifteen miles from San Diego, was little more than a gambling town for American tourists in search of cheap whisky and even cheaper women, its main street lined with saloons, brothels and gift shops. It was also the gateway to Lower California's Pacific coast, and the capital at Ensenada. The easiest and quickest route to Tijuana from Mexicali was to follow the old Butterworth Stagecoach trail north of the border, but that was now closed to the rebels by the presence of U.S. troops. This left the Magonistas facing a 90-mile trek, across desert as dry as the Sahara, then up the narrow Picacho Pass over a 5000ft mountain range of monstrous granite boulders piled at the desert's edge by some primeval force. On reaching the *mesa,* the trail wound its way across a flat upland plateau covered in waist-high mesquite and prickly desert plants that tore at the riders and their animals, before descending into the Tijuana Valley. Leading a force of heavily armed men and their wagons through such an inhospitable wilderness was a feat in itself, especially since it was likely to culminate in the insurgents confronting seasoned Mexican regulars in battle.

It would have been an early morning start, Pryce anxious to negotiate the Picacho Pass before the greatest heat of the day. In places, wagons could barely squeeze along the track clinging precariously to the mountainside, the pass so narrow, that if ambushed, the *insurrectos* stood no chance. But Pryce was determined to use the pass rather than struggle over the mountains as the ill-fated Rodriguez expedition had done a month earlier, so sapping the strength of the insurgents that they were in no condition for the fight at Tecate.

It was the first week of May 1911, the Sonoran desert already gripped by the withering heat of summer, its intensity fooling the unwary as convincingly as the sweet-water lake shimmering at the edge of every desert traveller's thirst-ravaged imagination.

One moment, there was a confidence and bounce in his stride; the next his lights were knocked out, and lying unconscious beneath that blistering sun he was as good as dead.

In the cool darkness before dawn, the ragged band of female camp followers prepared breakfast as they would have done a thousand times, slapping flat *tortillas* into shape between the palms of their hands. Although they rarely ever seemed to bathe, not even splashing water on their dust-caked faces during the heat of the day, the preparation of *tortillas* was always preceded by a ritualistic washing of the hands. This preliminary rite concluded, flour, salt, and lard was mixed with a little water into thick dough broken into balls the size of chicken eggs. One by one, these little spheres were rolled between the palms of their hands, gently kneaded between their fingers, then flattened into a pancake some twelve inches in diameter, an eighth of an inch thick. *Tortillas* were cooked one at a time on an iron griddle, not infrequently receiving a delectable further browning by being cast unceremoniously upon the embers. Easily digested, these little cakes would have formed as much a part of the *gringos* rations on the march to Tijuana, as hard tack and beans washed down with black coffee, occasionally supplemented by broiled doves and cotton-tail rabbits shot from the saddle. But there would be no recreational gunplay on this trip. The rebels had as much beef as they could eat – dried slabs of it strapped to the backs of the mules they had rustled from the C and M Ranch.

Before sun up, the Second Battalion, 200 men all mounted, set off at a Mexican trot, two by two, each carrying 200 rounds of ammunition slung on belts either festooned around their waists, over their shoulders bandolier fashion, or across saddles like so many hoops. Strapped to the flanks of their horses was an assortment of precious water canteens, all shapes and sizes. Every desert rider knew about thirst, that eight hours without water was the limit of a man's endurance before he divested himself of all clothing to plunge into the clear pool of sweat water splashing just beyond his reach. By nightfall, Pryce expected his Cocopah Indian scouts to have led the column to the first water, the ominously named Bitter Creek high on the *mesa*.

The trail west from Mexicali was clearly marked, meandering through thick clumps of green, spidery creosote bush poking through the salt-encrusted sand at stirrup height. Not far behind was the team of C and M mules hauling the army's provisions, and Doc Larkins' Red Cross ambulance, an even larger Red Cross stitched on its side this time so that it would be unmistakable the next time they ran into the *federales*. Following up the rear, were the female camp followers, their few belongings wrapped in bundles, and a handful of copper-hued urchins in tow. The women shuffled along in their *guarachas,* rawhide sandals worn to protect the soles of their feet from cactus thorns. Everything in the desert was prickly, the women carrying their town shoes strapped to their forearms, like badges of respectability.

On the way to Picacho Pass, the trail first brushed the edge of a great salt lake. Sixty miles long and ten wide, the white expanse of Laguna Salada spilled across the desert floor like drifting snow, all flickering mirages and treacherous quick sands. Fed by over-flows from the Hardy River (itself a geological freak born amongst a clutch of volcanic mud springs) and the Colorado Delta, Laguna Salada expanded and retreated. After that winter's floods it was at its deepest in living memory but that still only six feet. For the *insurrectos* seeing it for the first time, it must have seemed a terrifying obstacle but the more fascinating on account of the riches reputedly buried beneath its glistening surface. Many of those with Pryce – soldiers-of-fortune alert to their next profitable adventure – would have heard the legend of the lost Spanish galleon with its cargo of black pearls bound for Madrid, which had sunk there four hundred years ago when Laguna Salada was an inlet on the Sea of Cortez. Pryce knew the story from his second-in-command Melbourne Hopkins who chatted about it constantly. The route to the sea had since been closed by silt deposited by the ever-changing course of the Colorado, but the legend continued to entice treasure seekers.

After leaving the lake, the trail next wound its way through a desert of encrusted sand, from all appearances sound, but in reality so completely undermined by burrowing animals that any deviation from the path risked plunging a horse up to its belly. Then there were the sidewinders, a short, poisonous snake with a kick like a mule. If a horse scratching amongst the *mesquite* for a few green shoots was bitten on its nostrils, this was usually fatal, nostrils swelling, and the animal suffocating unless its rider had the presence of mind to force open the animal's nostrils. For such emergencies, seasoned desert riders always carried short lengths of stiff rubber tubing in their saddlebags.

Before midday the column arrived at the base of the rocky sierras. At first sight there seemed no way to ascend until the Indian scouts led the *insurrectos* up an indistinct and fearfully abrupt trail, the Picacho Pass. As they climbed, the rebels would have gulped on their canteens, the exertion of the ascent only alleviated by copious draughts of water. At every twist, the trail looked as if it were about to pinch out. The mules, more sure-footed than the horses, were best equipped for the climb until half way up the pass the majority bolted, stampeding down the trail and into the desert, carrying the army's provisions all the way back to Mexicali. Dried beef, biscuits and *tortillas* were all that was left for the rest of the journey to Tijuana, the rebels ravenous by the time they eventually got there.

As the column of men rose above the plain a magnificent view would have unfolded below: at their feet the desert, stuck fast between two towering mountain ranges, at its heart Laguna Salada, a shimmering amoeba swimming through air so hot, so heavy with suspended sand, that the haze seemed to coagulate into a wall rising thousands of feet above the plain. In the distance beyond, where the naked battlements of the Cocopah Sierras met the plain, drifting sand transformed giant boulders into so many pebbles on a beach. Then further, the muddy delta of the Colorado, the river rolling lazily into the Sea of Cortez along a dozen meandering channels.

After five hours climbing, and probably at least a gallon of water per man, the Second Battalion arrived at the crest and entered upon the flat *mesa* stretching for as far as the eye could see. Covered in mesquite, scrub oaks and stunted pinion trees, most of it never more than then the height of a horse, the high chaparral was broken occasionally by white granite stubs of ancient mountains worn down by time, looking like the weathered tombstones of some long-lost civilisation. A storm had been building over Laguna Salada as they neared the end of Picacho Pass, the white, fleecy clouds rising like a Doric pillar thousands of feet into the sky until the flat-topped thunderhead towered above the sierras. Suddenly, the stifling heat vanished; the air grew chilly, discoloured, heavy, possessed with strange uncanny moaning. Gripped by the icy cold, whipped by the wind, the rebel column moved slowly out on to the vastness of the *mesa* cloaked in a depressing yellow gloom. Then the storm broke, amidst crash upon crash of thunder and vivid flashes of lightning, a shower of hail stones the size of pigeons eggs beat down upon the men. Horses reared and bolted in every direction, their riders clinging on desperately as they crashed through the dense chaparral. For twenty minutes it raged, soaking the *insurrectos* crouched on the ground, steadying their panic-stricken mounts. Every cattle track became a rushing torrent, not one distinguishable from the next. When it finally abated, even the Indian scouts were unable to find the trail immediately. By the time they did, the terrifying heat had returned, a few tiny pools of water all that was left to mark the passing of the storm.

With night closing in, the *insurrectos* grew restless and filled with forebodings. While some jogged steadily on with fixed determination, others declared they had lost their way and would never find water again and perish. Then on reaching the brow of a steep sandbank they saw fires twinkling beneath them in the darkness, the Indian scouts motioning that below was Bitter Creek. Urging their horses forward through the deep sand, the rebels raced for the water, only to be driven back by the overpowering stench from the rotting carcasses of several mules scattered around the wells. The water was undrinkable except for one hole half filled with sand which, when excavated, produced sufficient to re-fill canteens and water the horses. That day they had covered barely twenty-five miles. The remainder of the journey, so Pryce was assured, would be easier, certainly when they entered the lush Tijuana Valley.[4]

Having no wish to attack Tijuana at the end of a long ride, Pryce planned to camp the following night at Tecate thirty miles from Tijuana, there to await the arrival of Berthold and reinforcements from El Alamo, unaware that by then Berthold was dead from gangrene poisoning and that the survivors were led by an American army deserter, Jack Mosby. The second day's ride was uneventful, until just short of Tecate when scouts reported that the Magonistas from El Alamo had recaptured the town, and were camped on the Morales Ranch. Not only was there no Berthold, but Mosby had also been wounded in an unplanned skirmish with a company of *federales*. Mosby and his Magonistas had been reconnoitring the area, when rounding a rocky outcrop they ran into the stage escorted by *federales*. The combatants had no choice but engage each other at point-blank range, during which exchange Mosby was shot through his left lung. Lying on the ground, and groaning loudly, he continued to direct the battle until the *federales* retreated leaving the stage behind. Bundled aboard, Mosby was rushed across the line to Things Store in American Tecate where he was treated by a U.S. Army surgeon and packed off to hospital.[5]

Besides the need to rest before the assault on Tijuana, there was another good reason to hang on at Tecate. The Liberal Junta had at last promised to send help, namely a Colt machine gun together with a rapid-fire expert named McDonald. For weeks Pryce had pleaded with Magon for weapons and ammunition, and at last the machine gun, one of two on order costing $600 each, was due to be delivered to the rebel camp. The problem with the rebel armoury was that it tended to go walkabout, the *insurrectos* a notoriously unstable bunch whose enthusiasm for the fight waned whenever times were hard, or the spoils of war better somewhere else. The Magonista revolution would always be a crazy merry-go-round of arms procurement.

The rebels waited a week at Tecate with no sign of any machine gun or the man McDonald. Growing restless as rations ran low and desertions increased, Pryce sent them out to raid the Morales Ranch abandoned by the Mayor of Tecate when he fled for the umpteenth time across the line into the United States. Morales was no friend of the Magonistas, and his stock was considered fair booty of war.' When at last McDonald arrived from San Diego, it was minus the machine gun. Once again, Magon and his Liberal Junta had failed to deliver. But Pryce could delay no longer. Dissension was spreading through the ranks and he was having great difficulty holding his army together. On the morning of 7 May after the women camp followers were locked in a saloon at Tecate, for their own safety, the rebel column set off on the last leg to Tijuana.[6]

West of Tecate the country changed dramatically, the trail descending from the scrub of the high chaparral into the green

Tijuana Valley. Where previously the prevailing wind had blown out of the hot interior of the Sonoran Desert scorching everything in its path, now it came from across the Pacific dumping thirty or more inches of rain in the Valley in most years. Blessed with a Mediterranean climate not unlike Southern California just across the border, Mexican farmers were able to grow five crops of alfalfa a year, winter barley and other grains, together with a bewildering variety of vegetables mainly for the American market. The richness of the land must have lifted the spirits of the *insurrectos*, most of whom would have been more than satisfied to settle for a slice of this on the conclusion of the revolution.

But there was something missing as the column drove on to Tijuana at the mouth of the valley where it met the Pacific Ocean. Like a grounded Marie Celeste, the fields were deserted, winter barley waiting to be harvested, acres of alfalfa flattened by herds of stray heifers. Where there should have been white pyjama-suited *peons*, heads bowed beneath oversize *sombreros*, hoeing and tilling rows of carrots and lettuces, there was no one. The population had fled; the doors of their *adobes* hung open; there were no copper-hued urchins playing in the dust. For almost thirty miles, Tijuana Valley had been abandoned as soon as word arrived that the 'Mexicali bunch' was on its way. Most had crossed the border, either to relatives, or to shelter in the refugee camps opened by the U.S. Army. There they would wait until the revolution passed by.

The poorest part of Tijuana was clustered around the usually dry bed of the river of the same name, a clutter of often temporary, ramshackle wooden buildings sloping up the hill towards the more permanent dwellings, the most prominent of these a white-painted old *adobe* mission, the *cuartel* (federal administration centre), a jail, the bullring – one of the most popular in all Mexico – and forty feet from the border, the most important building of all, the Mexican Custom House. Directly facing it on the American side stood United States Customs. For both countries, the collection of taxes on goods and people crossing the line was a lucrative business. By the time the Rio Tijuana reached the coast, it had vanished beneath the bed of the river leaving the town a desert island surrounded by sand-grey hills dotted with clumps of mesquite.

As early as 1911 Tijuana was a destination for thousands of American tourists lured by cheap goods, and in the days before Mexican cooking migrated across the border, offering a rare opportunity to sample foreign food. But most made the fifteen-mile journey by train from San Diego to the border for an adventurous night of non-stop revelry, dice, faro and roulette, Chuck-a-Luck and Klondyke. In conservative middle America where the majority blamed all the country's problems on the twin demons of liquor and gambling, Tijuana was an evil, wide-open frontier town, at a time when apart from Nevada, gaming was outlawed throughout the United States, the law as vigorously enforced and violently policed as liquor prohibition a decade later. For the professional gamblers driven underground by prohibition, Tijuana was just a train-ride away.

Although Tijuana's frightened citizens had been expecting an attack for two months, they were disinclined to abandon the town if it meant switching off the flow of tourist dollars. Instead, casino owners and saloon managers stuck to the business of fleecing the tourists while their wives and children crossed the border to safety every night.

Tijuana garrison numbered about 100 men, 25 of these *federales*, the remainder *rurales* (police) and pressed men. The commander, Governor Jose Marie Larroque, ordered a defensive wall of sandbags built around the Custom House, the *cuartel*, and bullring, above which he raised the red, white and green flag of Mexico. Laroque was not a happy man, believing himself isolated and abandoned when his superior Governor Vega of Ensenada refused reinforcements. Vega wanted every last soldier to defend the capital from imminent attack. The garrison's anxiety was clear to any visitor raising his camera to snap the defenders who, clad in their blue and white uniforms, paced nervously back and forth through the narrow alleyways. In the hills beyond Tijuana, the presence of Mexican scouts, their broad-brimmed *sombreros* bobbing up and down as they rode between the *arroyos,* was obvious from the occasional flash of the sun's rays bouncing off a rifle barrel.[7]

Margaret Holbrook Smith was one of those tourists who visited the town on the eve of the battle with the Magonistas:

It was Sunday May 7 and we were allowed to enter Tijuana for we were anxious to behold – in this age of peace – a town actually prepared for a siege, she wrote later. We were advised not to snap our cameras nor to comment on the breastworks thrown up nor to make laughing criticism of anything we should see.

The last warning was most unnecessary for no one with a ray of humanity could have felt anything but sympathy for the band of federales and rurales prepared to fight for their homes. For months they had been waiting for the attack, and it was pitiful to see their strained and anxious faces. Almost all the women and children had been sent on to American soil, so only the defenders were left in town. Everywhere the air was tense with expectation. All that night they kept watch, and with morning came the word the rebels were marching from the springs only two miles distant.[8]

The defenders of Tijuana were not the only ones to know battle was soon to be joined.[9] Spectators were streaming out of neighbouring San Diego to claim their grandstand view of the action, a convoy of model-T Fords snaking along the desert road to the border like a black reptile.

General Pryce had divided his Magonistas into three companies: A led by Captain LeClare of Wenatchee, B by Captain Paul Smith, otherwise Silent or Schmidt, and C commanded by Captain Sam Wood, yet another of the Boer War veterans with which the ranks of the *insurrecto* army were liberally sprinkled. Wood was sent ahead with fifty men to reconnoitre the defences, arriving two miles south of the town shortly before dawn on 8 May where they engaged a patrol billeted in Diego Aharadu's ranch house. One burst of gunfire sent the *federales* scuttling back to Tijuana, and into the trenches dug around the bullring.[10]

The first sign of the rebels, for the hundreds of spectators gathered with their picnic baskets at the top of the slope on the American side, was a line of men running and ducking through the sagebrush at the edge of Tijuana. Suddenly, as one, they dropped to their knees, opening up with Winchesters. Across open

111

ground, a Mexican woman carrying two children raced for her life. A man driving his horse through the deep sand in the river bottom towards the U.S. border crumpled and fell to the ground. Tiny geysers of sand kicked up around the trenches of the Mexican defenders as the rebel riflemen found their range. Through the crossfire, two Americans trapped in Tijuana by the rebel attack, tried to make their escape, appearing out of a cloud of dust crouched over a motorcycle heading at high speed for the border. Moments later in another explosion of screaming tyres, a model-T Ford raced own the main street for the line. The most inveterate gamblers had decided to leave![11]

Ricochets from the battle were whining across the line, scattering the spectators amongst the mesquite or diving for cover behind the nearest sand hill.

> When the bullets came our way and whizzed too near us, wrote Margaret Smith, we retreated to the canyons, and by lying down on the hillside could continue our vigil through the glasses. These bullets I was told were dum-dum bullets, which spread or flatten out as they strike. At first it did not seem possible it was a real war. The rapid shots sounded to me exactly like quail shooting, and the volleys as if some target practice were in progress.[12]

By now all roads led to Tijuana, San Diegans so excited by the battle that the San Diego-Arizona Eastern Railroad Company, which operated the small section of track to Tijuana, laid on special excursions to the front line. Soon the pressure of sightseers with their picnic baskets was such that the sheriff, fearing the situation was beyond his control, asked Captain F. A. Wilcox, and his 30th U.S. Infantry patrolling the border, for assistance. The frenzy of interest was also too much for the captain who, snatching up a loud hailer, bellowed at the crowd, 'You people had better get away from here before someone is shot.' His patience finally snapped when two Mexicans sharing the same horse, rode calmly out of Tijuana, explaining they were off to visit relatives in San Diego for the day. After that, the Captain closed the border, although too late to stop three escaped inmates from Tijuana Jail from crossing it in the confusion.[13]

Pryce and his Magonistas had easily secured the southern perimeter of the town, leaving the besieged garrison with its back to the wall, its only escape route into the United States blocked by Captain Wilcox and his infantry patrol. After the initial rebel thrust the two sides relaxed for the rest of the morning, occasionally exchanging fire, the Magonistas planting a 'rogue' bullet or two above the heads of the grandstand crowds on the hillside along the American side.

Pryce's waiting game was, however, too much for one young Mexican *federale* officer, Lieutenant Guerrero. Riding up to the border, and so clearly the worse for drink that he was barely able to remain astride his horse, but with another refugee from the battle, an American named Joe Mumford, clinging to his waist, Guerrero threatened the assembled soldiers and civilians with all manner of reprisals for the action of the *gringo insurrectos*. Fearing what might happen next, Captain Wilcox ordered his sergeant to seize the bridle of Guerrero's horse and arrest him. But the Mexican was having none of this, and had to be restrained when he appeared to reach for his Luger. With his pistol, cartridge belt, and horse now impounded, Guerrero hopped back across the line and, ignoring the exhortations of his Mexican comrades, stood toe-to-toe with Captain Wilcox screaming insults until a Mexican Customs officer raised his rifle as if to shoot the rebellious young officer. But Wilcox refused to be provoked, even when Guerrero defiantly threw down his last remaining weapon, his sword and, holding his arms wide, implored the U.S. soldiers to shoot him on the spot. Finally retreating towards Tijuana, Guerrero was last seen escorted by another *federale* who had ridden out to meet him, firing his revolver in the air as though shepherding the rebellious officer back to the corral.[14]

By 4.30 p.m. order was restored at the crossing point in time for the arrival of General Tasker H. Bliss, Commander of the Department of California, a motorised convoy depositing the General and his phalanx of staff officers at the line in a great flourish of salutes and ceremony. The General's last brush with the rebels was at Mexicali two months earlier when he was sent by President Taft to investigate whether they posed any threat to the United States. Then he had reported that the Magonistas were little more than 'organised bandits.'[15] Now they were knocking on

America's front door. For more than an hour, Bliss stood at the crossing point almost motionless, surrounded by his staff officers, all of them watching the rebels intently through field glasses. As night settled, the General and his entourage climbed aboard their vehicles and roared back to San Diego.

By then the fate of the beleaguered garrison was as good as sealed, and with no intention of missing the final act, the hundreds of spectators settled down in the surrounding hills to await the resumption of the battle. The only incident to relieve the vigil occurred at about 10 p.m. when an explosion of rifle flashes lit up the night sky along the slopes of a low hill east of Tijuana. Lieutenant Guerrero, now sober, had taken a detachment across the dry river bottom in an attempt to outflank the rebels. Realising this, Pryce sent Captain Sam Wood and his C Company in hot pursuit, Guerrero ambushing Wood and fatally wounding him in the engagement. Guerrero was also wounded in the skirmish, but managed to make it back to Tijuana.

Before insurgents and defenders settled down for the night a horse-drawn Red Cross ambulance arrived from San Diego, driven by Dr James Jackson, accompanied by an attractive young nurse. Although there were wounded on either side, Larroque refused the ambulance team permission to enter the town, so the doctor and his nurse spent the night with the hundreds of others waiting in the hills. The rebels were also without a medical orderly, Doc Larkins having deserted across the line as soon as the first shots were fired.

Just before dawn Pryce sent word to Larroque that the rebels were poised to take the town but if the *federales* surrendered they and all property would be spared. His peace overture was rejected, Larroque proclaiming he would never surrender. At first light, Pryce ordered the Magonistas into action, the rebels directing their fire into Tijuana from secure positions along the slopes of low hills south of the town, a strategy loudly applauded by the contingent of U.S. troops and spectators.

Slowly, the rebels moved off the hills, darting from one clump of mesquite to the next. On reaching the edge of the town, Pryce sent a squad of six volunteers commanded by Captain LeClare across the open main street, to secure a strong position on a bank at the rear of Savine's Curio Store, a prominent green-painted building in the centre of Tijuana. On the front porch of the store, they erected a barricade of wooden crates, which, they soon discovered were packed with bottles of local beer. From his vantage point, LeClare directed rifle fire into the Mexican trenches, the captain and his *insurrectos* showered with glass and beer when incoming fire ploughed into the stacked crates. For two hours he and his men held their position, until under cover from the sharpshooters, Pryce advanced with the remainder of the Magonista army.[16] Afterwards, describing the attack to reporters, Pryce boasted that his men, 'showed no quarter or mercy . . . fought like demons, time and again rushing trenches or strongholds in face of a veritable rain of lead.' Greatly outnumbered, the Mexicans fought to the last man. Three in particular caused the greatest number of casualties among rebel ranks. Lodged behind the thick walls of the old *adobe* mission, they picked off the *insurrectos* almost at leisure, leaving Pryce with no option but to set the building alight.[17] After an hour, four rebels got close enough to fire the thatch, two of the defenders being shot down by the Magonistas as they fled the blazing building. The third held his ground, dying in the fire.

Pryce's attention now turned to dislodging defenders from their positions in the bullring. Wasting no time, he ordered the wooden seats fired, the blaze quickly taking hold, two Mexicans perishing in the flames, another joining his comrades in the sandbagged trenches around the Mexican Custom House, their last line of defence. Despite the well-directed fusillade from LeClare and his men, the Mexicans were well dug-in at the Custom House. Then on the slopes across the line, spectators suddenly spotted four *gringos* crawling on their stomachs through the dirt of the main street, before sliding, apparently unnoticed by the defenders, into an abandoned trench, giving them a clearer shot at the remaining Mexicans hidden behind the Custom House breastworks. With their position seemingly lost, the surviving Mexicans broke cover. Pryce, suspecting an outflanking manoeuvre, checked his advance, but instead of a counter attack the *federales* kept on running towards the safety of the western hills. Larroque was dead and Guerrero wounded. The survivors led by Lieutenant Luerdo Gonzales surrendered to Lieutenant Emmons of the 30th Infantry on reaching the border.[18] The spectators who cheered the advance of the rebels now applauded the heroic defenders. William Smythe,

founder of the Little Landers Colony a mile across the valley on
the U.S. side, said after witnessing the action:

> Whatever the merits of the struggle in Mexico, the resis-
> tance offered by the men of Tijuana was worthy of praise.
> They were fighting for their homes and they fought with
> magnificent courage as long as their ammunition lasted
> apparently. Few realise what a frightful strain the people of
> Tijuana have undergone for months, moving their women
> and children across the border night after night while their
> men kept up their weary vigil . . . the fortune of war was
> against them but they added a bright page to the history of
> Lower California.[19]

At the final count the rebels lost seven men killed, the Mexicans
eighteen. Very soon the steady trickle of casualties arriving at the
U.S. Army border post was directed to a field hospital at nearby
Little Landers Colony. The first, a Frenchman only ever known to
his rebel comrades as 'Blackie' staggered across the line bleeding
profusely from a stomach wound. Dr Jackson of the Red Cross
tore couch seats from an automobile to improvise a bed erected
on the station platform but 'Blackie' died within minutes. The
next up was Lieutenant James Dunn with a shoulder wound,
closely followed by Lewis Wilcox, of Grand Rapids, Michigan,
formerly of the Sixth U.S. Infantry, hit in the right hip by a dum-
dum bullet. Luckily, the shell lodged in his cartridge belt and after
the flattened bullet was prised out, a greatly relieved Wilcox
refused an offer of $25 for it from a souvenir hunter.

Through the blackened and smoking ruins of Tijuana, Pryce
headed straight for one of the least damaged of the buildings, the
cuartel. Some instinct told the Welshman where he was likely to
find most booty. Sure enough there was a safe but one that was
very securely locked. At least until it could be opened, this would
be Pryce's headquarters, the general issuing orders that the most
comfortable bed in Tijuana should be found and moved into the
cuartel. If nothing else, he was determined to get a good night's
sleep. Meanwhile, Pryce was taking no chances with his light-
fingered comrades. 'Dynamite Bill' was called to the headquarters
to work on the safe mechanism. Suddenly Bill's fingers froze in

mid-air, hovering above the dials as he spotted wires leading from the back of the safe to beneath the floorboards. 'It's mined', he mumbled, choking on a warning that sent Pryce and company fleeing into the street before a loud explosion destroyed the safe, its contents – and the general's fine bed.[20]

With the winning of the Battle for Tijuana, Pryce and his Magonistas stood on the threshold of an even greater victory. The whole of Baja California beckoned. The Mexican army of Colonel Mayol, the only force capable of preventing the rebels from seizing Lower California, was a hundred miles away patrolling the Colorado River delta flood prevention works. Whatever were Pryce's intentions, the decision on the *insurrectos* next move would be his.

NOTES

1. Letter from President Diaz to President Taft after being told the rebels had captured Tijuana. Clearly, Diaz made the mistake of thinking they were Madero's troops.
2. Romulo Velasco Ceballos, *Se apodera Estados Unidos de Baja California* (Mexico, 1920), pp. 127-128. Since the *federales* captured this letter sent to Pryce at Mexicali, it is always possible he never received it.
3. *Buenos dias, Tijuana* (Phoenix, Arizona State University Library).
4. The journey from Mexicali has been reconstructed by the author from accounts appearing in the *San Diego Union, Calexico Chronicle, San Diego Sun, Los Angeles Times, Los Angeles Examiner* between 1-8 May 1911.
5. *San Diego Union,* 3, 7 May 1911.
6. ibid., 7 May 1911.
7. *San Diego Union,* 8 May 1911.
8. Margaret Holbrook Smith, 'The capture of Tijuana,' *Overland Monthly,* Vol. LVIII, No. 1, July 1911.
9. *San Diego Union,* 8 May 1911.
10. ibid.
11. *San Diego Union,* 9 May 1911.
12. Holbrook, 'The capture of Tijuana.'
13. *San Diego Union,* 10 May 1911.
14. ibid.
15. *Los Angeles Times,* 17 February 1911.
16. *San Diego Union,* 10 May 1911.
17. ibid.
18. ibid.
19. ibid.
20. ibid.

Chapter 6

The Cruise of *HMS Shearwater*

Within the same week that Pryce assumed command of the Magonistas Foreign Legion, events were to occur on the Pacific west coast of both upper and lower California that were to add a bizarre dimension to the deepening mystery surrounding the Welshman's involvement in the Mexican Revolution. The first was a cricket match in San Diego's Babloa Park where the local club were playing an Invitation XI from the British Navy's Pacific West Coast squadron, comprising just two ships, *HMS Algerine* and *HMS Shearwater*. From beneath a clump of lime-green cotton-woods glistening with the first flush of spring, a small group of mostly confused spectators watched the contest between the men in white. To them, the object of the game seemed to be to strike three wooden sticks, the wicket, with a very hard ball, and each time this was accomplished another member of the team would stride out with bat in hand to take his turn at defending them. Occasionally, when the men with the bats hit the ball extremely hard, they scampered between the sticks, an activity greeted with muffled excitement among those who understood what was happening.[1] The announcement of the name of each new batsman arriving at the wicket received polite applause, one of these, Lieutenant Robert Graham, from *HMS Algerine* – the brother-in-law of Caryl ap Rhys Pryce. Sitting among the spectators in Babloa Park was Graham's wife, Eileen, Pryce's younger sister. Since Eileen was hardly likely to have travelled half way round the world for the cricket, the opportunity of a reunion with her husband probably arose while she was on a visit to her sister Gladys who was still living on a chicken farm on Vancouver Island. Whatever the reason, it has to be seen as a remarkable coincidence, occurring at the very moment their brother was leading a revolutionary army towards Tijuana, only fifteen miles south of Babloa Park, San Diego!

Also among the spectators was Captain David Jones, the commander of *HMS Algerine.* If he had seemed anxious, it had nothing whatsoever to do with the cricket in the Park. His concern arose from a coded wireless message he had received that day from Captain George Vivian, Commander-in-Charge of the Pacific West Coast squadron, who was aboard *HMS Shearwater* which should have docked by then alongside the *Algerine* in San Diego Bay, directly opposite the U.S. Naval Station on Coronado Island. The *Shearwater* was delayed, and the coded message transmitted to Captain Jones by the Admiralty in London explained why: 'Contingent marines landed at San Quintin. Rebels attacking Mexican Land and Colonization Company.'[2] The British had intervened in the affairs of Central America for the first time in forty years. When the marines last landed, they refused to budge until British Honduras (now Belize) was added to the Empire. The reaction from the U.S. Government was predictable: it was a violation of the Monroe Doctrine of non-interference in America's 'sphere of influence,' while President Diaz regarded it as an invasion of Mexico's national sovereignty.[3] The incident had all the makings of an international crisis, occurring as revolutionary forces besieged President Diaz and 20,000 U.S. troops massed on the border. Had the British decided to strike first? That is what other interested parties, in Germany, France and Japan would ask once news of the landing leaked out. Almost as soon as it did, the U.S. dispatched a gunboat, the *Yorktown,* also with a contingent of marines, to Baja California to prepare the way, or so it claimed, for an exercise of the U.S. Fleet in Magdalena Bay, not far along the coast from San Quintin where the British were now lodged.[4]

Although the first attempt by the Mexican Land and Colonization Company to establish a British settlement at San Quintin had failed, and the first railroad had been abandoned, the town with its excellent natural harbour was still considered important to developing its interests. British investors, of which the company was the largest, were responsible for more than 20 per cent of all foreign investment in Mexico – after the United States the most influential investor country. The Land and Colonization Company owned cattle ranches the size of small fiefdoms in the immediate hinterland of San Quintin, and the success of these, and the leases to work the valuable salt flats fringing the bay depended upon its plans to develop the port. Neither had plans for railroad construction been entirely abandoned, the port destined to become an important terminal once the revolution was over. It was because of this the company retained agents at the Bay of Five Hills, the name given to San Quintin's fine natural harbour by buccaneers on account of the stumps of five extinct volcanoes guarding the entrance.

The *Algerine* and *Shearwater* had spent the first three months of 1911 patrolling the coastline either side of the 800-mile promontory that was the Baja Peninsula of Lower California, their presence clearly designed to remind the warring factions that Britain had an interest in the fracas. While their clipper bows and raked funnels gave the appearance of ocean-going yachts, both vessels were sloops-of-war, heavily armed with 25-pounders, and a nest of machine guns mounted on elevated deck platforms, protected by armoured shields. Coal-fired, they nevertheless retained elements of sail power for speed and versatility.

In 1911, the Mexican Land and Colonization Company was still generating a useful profit, mainly from its mining concessions, and of sufficient significance that any threat to the company's viability was a matter for real concern to its aristocratic London shareholders. The Maderistas were sufficiently distant, in northern mainland Mexico and Morelos State in the far south, not to worry foreign investors in the remote Baja Peninsula. But the Magonistas, even though their military success was small by comparison, were on the doorstep, their presence spreading panic throughout Lower California where it was imagined a rebel was hiding behind every cactus tree. On hearing Tijuana was being attacked, Mr M. C. Healion, the company's manager at Ensenada, had set off to investigate the situation for himself, arriving at the border town the day after it fell to Pryce and his insurgents. By then the border had been re-opened, and visitors were being charged twenty-five cents to cross into Tijuana where rebels lounged about the main street with their weapons and belts of cartridges, but 'sober and civil,' according to Healion. The only place open for business was a Chinese restaurant but Healion did get a ten-minute talk with Pryce whom he described in a report to his home office as:

> An intelligent, quiet and unassuming man of perhaps 36 to 38 years of age, an Englishman by birth and education,

living for some years in Scotland to told me, then to Canada for four years before coming to the United States. It is my impression that he was in service during the Boer War or during the Spanish-American War. At any rate, he evidently has had previous experience in warfare and is a man of more than ordinary executive ability. All of the rebels are hardy, adventurous fellows who probably outclassed as well as outnumbered the Federals. It was difficult to get any accurate information or to form an opinion as to what move would be made next. The General, however, and some of the privates with whom I talked, made no secret of their intention to next move on and capture Ensenada. They are now resting up, recruiting at Tijuana, and arranging for reinforcements on their way to Ensenada. It is their intention after taking Ensenada to establish a Government for Lower California. The enclosed manifesto, which may be of interest to you, was handed to me by General Pryce in explanation of the objects they have had and have in view. When I told him that with his permission I would send it to our London Office he said by all means do so, as they desire to have it known the world over what they are striving to attain.[5]

Healion estimated there were up to 250 rebels at Tijuana, 90 per cent of these Americans with a few Englishmen. Among the remainder were Mexicans and Afro-Americans. Pryce expected to be reinforced by a group of Cocopa Indians for the attack upon Ensenada. Two days later, the situation had so deteriorated that Healion telegraphed his head office a second time warning of imminent danger to the company's properties on the Baja Peninsula: 'Company fear all records will be destroyed. Marauders opposed to Madero and Government, said to consist of 90 Americans commanded by an Englishman (*sic*).' The reason the records were of particular importance was that they represented land titles and maps the company had spent many years proving in the Mexican courts. Without these, its interests were worthless.

Healion followed this warning with a more detailed report on the situation. No help could be expected, he said, from Governor Celeso Vega who was still recovering from the wound he had received at Mexicali. Vega had already told foreign nationals that if the town fell to the Magonistas, he would board the Mexican warship anchored in the harbour and, training its guns on Ensenada, reduce it to rubble. According to Healion, the town stood helpless and unprotected in the path of the rebels, and without Mexican Government reinforcements, would certainly be taken by the insurgents:

> The first thing they do on entering a place, no matter how small, is to destroy all public records, and if they enter Ensenada, it is thought that all the Court and other public records will be promptly destroyed, and it is likely they will take possession of or destroy all the Company's maps and titles. This we are now providing against and are having everything packed for shipment to San Diego by tomorrow evening's boat: by that time we will feel our most valuable records are safe unless the town falls into the hands of the rebels in the meantime.[6]

Located at the northern end of the beautiful Todos Santos Bay and blessed with a delightful climate, Ensenada was home to a substantial foreign community of entrepreneurs, American retirees, ranchers, and prospectors en route to the Sierra San Pedro Martir, the magnificent range of mostly uncharted mountains that formed the backbone of the Baja peninsula and the reputed source of the 'mother lode' that fed the gold workings at El Alamo. What they were unaware of at the time, was that while Pryce and his Magonistas were the nearest at Tijuana, Simon Berthold and a small force of rebels had arrived at the El Alamo mining camp after riding out from Mexicali at the end of March. As it happened, they would poise little or no threat whatsoever, Berthold dying slowly from gangrene after being shot in the thigh by an Indian boy whose pony he had stolen.[7]

While the revolution raged, few adventurers dared enter the interior, a land of soaring granite cliffs, and escarpments plunging thousands of feet on to a desert floor that vanished beneath a shimmering veil, shot through with sand and salt. Stepping back from the abyss, the explorer or prospector would just as quickly be enveloped by the scent of forests of pine and fir, filling his canteen from freshwater streams winding their way across flower-strewn alpine meadows. For the moment, however, the prospectors waited in the cantinas of Ensenada. Husongs was a favourite haunt, the oldest cantina in the Americas; a place where wide-awake Americans and well-bred Englishmen, outfitting expeditions for a push into the wild interior, swapped intelligence and gossip about the latest gold prospects, the raucous exchanges lubricated by copious quantities of *tequila,* occasionally conceding ground to the strumming of the wandering *mariachi* bands.

But now all the talk was about invasion. For Ensenada's 1,500 inhabitants the tension was becoming unbearable, no more so than for the American Consul George Schmucker on his first overseas posting. Feeling intimidated by Governor Vega's threats to blow up the town in the event of an invasion, while at the same time convinced there was a conspiracy between the British and the United States to annex Lower California, Schmucker was driven insane. In his fevered imagination he believed certain American residents in Ensenada were attempting to chloroform him; that the Magonista revolution was either the work of Freemasons, a plot by the Church of Rome, or an unholy conspiracy between American capitalists and left wing insurrectionists. All this he told Washington in a frenzy of insane telegrams, the last a paranoid plea for help:

> To comprehend political and social conditions at present moment, study and apply latter part of the Book of Revelation, Holy Bible . . . I have a plan that will result in bettering civilisation everywhere and in preventing my own assassination. Answer.

Schmucker suffered a total mental breakdown and was ordered home under escort. Left alone for a moment on the quayside at Ensenada while awaiting the arrival of the San Diego ferry, he set off into the Pacific, on foot, wading through the crashing surf, the water up to his neck before he could be rescued.[8]

Healion must have considered his precautions fully vindicated in transferring the company records to San Deigo when he read the headline in the *San Diego Union*: 'British Warship Lands Force at San Quintin'. This was not exactly what his company wanted.

True, it had been pressing the Foreign Office on London to intervene in Lower California, but in partnership with the United States.

HMS Shearwater had arrived off San Quintin in a gale on 8 April, the same day Pryce had been elected *generalissimo* of the Magonistas Foreign Legion. Before the *Shearwater* and her sister ship the *Algerine* had began their patrol across the Sea of Cortez to Baja California, the *Shearwater's* commander Captain Vivian had opened his sealed orders from the Admiralty. Although these orders cannot be found in the official records of the patrol held at the Public Record Office at Kew, Vivian said they instructed him to intervene if necessary to protect British lives and property. Gale force winds meant the S*hearwater* anchoring nine miles off shore at St Quintin. Despite heavy seas the thirty marines were disembarked by row boat almost immediately and not, as the British were later to claim, landed in direct response to a letter delivered to the *Shearwater* by local inhabitants.

Once ashore, the very first thing the marines did was to hoist the Union Jack above three buildings in San Quintin, and mount a Maxim gun on the roof of the hotel. San Quintin was deserted, a ghost town, but for two Englishmen and an American, the entire population having disappeared into the desert when it heard the 'Mexicali bunch' was on its way. At that time, Pryce had not yet left Mexicali, but his reputation had already spread to the west coast several hundred miles away! For twenty-four hours the marines commanded by Lieutenant Percy Newcombe stood ready to repel any rebel attack. When nothing materialised, the landing party re-embarked, taking aboard the *Shearwater* the English agents for the Mexican Land and Colonization Company and the American.[9] Unable to dock at Ensenada because of a smallpox outbreak, the *Shearwater* sailed on to San Diego where Captain Vivian discovered the *Algerine* had lost the cricket match – and he was at the centre of a diplomatic incident.[10]

The British had always challenged both Spanish, and later, United States claims to dominion over Central America. For two centuries buccaneers with the full support of the Crown had preyed upon Spanish galleons carrying Peruvian gold up the coast to Mexico. The uninhabited islands and bays of Lower California were perfect hiding places from which privateers like Thomas Cavendish swooped upon the treasure ships. There is even a wind that blows every winter from across the Sea of Cortez the locals call the 'Cromwell,' in the mistaken belief he had been one of those buccaneers. By the 20th century, the Mexican Land and Colonisation Company were considered by many to be the pirates representing British interests in the region.

But Diaz, his power melting away almost by the day, needed all the allies he could find. Britain had been one country he had been able to rely upon for support, and had, accordingly, rewarded its entrepreneurs with cheap land and mineral concessions. Not wanting to lose that support, Diaz was not disposed to fall out with Britain over the 'invasion' at San Quintin. Nevertheless, his Foreign Minister, Senor F. L. de la Barra was instructed to deliver a protest to the British *Charge d'Affaires*, Mr B. Hohler, in Mexico City:

> The Ministry have received news of the occurrence with profound astonishment, as they cannot conceive that such action was taken by orders of His Majesty's Legation, seeing that nobody had requested the disembarkation. It is evident the incident is nothing more than an error that must be attributed to the commander of the vessel in question but this in no way obviates the just surprise of the Mexican Government at so absolutely unusual and groundless an act, and still less at the incorrect action of the aforesaid seaman in ordering the disembarkation on Mexican coasts of the persons who arrived with that object. I beg that you will kindly bring this matter to the knowledge of His Majesty's Government, in order that, proceeding with their accustomed justice, they may inflict on the infringer (*sic*) of International Law the proper reprimand for his action.[11]

Between the diplomatic niceties, Diaz was asking why the marines were aboard *Shearwater* if not to initiate a landing? The Mexicans certainly wanted Captain Vivian reprimanded for his actions. The response from the British Foreign Office was an apology delivered to the Mexican Government by Mr Hohler, explaining that the commander had acted properly in difficult circumstances, and that the landing party had been instructed not to assist either side in the revolution, but only to protect British property and lives against insurgents who had already caused considerable damage further along the coast.[12]

In the United States, the *Shearwater* affair only fuelled widespread rumours of an imminent British invasion of Baja California, the incident at San Quintin described on the floor of the U.S. Senate as 'an act of war'. The Monroe Doctrine — U.S. opposition to further attempts at European or Asiatic colonisation of the Americas — was a fundamental plank of American foreign policy, and many now suspected that if the Japanese did not take the opportunity created by the chaos of the Mexican Revolution to invade, then the British would.

Senator Stone reminded the Senate of how sensitive were the people of the United States to the armed intervention by European or Asiatic powers in the affairs of the American nations. The United States, he said, had not yet assumed the 'office of a policeman patrolling those American Republics' but this might easily be thrust upon it by the actions of other countries.

The landing of marines by *HMS Shearwater* was the very first incident to corroborate reports of foreign intervention, said the senator.

> I have this to say about that incident: that the landing of that force was not necessary to enable the three men in question to board the vessel, and hence if the marines were landed merely to prevent a Mexican force attached to the revolutionary movement in Mexico taking possession of this Mexican town, the act was arbitrary, and being an hostile demonstration on Mexican territory was in effect an act of war if authorised or approved by the British Government.

For these reasons, Senator Stone said President Taft should send troops into Mexico to safeguard American interests before the conflict spilled across the border into the United States.

After this, the British Foreign Office adopted a strategy of damage limitation. Captain Vivian produced two neatly typewritten letters from the San Quintin refugees he had taken aboard the *Shearwater*, requesting his assistance, the more remarkable because the letters were allegedly delivered to the commander before he disembarked his marines in a storm, and despite the fact that by his own admission his vessel was anchored nine miles off-shore on account of the gale. A search of the log of the *Shearwater* shows an entry to the effect the commander's sealed orders from the Admiralty for the mission have disappeared. Had an attempt been made to expunge the official record? Significantly, Captain Vivian was not reprimanded in any way for invading Mexico; his record remained unblemished. The truth is that when the *Shearwater* landed its marines there was not a Magonista within fifty miles, the only threat to San Quintin being a bunch of Indian renegades who arrived a month later and robbed the grocery store.

News of Berthold's death from gangrene poisoning at El Alamo reached Ensenada by a curious route. A Mrs Nellie Meyers, a palmist and crystal ball-gazer with mining interests in the gold mining camp, arrived in Ensenada claiming she had spent the last few weeks nursing the wounded Berthold.[13] Only a single shot was fired when the Magonistas captured El Alamo, and that when a Mexican dropped his rifle as he tried to escape. Arriving at El Alamo, the wounded Berthold, his leg already ravaged by gangrene, was examined by a mysterious Dr Allen Foster, a man with a wicked past. Given the option of an amputation without anaesthetic, in which event he would probably have died from shock, or a slower but certain death from the infection, he chose the latter.

As their leader lay dying, command of the few *insurrectos* remaining at El Alamo passed to Captain Jack Mosby. He claimed to be the son of General John Mosby, one of the most famous of the Confederate Army raiders during the Civil War – that was until the real son walked into a newspaper office in Washington. For six weeks, Mosby orchestrated the most disgraceful episode of the Magonista Revolution, refugees from El Alamo arriving at Ensenada with accounts of robbery, summary executions, and gun fights between the *insurrectos*.[14] The occupying force found no gold. The richest mines had been exhausted years earlier, the remote mining outpost abandoned to those who had good reason to hide from their past. People such as Dr Foster, whose real wife was back in California where he was wanted for bigamy and abandoning his family. There were other Americans like the Fosters in El Alamo, hiding murky pasts behind aliases. Most found it easier to collaborate with the rebels, Governor Vega punishing them for

this a month later when his *federales* executed four of the collaborators.

Mrs Myers was probably Berthold's wife, although she insisted
she was only visiting her mining concessions in El Alamo when
the rebels arrived. According to her account, the rebel leader was
recovering from his wound and would soon assume command
from Mosby:

> A bullet had shattered his right thigh, she told Vega's inter-
> rogators on arrival at Ensenada. I aided in nursing him.
> Because the bullet had apparently gone entirely through
> the leg, the wound was not probed. A few days later they
> found the copper jacket from the bullet still in the wound.
> This was enough to have caused the death of an ordinary
> man but it did not even change Berthold's temperature.
> The jacket was removed and Berthold is now recovering.[15]

But by then Berthold, the socialist activist from the streets of
Los Angeles, and the Magonistas' political commissar, was already
dead and buried, and the rebels led by Mosby riding north to
rendezvous with Pryce's Foreign Legion.

If Pryce had been conscious of the wider international ramifications – the naval build-up in San Diego Bay and the U.S.
mobilization along the Mexican border, not to mention the
incident with the *Shearwater* and the perceived threat to British
interests – would he have led the Magonista attack on Tijuana,
from where he was preparing to march on Ensenada? Here was a
man who knew all about the sanctity with which colonial interests
were regarded, first in India and then again in Africa, as important
to him, one might have thought, as his mother's milk. While fighting for foreigners in a foreign land was something with which he
was comfortable, challenging the jurisdiction and property of
Britain was a quite different matter.

The ranchers at Mexicali may have dismissed the Magonistas
as a bunch of rascally rustlers, but the world beyond had been
persuaded by Magon's propaganda that his was an army on the
move – and commanded, not by a notorious bandit, or socialist
activist, nor by a deserter from the U.S. Army, but by Pryce, a man
with a military track record. Magon and Pryce had absolutely

nothing in common, probably not even common cause. But Magon had recruited to his cause, for whatever reason, and by whatever means, an able, professional soldier and leader of men, one who could actually make the difference between the revolution's success and failure.

NOTES

1. *San Diego Union*, 14 April 1911.
2. ibid., 15 April 1911.
3. Public Record Office. Letter from F. L. de la Barra, Mexican Foreign Minister, to Mr Hohler, British *Charges d'Affaires*, Mexico City, 19 April 1911, AM1 8255, No. 17283; *San Diego Union*, 27 April 1911; PRO, letter from Colonel Vega, Governor at Ensenada, to HM Government ship *Shearwater*, 15 April 1911, AMI 8255, enclosure No. 4 to letter No. 18, of 18 April 1911 from the Commander-in-charge, West Coast of America, *HMS Shearwater*.
4. *San Diego Union*, 16 March 1911.
5. PRO, Healion to Ireson, Secretary Mexican Land and Colonisation Company, London, 13 May 1911, FO371 1147, No. 20012.
6. PRO, Healion to Frank Ireson, 15 May 1911, FO371 1147, No. 18450.
7. *San Diego Union*, 10 April, 13 April 1911.
8. For account of Schmucker's actions and subsequent fate, see Lowell Blaisdell, *The Desert Revolution: Baja California 1911* (Madison, 1962), pp. 112-115, 164, 194-195.
9. PRO. 'Report of proceedings armed party landed in Mexico,' AM1 8255 No. 17/1911, No. 18/1911; 'Orders for landing party,' Commander Vivian to Lieutenant Percy Newcombe, 11 April 1911, AMI 8255.
10. *San Diego Union*, 10 April 1911.
11. Public Record Office. Letter from F. L. de la Barra, Mexican Foreign Minister, to Mr Hohler, British *Charges d'Affaires*, Mexico City, 19 April 1911, AM1 8255, No. 17283.
12. Public Record Office. Letter from F. A. Campbell on behalf of the Secretary of State at the Foreign Office, to Mr Hohler, British *Charges d'Affaires*, Mexico City, 18 May 1911, AMI 8255, 88/89/11.
13. *San Diego Union*, 13 April 1911.
14. ibid., 28 March 1911.
15. *San Diego Union*, 13 April 1911.

Chapter 7

Pryce's Kingdom

The capture of Tijuana by General Pryce and his *insurrectos* would prove to be the high point in the Magonista campaign. Magon and his junta urgently needed revolutionary success if they were to mount a serious challenge to their adversary, Francisco Madero whose brother had already denounced Pryce and his insurgents in the United States press as a band of outlaws. But the reluctance of Magon to assume military command was alienating sympathisers in the IWW and the American Federation of Labor.[1] As the divisions widened, and Madero's forces drew closer to a final showdown with Diaz, the Liberal Junta made a last desperate appeal to 'The Workers of the World.' Issued a week before Pryce entered Tijuana, the manifesto placed the struggle in Lower California on the global stage, the first act of 'the great universal tragedy which will soon have for its stage the surface of the whole planet, and whose final act will be the triumph of the noble formula – Liberty, Equality, Fraternity.' For five months, proclaimed the Magonista manifesto, the Red Flag had 'flamed on the battle fields of Mexico, carried aloft by emancipated workers whose aspirations are epitomised in this sublime war cry: Land and Liberty.'[2] Although it was evident to just about everyone the dictatorship of Diaz was about to collapse, the message from the junta was that to replace him by the millionaire capitalist Madero and a 'bourgeois Republic like the United States,' meant the revolution was not over. The propaganda, however, failed to measure up to the reality. The day after Pryce raised the Red Flag above three key buildings in Tijuana, Pascual Orozco's troops seized Ciudad Juarez, the largest town on the U.S./Mexican border in the name of Madero, immediately overshadowing the Magonistas' great triumph. Madero was now unstoppable, Diaz resigning on 25 May 1911, and leaving the country in the hands of a provisional government promising early elections. None of this would have been apparent to Pryce when he marched his ragged army into Tijuana and the short-lived Republic of Baja California.

The echo of the last shot in the battle had hardly faded before the spectators lining the hills across the border stampeded for the town, blinded to any danger by their anxiety to share in the spoils of war. None in the crush of tourists brushing aside the flimsy border barricades would have recognised Pryce, standing there amongst the wreckage, a wiry individual of about six feet with a large blond moustache, sporting no insignia of rank, his uniform a green sack coat, khaki jeans, and a grey fedora hat.[3] From his wrist dangled a *gueritta,* a short riding crop decorated with a sheaf of plaited horsehair. Perhaps he had a slightly less tattered appearance than the others. He also had Milton, his giant Afro-American bodyguard whose size was exceeded only by his reputation for bayoneting Mexicans.

Whatever the eventual outcome, for the moment at least, the Magonistas in control of Tijuana could not be ignored. Pryce, and his second-in-command, Melbourne Hopkins may have been considered a 'pretty pair of scoundrels' by the British Foreign Office, but they very quickly became front page news across the United States.[4] If they realised the world was watching, this did not seem to prevent them running up the Red Flag in defiance of the hostility confronting socialist revolutionaries from across the border.[5] After the fall-out from the bombing of the *Los Angeles Times* office, and the bitter war waged against unionism that ensued, this was not a good time to be an anarchist camped on America's doorstep.[6]

The very first thing to greet the sightseers streaming across the border into the still smoking ruins of Tijuana was the sickly smell of liquor from the bottles ground into the dust on the orders of General Pryce. Beer and wine were spared but the *insurrecto* leader had no intention of allowing his force to disintegrate in an orgy of drinking and gunplay.[7] Among the first to arrive in an automobile flying the Red Cross was Dr Jackson accompanied now by two pretty nurses. The doctor, it transpired, was not official Red Cross, but a freelance, and so were his nurses whom he introduced to Pryce as 'just friends.' Pryce assured them they would not be molested; that they would be safer in Tijuana than on the streets of San Diego. Then pointing towards the *cuartel*, he directed them to where 'some of the other boys' were requiring attention.[8]

Half way up the hill to Pryce's headquarters in the administration building, now acting as a makeshift hospital, Dr Jackson counted the bodies of eight Mexican defenders, surrounded by the empty shells of wicked dum-dum bullets. Another pile of bodies was stacked behind the *cuartel* in full sight of the tourists streaming into town. The town's solitary public telephone booth had been peppered by rifle fire, the black receiver hanging forlornly from its hook. In a room at the back of the administration block, the doctor found an American woman lying on a bed, bleeding from a leg wound. Refusing to give her name, she would only say that when she saw Pryce and his insurrectos shaking hands with the Mexican wounded she assumed the battle was over and stepped into street only to be shot by a retreating *federale*.[9]

As the wounded were treated and bodies collected for burial, the rebels continued their bottle-smashing spree, clearing Tijuana of its entire stock of hard liquor. A *San Diego Union* reporter, the first newsman to re-enter the town, reported that hardly a window pain had survived the battle. Even fences were cut and clipped by the rebel fusillade, the shingles on the roofs of houses torn or shot away, he reported:

> The odour of spirits was perceptible everywhere. General Pryce had given orders to have every bottle of booze in Tijuana destroyed. And every bottle was destroyed. It made no difference whether the case contained the finest champagne or the best of whiskey. It was broken open and its contents spilled upon the ground. While men were busy breaking open the cases others were busy on the inside of the saloons and stores breaking the bottles on the shelves and elsewhere in the rooms. In several instances so much liquor was destroyed that it ran out of the saloon doors, trickled down the steps and was absorbed by the ground.

Destroying the gambling town's stock of booze would have registered well with those Americans who saw all problems in terms of the demon drink. But Pryce made no attempt to stop the looting, what he himself regarded from his ten years in Africa as 'the fair spoils of war'. Very soon, the army of sightseers were also involved, taking whatever they could get their hands on. Describing the 'shopping frenzy,' *San Diego Union* reported:

> They were going through the stocks of goods in the various stores, selecting what they wanted and packing it away. In hundreds of instances articles of all kinds that were not wanted were thrown upon the floor only to be ruined by being walked upon. Thousands and thousands of dollars worth of costly goods were stolen. At first the soldiers invited visitors to step right up and 'help yourself' but later in the day charged every man and boy who entered a dollar saying, 'help yourself; take anything you want'. None of the private houses were entered by the rebels except here and there to get pillows and some bedding for the wounded.

The fall of Tijuana would rapidly descend into farce: a comic opera wounding the rebel cause more seriously than enemy bullets. The revelry spilled into the main street, victorious *insurrectos* swathed in looted Indian blankets, coloured shawls and sombreros strutting their stuff like circus clowns mimicking bullfights, while others raced their horses up and down to entertain visitors. But when asked who they were and where they came from, it soon became evident this was an 'army of Smiths' – J. C. Smith and Roy Smith from San Diego, Paul Smith was captain of A Troop, and Lieutenant 'Bulldog' Smith had been killed in battle. Only 25 of Pryce's 200-strong rebel force were Mexicans, the remainder mostly American renegades, Wobbly anarchists, and Boer War veterans like Pryce. Not all joined in the fun. After 24 hours with only a scoop of beans and half a mug of coffee, some just settled down to eat, one pair seen squatting in the dust assiduously gnawing their way through large bread loaves.

In the middle of this carnival lay the dead; and beside them twenty or more wounded, swathed in bandages. Around midday Pryce called a halt to the victory celebrations, ordering the *insurrectos* to parade in front of the Custom House where a trench had been dug to bury their eight fallen comrades, the last of whom, an unidentified Irishman, killed when his rifle exploded. After the

General had read the Episcopal Church burial service, and as a platoon of Magonistas fired a three-volley salute over the mass grave, a rebel scout arrived at a gallop, exploding to a halt in a cloud of dust beside the open grave. Excitedly, he told Pryce two *insurrectos* had been killed during a skirmish with *federales* in the bush at Tijuana Hot Springs health spa two miles outside town. Before the General could send someone to investigate further, another of the rebels leaped on his horse and rode through Tijuana shouting, 'Get out of town; get out of town.' Bargain hunters poured from the stores, many abandoning their purchases in the panic to reach the border, one party of women shoppers tearing their dresses and scratching their hands scrambling through the barbed wire fence the U.S. Army had now erected along the line. In the confusion, frantic tourists found themselves stopped by American customs officers and charged duty. The freelance Dr Jackson was stripped and searched on suspicion of being a smuggler. By then 500 sightseers were struggling to get back into America.

Meanwhile, in Tijuana, the rebels crouched in their trenches awaiting the anticipated counter-attack. There was no shortage of rumours. Colonel Mayol who had whipped them at Mexicali was reportedly at the edge of town, with his 500 regulars after a forced march from the Colorado River works; another battalion of Mexican regulars had been landed with two field guns at nearby Rosario. The *insurrectos* began digging furiously to extend the sand-bagged fortifications built by the Mexicans. In the very middle of all this activity, Montana Gomez, a Customs agent for the San Diego-Arizona Railroad crawled out of a dugout beneath one of Tijuana's bullet-riddled houses. Caught on the wrong side of the line when the battle started, Gomez had dug a shallow hole, climbed in and covered himself with dirt, remaining there for two days until his chance came to escape in the confusion following the *insurrectos* funeral. Ghost-like, and weak from hunger, he staggered across the line pleading for food and water.[10]

When no counter attack materialised after more than an hour, the rebels realised it had all been a misunderstanding. The scout who had raised the alarm was a Mexican whose patrol commander was a Swedish-speaking corporal. Not for the first time there had been a language breakdown in this multi-lingual army. A German sergeant, his accent several inches thick, demonstrated the problem graphically as he assembled the rebels following the emergency: 'I vant you rascals to know dat ven I calls you, you come. I don't run my legs off hunting you. Ven I wants you, I vant you. Ve haf no bugle in dis army, but ven I blows did vhizzle it means you are vanted, and see dat you get here.'[11]

The panic over, Pryce sent word to the refugee storekeepers of Tijuana it was safe to return to their businesses. Among those trickling back across the border was a San Diego undertaker with eighteen coffins to collect the Mexican dead. Lieutenant Governor Larroque was being lifted into a coffin as General Pryce gave his first Press Conference. Leaning against the corner of his head-quarters, the general was at pains to deny the latest allegation of barbarity levelled at the Magonistas by the Press: that they had burned at the stake two Mexican Government spies captured at Tecate:

> My men have always conducted themselves as you see them now, orderly and quietly. When we have any fighting to do, we do it, and when we are through fighting we don't go around raising hell as the papers have stated. Of course, war is war, and we must live by what we can find or take.
>
> I suppose you are more anxious to know what my future plans are. I understand that about 100 federales ate break-fast this morning at the Dupee Ranch. They are expected to reach here probably tomorrow. We will be here to receive them. The reception will be a little more stubborn than the one we received last night.
>
> After we have disposed of them I will leave a sufficient number of men here to protect the town and then go down to Ensenada. By that time I will have reinforcements. We expect to have more trouble down there than we did here because we will probably be up against a much larger force.
>
> After Ensenada has been taken then the work of estab-lishing a stable government will begin. Just who may be at the head of it I do not care to say. But I want to impress upon the minds of everybody that my men are not cut-

throats, neither are they bums or fiends. They are simply men fighting for a cause. And you can also impress upon the minds of everybody that they are just as safe in Tijuana as they would be in San Diego, provided, of course, they behave themselves and recognise the authority of our men.

The merchants are free to come, reopen their stores and resume their business. You might also add I have destroyed every drop of liquor in Tijuana, excepting some beer and light wines which we found. There isn't a drop of whiskey or champagne in Tijuana this minute. You know that because you saw my men destroying it in every saloon. And you have not seen a drunken man since you have been over here. And you won't see any more over here so long as we are in control for I don't propose to let another drop of liquor of any kind be sold in this town.[12]

Pryce left the press conference to deal with a particular dilemma: what to do with their solitary prisoner, Mario Alonso. Instead of retreating with his comrades, Alonso had put up a stubborn resistance from behind the barricades around the Custom House until eventually winkled out. Pryce was inclined to release him across the border, until one of his officers butted in, suggesting, 'Wait general, there is work to be done. Why not make this man do it?'

'It is true I have not had any dinner,' laughed Pryce. Then turning to Alonso, asked, 'Can you cook?' Ready to do anything to save his life, the terrified Mexican was taken away to prepare a meal for the rebel officers' mess. It was good, so good in fact he was given $2 before being hauled outside again, handed a shovel and told to dig a grave to bury the bodies of his dead comrades. Afraid this was intended to be his own after a rebel officer called out mercilessly, 'Make the grave big enough so there's room for you,' the poor Mexican was in a state of collapse by the time he had finished. Only then did he discover the 'grave' was an extension to the Magonista fortifications. Last seen, Alonso was disappearing across the border in a cloud of dust.[13]

Over the entrance to his headquarters, Pryce had hung the sign 'Tierra y Libertas, Headquarters Second Division Liberal Army.' Above it flew the Red Flag, although the Stars and Stripes fluttered

The Red Flag flies above the Post Office in Tijuana in May 1911 after General Pryce and his "insurrectos" captured the border town from the Mexicans.
(San Diego Historical Society).

*A group of men from Pryce's Second Battalion pose for
photographers in Tijuana.*
(San Diego Historical Society).

138

below that, an indication perhaps the general had himself become confused about the political direction of the uprising, if indeed he had ever cared. When a reporter suggested the Stars and Stripes would soon float alone over the whole of Lower California, he commented, 'It sounds good to me.' Always available for Press interviews, Pryce expressed himself well satisfied with headlines proclaiming, 'American Flag is Floated by Rebels,' and 'General Pryce Does Not Deny Desire to Give Peninsula to United States.'[14]

From the moment Tijuana was captured, the speculation about a filibuster drowned out all of the Liberal Junta's propaganda about a socialist revolution sweeping victoriously across the Sea of Cortez to engulf the whole of Mexico. In spite of Pryce's some- times calculated ambiguity about his real intent, it was generally believed that after the Foreign Legion had taken Lower California for itself it might be persuaded to annex it to the Union. Many saw no other explanation since with his success at Ciudad Juarez on the very same day, Madero had put both hands firmly on the throne. No one doubted the Welshman was the most competent general the Magonistas had acquired. But why should Pryce con- tinue the struggle for the 'poor peons' when most people thought the revolution was as good as over, unless it was the mercenary's age-old determination to profit from bearing arms. Interviewed again by a *San Diego Union* reporter after the fall of Tijuana, Pryce admitted he was considering 'the idea of making Lower California a republic with which the United States will be glad to deal as a valuable addition commercially and in republic form of government,' adding ambivalently, as though anxious not to forget the script written by Ricardo Flores Magon, '. . . where white men as well Mexicans can secure justice.'[15]

Such a statement would only have fuelled patriotic passions on either side of the border. Newspapers in southern California depicted the rebels as lusty young Americans, moved by the spirit of adventure, and while naturally wayward on occasions, were, nevertheless, only following in the footsteps of those who took Texas from the Mexicans. On the other hand, others warned from the outset of the emergence of a 'filibuster republic' on America's doorstep, run by desperadoes with good reason to remain south of the border. For their part, the Mexicans were convinced the rebels were financed by American big business supported by Wall

Street financial interests as part of a conspiracy to seize another large chunk of their country. As evidence of this, they had only to point to the vast stretches of land and properties already owned by the newspaper tycoons Otis and Hearst, the sugar baron Sprekles, and the Cudahy meatpacking family from Chicago.[16] Apart from bribes paid by Imperial Valley farmers to protect their water supply from being sabotaged by the insurgents, Pryce and the Magonistas received very little 'foreign' financial support. Even these farmers wanted a more enduring guarantee for the future, two local newspapers, the *Calexico Daily Chronicle* and the *Imperial Valley Press* echoing their longer term concerns when, with the rebels on the brink of success after the capture of Tijuana, they advocated the surreptitious annexation of Baja California by the United States. The liberal-minded Scripps-owned *San Diego Sun* took much the same line, commenting, ' If Lower California should wake up some morning to find the stars and stripes floating over it, San Diego would suddenly become more than ever a City of destiny.'[17] A year later, however, a Senate Sub-Committee found no evidence of complicity in the revolution by American business and financial interests. Allegations that the industrialist John D. Sprekles had financed the campaign to protect his interests were shown to be farcical, serving only to discredit those who led the uprising.[18]

The still unresolved mystery was how exactly did the Welshman Pryce, whose foot had wedged open the door to Lower California, fit into all of this? Because of his ten years in Africa, there was a widespread assumption Pryce was nothing more than a rascal, a scallywag – albeit well-trained in the art of warfare – who had joined the Magonistas on the off-chance of sharing in the spoils of war, although 160 acres would not have seemed that good a deal even in 1911. In Mexico, Pryce was never to escape the accusation of being a villainous subversive, while Magon, his leader, would eventually be elevated to Mexico's Rotunda of Illustrious Men.[19] Any detailed analysis of the Welshman's life, before, during and after the hiatus in Baja California, cannot escape the conclusion Pryce was too able, too intelligent, and too loyal to his class to be dismissed as a mere mercenary. Those who choose to do so, ignore the most significant fact of all: that aside from his part in the Mexican Revolution the Welshman spent most of his life as a *policeman,* first in Africa enforcing the holy writ of the British Empire, and later, as will be seen, in Palestine. Such was his interest in law enforcement that he had even applied to become the Chief Constable of an English county. Apart from Lowell Blaisdell in *The Desert Revolution: Baja California 1911,* generally considered the standard work in the English language on the uprising, most writers skate around the possibility that Pryce always had a quite different agenda to the Liberal Junta.[20]

Whatever his intentions, in the immediate aftermath of the battle for Tijuana Pryce struggled to control his unruly band of *insurrectos.* Despite leading them to a glorious victory, he knew their loyalty would evaporate as quickly as rain in the desert unless offered immediate rewards. Already there were those, who having looked upon their own dead after the battle of Tijuana had deserted, taking horses, saddles, weapons, and supplies. Pryce caught another bunch driving stolen cattle across the line to sell to American ranchers. As for Magon and the Liberal Junta in Los Angeles all they did was to send, not the weapons so desperately needed to continue the struggle, but the Party Secretary Antonio Araujo to superintend the collection of tolls and duties from the thousands of excited tourists passing through Tijuana's Custom House. Magon's greatest mistake was in not setting aside his propaganda machine to assume the military and political leadership of the Liberal Army from a man he himself would eventually brand as a 'thief.' By failing to do so, and becoming more openly anarchist in his ambitions for Mexico, he so alienated American socialists they began withdrew their support from the revolution. The last to desert the cause would be the IWW, the Wobbly members among Pryce's *insurrectos* who had always believed the fight was about establishing an anarchist Utopia south of the border. Since Magon had effectively abandoned the destiny of the revolution to General Pryce, the Welshman would prove to be the deciding factor in its outcome. While the majority of insurgents were prepared to fight on under his leadership, they had already lost confidence in the political leadership in Los Angeles.

With appeals for weapons ignored, and his commitment to the Junta's anarchist/socialist doctrines never very great, Pryce was unsure which way to jump. Although the opportunity for a filibuster by attacking the capital at Ensenada could never have been far from his mind, publicly he continued to insist his only interest was to help the 'poor peons.'[21] By now the international ramifications with their implications for British property interests in Lower California would have been evident to him once the Magonistas were exposed to the attention of the world's Press. Pryce's involvement with the rebels was beginning to appear, if not a monumental mistake, certainly an adventure too far.

The General's struggle to retain control of his command meant the liquor ban did not last long. On the third day there was a free distribution, the *insurrectos* crowding into Savine's bar every morning for their daily allocation of beer and wine, together with a daily shot of cognac or a cocktail of their choice, rather like the Royal Navy's daily rum issue.[22] Having nothing with which to occupy their time once the fortifications were in place, the rebels laid on a rodeo to entertain tourists, tossing their lariats at a craggy burro squatting on its knees in the middle of the main street. The festivities were interrupted when a herd of 57 wild horses caught in the hills were driven into town as mounts for the new recruits, kicking up a great cloud of choking dust rolling across the sidewalks into the saloons where *insurrectos* and visitors elbowed each other aside to shoot dice across green baize billiard tables. Tijuana was again a wide-open frontier town, the editorial writer for the *San Diego Union* commenting:

> The lid is off. The whir of the marble will be heard in the land once more; the hypnotic gyrations of the varicolored wheel will hold the fascinated gaze of the 'sucker'; the faro fiend will once more have a chance to try his 'system'; candidates for the home of the feeble-minded will tackle the Klondyke; the man with a passion for throwing his money away will take a whirl at Twenty-one; the scientific gamester will play 'cases'; free wine will flow like water; the lights will be burning night and day, and the deuce generally will be to pay, for the lid is off at Tijuana.[23]

At the border crossing, Colonel F. A. Wilcox in command of the American troops was at his witsend trying to control the tourists and gamblers flooding into Tijuana. When told by the War Department after a formal complaint from the Press that he had no right to prevent legitimate access, Wilcox promptly handed over responsibility for controlling the chaos to the U.S. Marshall.[24]

Through the shattered window of a restaurant where he sat eating a meal with his fellow officers, General Pryce watched as Tijuana came back to life. From a lean, leathery face, grave, sardonic eyes scrutinised events like a searchlight perched on top of his large blond moustache. In the fields beyond the edge of town the 'poor peons' were back at work, heads bowed beneath large sombreros, hoeing the plots they had abandoned three days previously.

But to the reporters visiting the *insurrecto* camp that day the situation seemed to be deteriorating rapidly. The Magonistas were behaving as badly as had been expected, like a bunch of thieving bandits. Challenged about this, Pryce's response was a robust, 'You know yourself it's all piffle, don't you . . .?' The goods they had commandeered from the stores were being sold to raise money to fight the war, he explained. At an impromptu Press conference, the General elaborated a little on his plans for Lower California, adding, 'As far as I am aware, I am the only general of rebel forces in Lower California.' Afraid perhaps he had gone too far in revealing his intentions, Pryce the next day distributed to the Press copies of the Liberal Party manifesto and its promise to return the land to the peons.[25]

The most frequent question was how soon before the Magonistas moved against the capital Ensenada. Pryce refused to say but knew a decision would have to be taken soon. Nothing succeeds more than success, and recruits were pouring across the border, among them quite a few deserters from the U.S. Army and from the naval armada assembled in San Diego Bay. Even the bellboy at San Diego's Brewster Hotel packed in his job to join the war after listening to the stories spun by the *insurrectos* who soon became frequent visitors to the taverns and brothels of the downtown area. There were also other recruits, like the forty Italian anarchists who arrived from San Francisco their eyes blazing with political righteousness; and a gang of outlaws who made no secret of the fact they would fight to the death rather than be hauled back to the United States. Among these was Marshall Brooks, the cattle rustler from Campo who with Henry Hall, a railroad thief, had been on the run for ten years after escaping prison, surviving for two of these hiding on barren Tiburon Island in the Sea of Cortez. More alarming was the reported appearance amongst the rebels of James Dunham, the man who butchered the McGlincy family in Los Gatos sixteen years earlier. On the run all that time, it was said he had become a sergeant in the Magonista army. At least one convicted murderer, 'Mojave Red,' was pushed back across the border by the *insurrectos*. Nevertheless, as a haven for southern California's 'most wanted,' it also attracted the attention of San Diego's sheriff's office.[26]

The supply of recruits could not be matched however by weapons procurement. When Araujo, the junta's man in Tijuana, was not collecting customs dues, he was guarding the army's war chest day and night. Not surprisingly, there was huge jubilation after Second-in-Command Captain Melbourne Hopkins discovered a cache of 85 *federale* Mausers and 2000 rounds of ammunition buried in the ground where a detail were extending the town's fortifications. There was an even greater yelp of excitement when he also unwrapped a machine gun.

'Nothing to it now,' yelled the *insurrectos* working on the trench as Hopkins held his find aloft, observing, 'Guess that will hold them for a while.'

Pryce was as excited as his men, ushering his second-in-command away to headquarters. But it was a glum-faced, tight-lipped Hopkins who emerged some minutes later. General Pryce also had nothing to say about the discovery of the machine gun, other than to advise visiting newspapermen 'there was a great deal of josh about it.' What he had realised was that the weapon had been buried by the *federales* and never used in the defence of Tijuana, because there was no ammunition for it![27]

NOTES

1. *Los Angeles Times,* 20 March 1911.
2. *The Industrial Worker,* 4 May 1911.
3. Margaret Holbrook, 'The capture of Tia Juna,' *Overland Monthly,* No. 1, July 1911, p. 5.
4. Public Record Office, Kew, FO 371 1147, 25 May 1911.
5. *San Diego Union,* 10, 11 May 1911.

6. Grace Heilman Stimson, *Rise of the Labor Movement in Los Angeles* (1955, University of California Press), p. 380: During the five years 1906-1911, 87 bombs were exploded in various parts of the United States by the Bridge and Structural Ironworkers Union against structures erected by non-union labour.

7. *San Diego Union,* 10 May 1911.

8. ibid., 10,11 May 1911.

9. ibid.

10. Close reading of the *San Diego Union, San Diego Sun, Los Angeles Times,* 10-13 May 1911.

11. Holbrook, pp. 6-7.

12. *San Diego Union,* 10, 13 May 1911.

13. ibid., 12 May 1911.

14. ibid., 14 May 1911.

15. *San Diego Union,* 13 May 1911.

16. Carleton Beals, *Porfirio Diaz, Dictator of Mexico* (Philadelphia, 1932), p. 428; *U.S. Senate Foreign Relations Committee,* 1911, p. 543; *New York Times,* 8 April 1911. In 1911, Otis owned 832,000 acres.

17. *Calexico Daily Chronicle,* 16 May 1911; *Imperial Valley Press,* 20 May 1911; *San Diego Sun,* 12 May 1911.

18. *Revolutions in Cuba and Mexico,* 62nd Congress, 2nd session, Report of a Sub-Committee of the Senate Committee on Foreign Relations (Washington, 1913), pp. 203-255, 373-386.

19. Teodoro Hernandez, *La Historia de la revolucion debe hacerse* (Mexico, 1950), pp. 114-125, for controversy surrounding the elevation of Ricardo Flores Magon to the Rotunda.

20. Lowell Blaisdell, *The Desert Revolution: Baja California 1911* (Madison, 1962, University of Wisconsin Press); also Lowell Blaisdell, 'Was it revolution or filibustering?' *Pacific Historical Review,* Spring 1962, Arizona State University, for assessment of role of Pryce, pp. 160-164.

21. *San Diego Union,* 13 May 1911.

22. ibid., 18 May 1911.

23. ibid., 14 May 1911.

24. ibid., 13 May 1911.

25. ibid., 14 May 1911.

26. ibid., 17, 18 May 1911.

27. ibid., 13 May 1911.

Chapter 8

The Dick Ferris Show

Whatever might be the eventual outcome of the Magonista Revolution, its fighters and General Pryce in particular, were for a while at least, to enjoy celebrity status in neighbouring San Diego, even as far as Los Angeles and San Francisco. This did not escape the attention of Dick Ferris, a man small in stature but larger than life in the publicity business. Publicity agent, actor and showman, all at the same time, Dick had jumped upon the revolutionary bandwagon when it first rolled into Mexicali back in February 1911 by writing to President Diaz offering to buy Baja California. If Diaz were to agree, then in recognition of the president's co-operation the new state would be named the 'Republic of Diaz.' But if he refused then Ferris would lead a filibuster army to seize Lower California.[1] When Diaz made the mistake of dignifying this preposterous idea with a reply, Dick waved his letter around the Press as evidence of recognition by the 'leader of a world power to the possible head of a possible near republic.'[2] It was pure pantomime and everyone was enjoying the fun, especially Dick, who encouraged by the column inches of publicity the stunt generated, refused to let go of a good idea, following up with a second letter to Diaz claiming Lower California belonged to the United States anyhow:

> Our occupation is a legitimate conquest in the cause of civilisation and the ambition of patriotic American citizens who recognise its geographical importance to this country in view of the completion of the Panama Canal . . . Unless peacefully ceded . . . the Panama Pacific Expedition will sail from San Francisco at an early date.[3]

Nor did Dick stop at this. To prove his threat was serious, Ferris placed advertisements in the *Los Angeles Times* and *New York Times* for Spanish-American War veterans to serve in an 'army of a thousand men' to mount the invasion of Lower California. And as with all his outrageous stunts, Dick claimed to have the backing of prominent Wall Street financiers, peppering his Press interviews with names like J. P. Morgan, and other multi-millionaires he said were lurking in the shadows.[4] Magon was another of those who fell into the trap set by the Ferris pantomime by using the pages of *La Regeneración* to ridicule the stunt, labelling Dick '*El millionario*':

> If Dictator Dick, alias Ferris the Fearless, will only wait a little while before starting out on that filibustering expedition to take Lower California, he'll probably get Diaz to sell and sell cheap. But will Diaz be able to deliver the goods? We think not.[5]

But Dick was not a complete fool. His bid to buy Baja California was initially designed to promote the Panama-California Exposition Pageant – for which he had only recently been appointed manager – to celebrate the planned opening of the Panama Canal in 1914, an engineering achievement, which was expected to transform the fortunes of the West Pacific Coast cities. Having discovered a promotional platform in Lower California, Dick was determined to milk it for all he could.

His next step was to enlist the support of a beautiful young Los Angeles socialite and suffragette campaigner, Miss Flora Russell. The *federales* in Tijuana were preparing their defences against the imminent attack by Pryce and his Magonistas when Miss Russell, astride a high-spirited white mustang, boldly bearded the American troops guarding the border, before plunging southwards towards the Hot Springs just beyond the town where the proprietor, Ed Hayes, another of Dick's clients, had arranged a formal welcome. Fluttering above Flora's shoulder was Dick's latest creation, his new Republic's 'flag for freedom,' a rising sun flashing its brilliant rays across a field of azure blue, and its crest a set of scales symbolising equality between the races.

Planting the flag, Miss Russell proclaimed to a gaggle of waiting reporters, 'Lower California, I claim you in the name of equal suffrage and of model government, which I hereby christen as the future 'Republic of Diaz'. May the great ruler of all things nourish the little plant typified by this flag that I raise over this troubled land and in his goodness bring to fruition the hopes and dreams of my sex for fullest liberty symbolised in the scales of equality and justice.' Dick had scored another publicity coup, but with nothing much left for an encore the Ferris Filibuster slipped out of the headlines for the next few months, until the arrival of General Pryce allowed him to resurrect his crazy scheme.[6]

After weeks of badgering the Liberal Junta for rifles and ammunition, Pryce finally received news that an emissary was being sent to San Diego to discuss the situation. It was the author John Kenneth Turner, again. Turner and his wife Ethel, who edited the English-language section of *La Regeneración,* were long-standing allies of Magon, advising the Los Angeles Junta on how best to circumvent the strict U.S. neutrality laws. A secret meeting was arranged in a San Diego saloon. For this, Pryce would travel across the border incognito as 'Mr Graham,' assuming, incidentally, the name of his brother-in-law, the Lieutenant aboard the *HMS Algerine,* sister ship of *HMS Shearwater,* the two vessels only recently having left San Diego after the incident at San Quintin.[7]

On the eve of the meeting with Turner, the ubiquitous Dr Jackson, still accompanied by his 'nurses' although they had all been repudiated by the Red Cross, returned to Tijuana having invited an ex-British Army officer resident in San Diego, a Lieutenant A. S. Milburn, to join them for dinner in a gambling town once again in full swing, day and night. Another mystery man to cross Pryce's path, Milburn was honorary part-time agent for a British shipping company at San Diego. Judging from his home at Redondo Beach and his fondness for imported wines and French cognac, the British community always suspected he had other, more lucrative, sources of income. One of these might have been the British Vice-Consul, Allen Hutchinsen, who saw Milburn as a man with his hand on the pulse of the British in San Diego and as such a valuable source of information.[8]

Dr Jackson suggested that since Pryce and Milburn were compatriots, the General should join them for dinner in Tijuana's Hotel de Paris, now re-opened after its Mexican owner had finally plugged all the bullet holes. So much alcohol was consumed that evening, Milburn spent the night at Tijuana after falling off his horse at the crossing point. The next morning, Pryce, Jackson and Milburn took their hangovers off to Tijuana Hot Springs, relaxing in the warm spa waters with Ed Hayes, the proprietor, and Second-in-Command Captain Hopkins. Feeling refreshed, and mindful of his rendezvous with Turner that day, Pryce suddenly declared he wanted to visit San Diego.[9]

Jackson, Milburn and Hayes jumped at the opportunity to escort the celebrated rebel leader on his very first visit to town. After some argument over whether he should remain behind in command of the rebellious *insurrectos*, Hopkins was also allowed to join the excursion into San Diego. A black, chauffeur-driven automobile then delivering medical supplies to the camp hospital was commandeered, and after the general, by courtesy of Savin's General Store, had discarded his drab rebel attire for a natty grey suit, white shirt and collar, and dark fedora hat, the party set off for town. Hopkins chose to stick with his ragged rebel clothes and sun-bleached sombrero.

The immediate destination was the prestigious U.S. Grant Hotel on Third Street. In the oak-panelled lobby beneath the sparkling chandeliers, Pryce checked in as 'Mr Graham', Hopkins as 'Mr Milburn', the pair retiring to their rooms to sample the luxuries of civilisation for the first time in many months. That evening, joined by Jackson and Milburn in the lobby of the U.S. Grant, the famous rebel leader was soon the centre of attention, among those crowding around, hanging on his last word, none other than the Mayor of San Diego, Louis J. Wilde. By the time the wellwishers adjourned to the Brewster Grill for a sumptuous and noisy meal, it had become a very large party, indeed. Back at the hotel much later, the Welshman revelled in his notoriety as he held court in the lobby. Relieved of the rigours of command and his war-stained garb, Pryce was an urbane and intriguing companion, a real-life adventurer full of stirring tales drawn from an action-packed life.

Among his attentive audience hanging on on to every last word were Dick Ferris and his actress wife, Florence Stone. The pair had hurried to the U.S. Grant on hearing on the San Diego grapevine that Pryce was in town. The general's future plans for creating a 'Republic of Lower California' were of particular interest to San Diegans who had always regarded the Baja Peninsula as part of their backyard. Dick Ferris now snatched at the chance of resurrecting his earlier scheme by making sure that by the end of the night he and Pryce had become good friends. The Ferris Filibuster was back on the road.

The next morning dawned a perfect summer's day in California, the early mist that rolled in off the Bay already lifting when Pryce and Hopkins, refreshed and eager for their day in town, were collected from the U.S. Grant by Dr Jackson, still accompanied by his 'nurses', and Lieutenant Milburn. Ostensibly, this was to be a leisurely sightseeing drive around town in the hijacked chauffeur-driven auto, at some pre-arranged time and place the rebel leaders dropping off for their clandestine rendezvous with Turner. Neither Pryce nor Hopkins made any attempt to conceal their real identities and, calling at several taverns, were warmly welcomed by San Diegans. News of their excursion had spread quickly, and the *San Diego Union* assigned a reporter to follow the pair for the rest of the day.

First call was the United States Military Hospital at Point Loma, across the Bay from where the U.S. Pacific Fleet was awaiting orders to intervene in Mexico to protect U.S. interests. Armed with baskets of fruit for the seven *insurrectos* being treated at the hospital, Pryce and Hopkins were allowed to talk freely with their wounded comrades. Pryce even shook hands with his old adversary, the wounded Lieutenant Guerrero, congratulating him on his bravery. According to the *Union* reporter: 'Guerrero couldn't speak English and Pryce couldn't speak Spanish and the nearest they came to understanding each other was in the offer of a cigarette by Pryce. The general also shook hands with three other wounded *federales* in the hospital.'

After visiting another group of rebel wounded at the Agnew Sanitorium, the pair slipped quietly into a saloon for the crucial meeting with the Liberal Junta's emissary, Kenneth Turner. Since the general's progress through San Diego had been almost regal, his whereabouts were no secret, so that the conference with Turner was frequently interrupted by the arrival of *insurrectos* who had also taken the opportunity of the lull in the fighting for an excursion into town. Most left after a few hurried words with Pryce whose eagle-eyed Second-in Command, Captain Hopkins, watched the saloon entrance for intruders. Suddenly, two U.S. soldiers were seen hovering just outside. Cutting short their meeting with Turner, they took the advice of an *insurrecto* visitor to 'beat it while the going is good and the going is getting worse every minute.' Pryce, Hopkins and Milburn hurried back to the U.S. Grant Hotel, the *Union* reporter following them across Fifth Street and into the Scripps Building as they tried to shake off their pursuers. Instead of taking the elevator, the fugitives dodged out through the Hamilton Grocery Store, doubling back across Fifth Street into the Five and Ten Cent Store. Only when satisfied they were no longer being followed, did they enter the hotel through the Third Street entrance, ducking out again immediately through a staff door to their waiting auto, and speeding off towards Tijuana. Following closely behind was another car carrying Ed Hayes, Dr Jackson, his two 'nurses', and the reporter from the *San Diego Union*.

The getaway was going well until two miles from the U.S. side of the border four American soldiers stepped from the brush at a place known locally as Smugglers Gulch, blocking the road and halting the Pryce auto with their rifles. Told they were being arrested on the orders of General Bliss – commander of U.S. forces in Southern California – Pryce, Hopkins and Milburn were marched off to Army Headquarters at the U.S. Custom House to await transfer back to San Diego and the military prison at Fort Rosecrans. Milburn's angry protests that he was a non-combatant were ignored. The Jackson party, arriving minutes later in the second car, were refused permission to approach the prisoners.

The transfer of the prisoners to San Diego was a solemn affair, exercised with a military precision normally reserved for the most dangerous desperadoes. The back end of the train back to San Diego's National City stop was cleared of all civilian passengers, before the prisoners were boarded. When it arrived at the National City stop, the escorting officer, Lieutenant Ord, shouted, 'Make way for the prisoners', the military escort clearing a way across the busy platform. An electric car was commandeered for the next stage of the journey to the end of D Street, the transfer to the army's H Street Barracks finally completed aboard a mule-drawn ambulance escorted by armed soldiers at front and back. Anticipating their arrival, curious San Diegans gathered outside the compound at the H Street Barracks shouting encouragement to the rebel general.[11]

At the barracks the three were given cigarettes and supper while telegrams were sent to Washington and calls made to Fort Rosecrans to prepare the Military Prison for its new inmates. Eventually it was agreed Lieutenant Milburn was indeed an innocent bystander and could be released, his last word to his captors that he would sue for false arrest. Shortly before Pryce and Hopkins were transferred by naval tug to Fort Rosecrans, the *Union* reporter was permitted by the duty sergeant to speak with them:

General Pryce smiled his real, broad, camp smile of welcome . . . he shook this reporter's hand heartily and for the first time in a week of daily interviews failed to say at the beginning of his talk that there was "nothing very exciting." We have protested against our arrest and do not believe we can be held for any length of time without charges against us. I have asked twice if there was any charge and was told each time that if there was the nature of it was not known to my captors. They cannot make any charge against us that will hold. We came into the United States as gentlemen and as perfect tourists to get a dinner and to remain no more than 24 hours. We came unarmed and were returning to Tijuana when we were arrested. I guess that's about all there is to say.[12]

The arrest of Pryce was another opportunity for Ferris to inveigle himself further into the General's confidence. Very quickly he found Pryce and Hopkins one of the best lawyers in town, although there was no shortage of volunteers eager to help. The U.S. Army soon realised the man it had arrested was considered more a celebrity rather than a villain. The readers of the independent *San Diego Sun* had warmed to the 'boss of Tijuana,' the Welshman's admirers preferring to cast him as some sort of Mexican Robin Hood, a role he would reprise when embarking some months later on a new career in Hollywood. Almost overnight, Pryce was the 'most talked of man in California' but a man whose life everyone knew would not be worth a snap if the American Government connived with the Diaz regime for his extradition. Back in Mexico it would be only a matter of hours before he was lined against an *adobe* wall to dance with the *fusillado*.

To make matters worse for the authorities, the arrest of the rebel leader was interpreted as intervention by the United States in support of President Diaz against the revolutionary forces. There seemed to be some justification for this when the *San Diego Sun* claimed that General Bliss had been leaned upon by the Mexican Consul in San Diego, Dr J. Dias Prieto, to arrest the two men to await the issue of an extradition warrant. The *Sun* was not alone in demanding to know whether the arrest of the rebel leader was the prelude to an American invasion of Mexico designed to protect the interests of Spreckles, Hearst, Cudahay, and Otis. Across its front page the *Sun* asked boldly: *IS IT INTERVENTION?* The newspaper noted that Pryce in visiting San Diego had acted no differently to Madero's commanders who had visited El Paso in Texas after the battle of Juarez:

> What have the American people to say about it? Will they stand for the act of General Bliss in striking a severe blow at the revolutionary cause at the moment when Diaz is on the run . . .
>
> The Diaz Government declares that Pryce is not an insurrecto but a filibusterer. If that is so then every Englishman and every American now fighting with Madero is a filibusterer. Pryce like the foreigners with Madero stands on a manifesto issued by citizens of Mexico. He is in the service of the Junta that has its headquarters in Los Angeles, as the foreigners with Madero are in the service of a Junta that has had its headquarters in El Paso and Washington DC. One Junta has as much standing as the other. Both are revolutionary. Both have conquered the region where they fought. Both have established a Government and exercise the military and fiscal powers of Government, not only ruling with the sword, but imposing and collecting taxes as well as customs.

The *Sun* had no doubt General Bliss intervened to save the despot Diaz, because Diaz most suited American interests in Mexico. 'General Bliss did not take Pryce in a battle – he 'pinched' him on the road,' it concluded. [13]

The arrest of Pryce was crucial to Diaz's last ditch plans to stop Madero's advance in eastern Mexico. With the Welshman removed from leadership, the Magonista army would collapse, allowing Mayol and other hard-pressed federal forces to concentrate on the main threat from Madero and Pancho Villa. In pursuit of this strategy, and immediately following the Magonista leader's arrest on 19 May (only six days before Diaz was forced to stand down), the Mexican Ambassador in Washington, M. de Zamacona, telegraphed U.S. Secretary of State Knox alleging Pryce had 'committed great depredations and various robberies.'

> The imprisonment of this criminal will aid materially to check the filibustering expeditions, which are constantly being organised on American territory against Lower California; but should he be set at liberty . . . the effect of this immunity will undoubtedly be to encourage still further the filibusterers in their criminal machinations. I hope, therefore, that your Excellency may see the way to prevent this great evil.[14]

Luckily for Pryce, Knox would have none of this. The ambassador was told the general could not be held unless it was shown he was guilty of violating American neutrality, which seemed unlikely. And if the Mexicans wanted him back they would have to prove him guilty of an extraditable offence.[15] Indeed, it appeared to some observers the U.S. Government was showing more concern for the Welshman's life than ever it had previously for the lives of its own nationals caught up in the Mexican revolution. Was someone somewhere pulling strings?

The special interest shown by Washington in Pryce failed to register immediately, with General Bliss now facing mounting criticism of his actions from a San Diego public that stood squarely behind the imprisoned rebel leader. Bliss was not the only one in trouble. Back in Tijuana, the now leaderless *insurrectos* turned against Dr Jackson who they blamed for enticing Pryce to cross the border. Fearing for his life, the doctor fled to the U.S. Grant Hotel where he announced he would be leaving soon for Europe with his wife for a very long visit. His 'nurses,' now abandoned, wandered around the hotel looking for someone to buy them supper.

Pryce learned that all was not well at Tijuana when visited at Fort Rosecrans by John Kenneth Turner. As he left the military prison Turner was pounced upon by reporters wanting to know about his secret meeting with the rebel leader, and to explain how it was he was also staying at the U.S. Grant Hotel. It was all purely coincidental, Turner insisting he was only in town to present a slide show about the revolution at the Germania Hall and would shortly be returning to Los Angeles. At Fort Rosecrans, Turner who was accompanied by Attorney Ernest Kirk, counsel for the Anti-Interference League, found Pryce and Hopkins not locked in cells, but squatting on chairs in the centre of the prison gymnasium, watched over by a ring of guards stationed around the walls. The prisoners each had a bedroll and were chatting amicably with their warders, their only complaint that the lights of the gymnasium were not switched off at night. Pryce was concerned not about himself but about reports that news of his arrest had led to wild bouts of drinking amongst the insurgents; that without its leader for barely twenty-four hours the Foreign Legion was, as the Mexican Government had predicted, already close to disintegration.

His face flushed with excitement, Pryce turned to Turner and said, 'Tell the boys to stand pat. Tell them I will be back on the firing line in less than twenty-four hours. Tell them not to worry.'[16]

Predictably, Dick Ferris was not far behind in offering succour to the prisoners, arriving with shirts and collars and other personal accessories purchased from the Army Store, plus additional legal advice in the shape, this time, of a Circuit Judge, Judge Lamme. Dick followed this later with a selection of food and drink from San Diego's finest restaurants delivered by a motorcycle despatch rider.

Eventually, the prisoners and their legal advisers settled down to the serious business of drafting Pryce's affidavit for submission to the District Court of Southern California in support of his writ of Habeas Corpus. All this took place in the middle of the prison gymnasium. Two attorneys, one a San Diego judge, an author, a publicity agent and his actress wife, several reporters, and the motorcycle dispatch rider gathered around Pryce as he dictated his statement, watched over by a ring of troops stationed along the walls of the gym:

> I came across the line of my own volition, and as a tourist would enter the United States from Mexico. I made the visit attired in civilian clothes and with no weapons of any kind

or documents bearing on any war or other disturbances. I held no meetings about the insurrection while here and did not buy or place orders for any supplies to take back across the line, or make any effort to secure recruits. I committed no crime or breach of international law and have as yet to be told what charge, if any, has been made against me. I insist I am being illegally held and there is no charge upon which I can legally be convicted or further detained.

This done, Pryce and Hopkins were confident of release within hours, until one of the reporters stunned everyone by asking the general about the 'missing $7,000'. Back in Tijuana, some of the *insurrectos* were alleging this amount had disappeared from the rebel army's war chest, the finger of suspicion pointed at Pryce by Antonio Araujo, the man Magon had sent to Tijuana to handle the collection of customs duties and tolls. Shaken by the allegation, Pryce took a dollar or two in small change from his pocket and said, 'This is the nearest to $7000 that I have or have had since my arrest.' His denial failed, however, to stop newspaper speculation, one reporting a U.S. Federal source as saying Pryce had banked the money in San Diego before his arrest.

No attempt was made by the military authorities to interfere with the procession of visitors. One of these, Allen Hutchinsen, the British Vice-Consul, insisted on speaking to Pryce privately. Emerging from the parley, Hutchinsen announced that he believed they had met before, and because of this could vouch for Pryce's honesty and decency. The Vice-Consul also revealed that some weeks earlier, when HMS *Algerine* was at San Diego, he had escorted Mrs Eileen Graham, Pryce's sister, aboard to meet her husband, Lieutenant Robert Graham.[17]

The following day, Saturday 20 May, Judge Sloane had a full house in his District Court. Among the spectators, Magonista rebels who had crossed the border during the night to witness the fate of their leader, rubbed shoulders with the *crème de la crème* of the San Diego legal community. The hub-hub of anticipation was such that Sheriff Jennings was obliged to call for order on several occasions. This exploded into uproar when Major George McManus, representing the U.S. Army, refused to produce Pryce and Hopkins, claiming the court was not qualified to adjudicate on the writ of Habeas Corpus. The Welshman's legal team, so numerous some were falling off the end of the appellant's bench, were indignant. In the well of the court Ferris and Turner led the chorus of dissent. In contrast, Major McManus, opposing the writ for the army sat alone and isolated.

Pressed by Judge Sloane to explain on what authority Pryce and Hopkins had been arrested, the major pleaded the Hague Convention's resolution that 'a neutral power which receives on its territory troops belonging to the belligerent armies shall intern them, as far as possible, from the seat of war.' Pryce's attorney Kirk was apocalyptic, wagging his finger at the major and insisting that since it was no crime to cross the border, the Army needed to prove the pair were in fact *insurrectos*. To this McManus replied:

> It may be contended that Pryce and Hopkins are here in a legal manner but where are we to draw the line? If something was not done to prevent it, they could all come up when hard pressed. They could cross this country from Tijuana under protection, and rush down to Mexicali. They could go all the way to Los Angeles, if necessary.[18]

Perhaps someone had pointed out to him those little red badges worn by the Wobbles crowding the court, with the slogan, 'Los Angeles in 1912'.

It looked certain Judge Sloane would grant the writ of Habeas Corpus, when the hearing was interrupted by a telegram from U.S. District Attorney McCormick in Los Angeles asking for an adjournment. That same morning McCormick had been told by the U.S. Attorney General in Washington to involve himself more directly in the proceedings. Anxious to avoid a jurisdictional conflict between the State and Federal judiciaries, the Judge adjourned until the Monday so McCormick could be present.[19]

The court had barely emptied, the presses of the *San Diego Sun* just plated for the evening run, when a flash arrived at its offices from the United Press Washington Bureau announcing that the War Department had decided there was insufficient evidence to hold Pryce and Hopkins for violating the neutrality laws and that they should be released immediately. General Bliss felt humiliated. This was tantamount to a reprimand for acting without authority. Refusing to believe the report, Bliss wired the War Department for confirmation. At the H Street Barracks Major McManus sat by the telegraph wire throughout the Saturday night waiting for the final word from Bliss. The army compound was packed with reporters and wellwishers awaiting Pryce's release.

The release order from Bliss came at 9 pm, and the Government tug *General De Hussy* sent to collect Pryce and Hopkins from Fort Rosecrans. As they disembarked at the Navy wharf at the bottom of H Street, Major McManus stepped out of the shadows and shook their hands, addressing the *insurrectos* in turn by rank as he wished them good luck. Their arrest, he said, was 'nothing personal.'

Waiting around the corner in a chauffeur-driven automobile, its engine running was Dr Jackson. After fleeing from angry insurgents the previous day, the doctor now saw an opportunity to rebuild his bridges. Bundling the pair into the car, he drove directly to the U.S. Grant Hotel. Since it was just possible they were being followed, the doctor dropped Pryce and Hopkins at the hotel, before leading them out through a rear entrance across C Street to Reading and Woolman's funeral parlour where they waited while he reconnoitred the area. Some thirty minutes later he returned to the funeral parlour on foot accompanied by Mrs Ferris, evidently relieved to see Pryce was safe. Then down the street roared the hired auto, stopping momentarily for the four to jump aboard before heading at top speed for Tijuana.

Alerted by Dr Jackson to Pryce's release from Fort Rosecrans, Dick Ferris was already on his way to Tijuana to organise the homecoming. Dick could see the headlines as he sped to the border, accompanied by Lieutenant Milburn and the omnipresent reporter from the *San Diego Union*. Later the *Union* reported the rebel homecoming under the headline: 'General Pryce back with rebels; volley for him and Ferris.'

According to the *Union,* the rebel leaders had a rousing reception from fifty mounted *insurrectos* waiting at the crossing point. There were cheers also for Dick Ferris when they recognised the man 'whose kindness to the general and captain while they were at Fort Rosecrans was known in Tijuana.'

The rebels fired their rifles and revolvers in a welcoming volley and shouted "Viva Libertad", "Viva Pryce" and "Viva Ferris", and surrounded their returned leader and escorted him to the town where there was further demonstration and rejoicing. Pryce told his men he was glad to get back, that they had kept the camp in good shape, had behaved well, and that he did not intend returning to San Diego unless in emergency or guaranteed proper protection. Ferris and his party left Tijuana at about 1 o'clock this morning on the return to San Diego. The rebels cheered and fired a volley in his honour as he left.[20]

News of Pryce's release was telegraphed to his brother-in-law Lieutenant Graham aboard *HMS Algerine* by the British Vice-Consul in San Diego, Allen Huchenson, who remarked on how successful the Magonista leader had been:

> I think it is very likely that you heard about it, but I mention it in case you did not as I have no doubt Mrs Graham must have been very anxious about her brother. He has done wonders in the fighting way so far and he now has a free hand to go ahead again and take the peninsula for the junta if he can.[21]

If this were to happen Pryce needed to do something about the morale of his troops, by then at rock bottom after news that Madero had overthrown Diaz and was on his way to Mexico City.[22] Next day the Magonistas suffered a body blow from which they were never to recover when Diaz fled into exile in France after signing a peace treaty with Madero. Foreign Secretary Francisco de la Barra was appointed provisional president while elections were organised that would almost certainly put Madero in the presidential palace.

Only Magon and the Liberal Junta denied the significance of these events. Defiantly, they issued yet another manifesto denouncing Madero as a representative of 'money power' in Mexico, a member of the 'slave holding class.' The message to Pryce from Los Angeles was to fight on until 'the natural resources of Mexico have been restored to the people for their free and equal use.'

Invective was about all Magon had to offer the insurgents at Tijuana. On hearing that General Viljoen was marching on Lower

California with orders from Madero to eliminate the Magonistas, the junta leader was at his most bombastic, warning Madero's general to expect a warm reception, war to the bitter end. 'You may rest assured of that,' screamed Magon across the pages of *La Regeneración*. 'Madero has proven he is of the same calibre as Diaz. That is sufficient for us. We will not stand for it.'[23] Nonetheless, they had no plans to leave their Los Angeles redoubt to man the barricades of Tijuana. That would be left to Pryce and his assorted bunch of mercenaries and Wobblies, deserters and desperadoes.

With every rumour of imminent attack, the mood in Tijuana grew blacker, even the professional gamblers scenting danger, and leaving town. The first crack in the ranks appeared when a murderous Mexican called Tobe rounded up thirty of his compatriots and rode out of town, having decided to go into business on their own account, raiding and looting ranches along the border as far as Campo.

Weapons, horses and supplies were disappearing at an alarming rate and it was time to pay another visit to the construction camps along the San Diego and Arizona Eastern Railroad. This time the *insurrectos* went by train after commandeering one hauling supplies out to the camps. After seizing it at Agua Caliente, the Conductor W. G. McCormick and the company agent C. E. Crowley were hauled before Pryce and asked them to confirm that Spreckles the sugar baron and landowner was building the line, Pryce adding, 'Well, Mr Crowley, war is war, and we must have supplies for man and beast, and I will not draw on you for more than is necessary and will receipt for everything taken but as Spreckles has millions and large interests in this section, it is my intention to make him and other large holders contribute heavily to the support of my army.'

But Pryce knew that living off the railroad and ranchers along the border could not last. Soon the ranchers would demand protection from the U.S. Army, against which the Liberal Junta's propaganda would be no defence. As for Madero, once in control of Mexico City he would his guns on the Magonistas. Perversely, the only thing that rung true in the junta leader's verbal onslaught was that the Magonistas had contributed to Madero's success, by forcing Diaz to divert essential military resources away from his

Rebels from General Pryce's Second Battalion, or 'Foreign Legion' as it was known, commandeer a train to take them into battle against the Mexicans. (San Diego Historical Society).

main threat to deal with Pryce in Lower California. For that reason alone, the Liberal Junta could justifiably argue it had shared in the victory over Diaz.

But with the signing of the peace treaty, the Foreign Legion was for all practical purposes left high and dry. The mercenaries among them were becoming more inclined to the view their only chance of salvaging anything from the revolution was to throw in their lot with the Ferris Filibuster. And for this to succeed they needed to take the capital Ensenada. Another battlefield victory would restore their position as a serious revolutionary challenge to Madero at a time when peace was fragile, and the Maderistas were quarrelling among themselves over the leadership. But Pryce for all his leadership qualities was paralysed by the volatility and unreliability of his rebel force, unable to say with confidence from one day to the next how many he commanded, and whether they would stand their ground in a fight. Asked by reporters about moving on Ensenada, his answer was always the same, 'Oh well, I don't believe I'm ready to announce that.' The fate of what remained of the Liberal Army in Mexico hung by a thread.[24]

Madero's victory over Diaz did not relieve the British Foreign Office of its concern about a possible rebel attack on the vast property interests of the Mexican Land and Colonisation Company, with its headquarters at Ensenada. Neither was the situation helped by the continuing presence of a British national at the centre of the uprising, this leaving HM Government exposed to persistent allegations of collusion, especially after the Shearwater incident. London instructed its Consul-General in Mexico City, Mr Hohler, to intercede with the Mexican Government on Britain's behalf:

Mexican Land and Colonisation Company complain that marauding has increased in Lower California. Tijuana reported captured by brigands; stores and records destroyed. Brigands are expected to move next on Ensenada where defence cannot be depended upon. Conditions much more serious than was anticipated. Company fear all records will be purposely destroyed. Marauders, opposed to Madero and Government, said to consist of 90 Americans led by an Englishman (sic). Company anxious that British or joint

British and United States naval action be taken for their protection.[25]

Pryce hesitated. His rebel force might have been poorly armed and weakened by desertions, but was still strong enough to capture Ensenada from the Mexican Governor Vega whose position was especially precarious after Madero's victory. Unpopular with Diaz because he failed to take decisive action to deal with the Magonistas after Mexicali, Vega was certainly no friend of Madero. There was bad blood between the two. Vega believed the president-in-waiting had conspired to block his promotion, which was why he was posted to a remote corner of the country. This probably explains his indifference to the defence of Ensenada, preferring to evacuate rather than face a rebel attack. With nothing to gain from a Madero presidency, there was always the possibility the Governor would have joined forces with Pryce and his Magonistas. Madero might have been victorious at Juarez but still had plenty to do to persuade all his generals to sign-up to the peace. In the southern state of Morelos, Emiliano Zapata had already broken with Madero over his failure to place agrarian reform at the top of his political agenda.

Pryce had his hands full repairing morale in Tijuana, and equipping and training a steady stream of recruits to plug the gaps left by deserters. As far as anyone could see, the general was continuing to prosecute the revolution of the Liberal Junta by preparing the army to march on Ensenada. The Red Flag still flew above the main buildings, while the collection of border tolls and duties was organised more efficiently. The postal service with San Diego had also been restored; a minimum wage of $1-50 for an eight-hour day imposed on employers in the immediate vicinity of Tijuana; and the San Diego and Arizona Eastern Railroad was forced to reduce its working hours from ten to eight, necessitating the employment of another sixty men. Behind this socialist front, however, there were those who suspected Pryce and Ferris were plotting a filibuster that would reward the *insurrectos* in other ways. Ferris and his wife had become frequent visitors to the camp, Mrs Ferris sometimes arriving unaccompanied in husband Dick's big blue automobile.

A visit from the attractive young actress was always good for morale. On one occasion after Pryce had escorted her around camp, introducing her to his men, Mrs Ferris was about to leave when a young rebel soldier approached, handing her a package. Surprised by the gift, the actress stood for a moment hat in hand, fluttering her eyes at her admirer who said shyly, 'I don't know whether you remember me, but I was a member of your company when you were playing "Cleopatra" in Los Angeles several years ago. I was not a very big member of the company, a Roman soldier, and one of the many Roman soldiers – but I knew you the minute I saw you.'

No one in the Ferris family it would seem could miss a cue, Mrs Ferris replying, 'You're a soldier of fortune now and have a some-what larger stage to work on.' The young *insurrecto* tipped his sombrero as the lady drove away, his gift to her: a Mexican water bottle wrapped in a piece of cloth torn from his shirt.[26]

Moments like this were rare in Tijuana. Every day there was some kind of fracas. Unwisely as it transpired, Pryce had decided the best way to deal with the potentially dangerous rivalry between the Mexicans and gringos was to issue the leaders of the rebel factions with 'franchises' to police the various saloons in return for which they retained a share of the takings. The protection racket was alive and well in Tijuana, thriving on the lawlessness Pryce and his officers were proving powerless to prevent. One visitor during these final days reported to the *San Diego Union* that a visit to Tijuana was like living on the brink of a volcano; there was not a sane man in the entire town, just anarchy. The only protection a tourist had was daylight; after nightfall people mugged and killed, the rebels taking the opportunity to settle old scores. Every time a shot was heard the *insurrectos* snatched up their weapons and rushed into the street expecting to find the town under attack. One night when this happened, a German insurgent who, crazed with liquor had made himself thoroughly unpopular, simply never returned. His body was found the fol-lowing morning hidden in the brush.

With control slipping away, sooner or later an incident would occur which would convince Pryce it was time to extricate him-self from a seemingly hopeless situation. That moment was pre-cipitated by another murder: a Mexican with the franchise to run one saloon accused another of moving in on his territory during an absence. When Captain Tony Vegas took a trip to San Diego on Sunday, May 28, trouble broke out among a group of drunken Mexicans in his saloon. Another rebel, Jose Pacheco stepped in and ordered the saloon closed. On his return Vegas saw this as an attempt by Pacheco to seize his property and challenged him to a pistol duel. Refusing, Pacheco backed away, slipping to the ground in front of the saloon at which point Vegas whipped out his pistol and shot him through the chest in front of a crowd of tourists. As he lay dying, Vegas fired another bullet into his neck.

General Pryce was quite fond of Vegas and was inclined to ignore the affair. He had already executed one *insurrecto* for raping a 12-year-old Mexican girl on a ranch twelve miles away, then horribly mutilating her with a knife. The young girl was dead by the time rescuers arrived, and Pryce, in no doubt of the rapist's guilt, lined the Mexican against an *adobe* wall and shot him. Vegas on the other hand was well liked by the *gringo insurrectos*, several of whose lives he had saved earlier in the campaign. The Mexican friends of Pacheco, however, demanded revenge, so a court martial was held, and Vegas sentenced to be executed by firing squad at dawn the following morning. This grieved Pryce more than any other decision he had taken during the campaign in Lower California, the Welshman writing to Attorney Kirk of his regret that two good men of his command should go to their deaths by violence and execution in their own camp.

Woken just before sunrise, Vegas was marched out to face the *fusillado*. Witnessing the execution was Fred Williams, a reporter from the *Los Angeles Herald* who had quit his job to enlist in the Magonistas a few weeks earlier:

> There were the usual grim preparations, the formation of the hollow square of soldiers, the march to the *cuartel* where the condemned man was imprisoned, the death march to the scene of execution, the advance of one of the firing squad to blindfold the doomed soldier, after he had been stood against a wall, and the offering of an opportunity to the condemned man to say farewell.
>
> From the time Captain Curtiss began reading the death sentence until the volley was fired, Captain Vegas, refusing

to be blindfolded, showed not the slightest sign of fear, but the passion which made of him a murderer flamed up within him again as he faced the squad that was to kill him. He had folded his hands across his breast, unconsciously an attitude of defiance it seemed, for almost immediately he spread out his hands and called out to the soldiers.

"Shoot me in the heart: remember no bullet in my head. If you are men don't let the Americans shoot; the Americans are my friends – let the Mexicans shoot me down."

A sneer came over the doomed man's face as he continued to talk. He called his executioners by name and scorned them. Then he said, "I'm ready."

There were five shots, almost as one. Vegas fell to the ground pierced by four bullets, but he was not dead; it was doubtful even if the four shots were fatal, so a fifth was fired into his heart. The body was allowed to lie where it had fallen until an hour or two later when it was rolled in a blanket and buried in a shallow grave nearby.

Prior to the execution there was a pathetic incident – the farewell at the *curatel* between the condemned man and his 14-year-old adopted son of whom he was as fond as if he had been the lad's father. The soldier of two battles took the boy into his arms, held him closely as he whispered words of endearment to him, and the guard saw tears roll down the man's cheeks as the boy said simply, "Goodbye, papa."[27]

The following morning the camp was in uproar. General Pryce and his adjutant, Captain Melbourne Hopkins were nowhere to be found. The immediate reaction of the bleary-eyed *insurrectos* was to hurry to the *cuartel* to check whether the army's war chest had been rifled. As Junta Secretary Araujo went through the books, others telephoned banks in San Diego where the army had placed deposits, issuing instructions not to honour any cheques presented by their missing general. Poor Araujo was at a loss to say if anything was missing. While most border taxes were entered in the books, much of the cash generated from the 'protection services' provided for the Tijuana saloons wound up in rebel pockets not ledgers.[28]

Pryce and Hopkins had quit camp under cover of darkness the previous evening to meet Dick Ferris waiting at the border with his automobile. The vehicle had a full load. Besides the rebel leaders, there was Mrs Ferris, a woman friend, and another two male companions. Before the over-laden auto had travelled any distance it blew a tyre, Ferris, unperturbed, driving the fifteen miles to San Diego on the wheel rim. On arrival, the group headed for Crane's Restaurant and a meal before Ferris delivered the fugitives to the rail station to catch the 5 a.m. 'Owl' for Los Angeles.[29]

Pryce was on his way for a showdown with Ricardo Magon. As far as anyone has been able to tell, the pair had never met, the only communication from Magon the occasional letter either congratulating the Welshman on a victory or reminding him to forward the revenue from customs tolls and duties to junta headquarters in Los Angeles. Thousands of dollars were shipped north, but not a single rifle or round of ammunition were delivered to the rebel army by the junta, the money appearing to disappear either into a huge black hole of political propaganda or diverted into supporting the life style to which the junta had become accustomed. Pryce and his army were left to live off the land.

The meeting between the revolution's two main leaders would be a defining moment, the veritable eye of the storm. Pryce planned to put three propositions to Flores Magon: either they join forces with the new de la Barra Government, form a coalition with General Ambrosio Figueroa, one of the Maderistas dissident generals, or disband the Liberal Army. The Welshman had abandoned any idea of marching on Ensenada. Unknown to Ferris, Pryce by this time had probably also decided to pull out of his filibuster deal. Dick certainly thought he was returning to Tijuana, because he heard him buy a two-way ticket, and leave orders for a hired car to meet him at the station on his return that same evening.[30]

There is only the word of the socialist writer John Kenneth Turner that there was ever a meeting between the two. Magon and other members of the Junta never mentioned it. Not long after the meeting was supposed to have taken place, Magon accused Pryce publicly of looting the rebel war chest and in so doing wrecking the Magonista Revolution, an accusation seized upon by the Junta's Wobbly supporters who from that moment onwards cast Pryce as the villain of the piece, no better than the worst of the desperadoes he commanded.

The two men could not have been more different. The battle-hardened veteran of the British Empire, Pryce was a well-bred adventurer, imbued with a sense of inherent privilege, characteristics of the very society Magon had spent his life fighting. Pryce's path may have been crossed by more vicissitudes than most men but his ties to his ancestral past were ultimately unshakable. He might have ridden freight cars with the Wobbly socialists of West Coast America, and stood beside them at Mexicali and Tijuana, yet he would never have counted himself one of them. Their socio-anarchist goals would have appalled the former policeman with a life-long respect for law and order. In view of all of this, his justification for involving himself in the revolution – the 'poor peons' – somehow seems totally inadequate. But at the same time Pryce was enigmatic, raising the Red Flag in Tijuana and issuing a proclamation fixing a minimum wage for peasant workers.

To make matters worse, the revolutionary duo could barely converse, Pryce not speaking a word of Spanish other than what was needed to acquire the basic necessities of life, food, drink, and shelter. The political theorist and avowed anarchist, Ricardo Flores Magon, on the other hand, grew in stature *after* the uprising collapsed, and was eventually elevated to the same revolutionary dais as Trotsky and Che Guevara. The small, rotund, middle-aged Mexican born of an Indian father and *mestizo* mother who spent half his life in jail, would be immortalised when his birthplace in Oaxaca Province was re-named *Ricardo Flores Magon*. But his Magonistas would never have marched off the pages of *La Regeneración* had not the Welshman proved, when Mexico was at the crossroads, that given support he was capable of seizing the whole of Baja California. Whether this would have been for the Magonistas or as part of a Ferris filibuster to add a new state to the Union – or even for Britain whose concern for events was not entirely altruistic – we will probably never know, because the uprising ended in farce as one of the most poorly conducted in the annals of revolutionary history, due largely to the incompetence of Magon and his Liberal Junta. Back in Tijuana, the now leaderless rebels were at odds over their general's presumed betrayal, especially after they discovered a letter dated 1 June (with footnote dated 3 June), Hopkins had sent to a friend, James Dunn at the military hospital at Pont Loma:

Dear Friend:

I am writing these few lines to give you the facts of my case. I was unable to call on you when I passed through San Diego. I just received your letter the last evening in Tijuana. Pryce and I left there to confer with the Junta. The officers all knew Pryce was coming up. We did not think it advisable to inform the boys. I decided to come up at the last minute. Neither one of us took a cent from the funds. I had a few dollars, which I made by selling a plant of curios, etc., which I had discovered. On account of the Junta not assisting us, we have had a hard time to get ammunition, etc. We raked in about $850 from license fees etc, and were holding it with the intention of getting field pieces and machine guns, expecting the Junta to come through with rifles and ammo. They have been receiving contributions right along, and never came through with a gun or cartridge. But that was not the worst. They did not send anyone down to transact the official business of the town, except towards the last they sent one down to handle the customs. All they ever did was to write letters of congratulation. Mayol got away from us on account of lack of ammunition. When we marched from Little's Ranch Pryce sent a letter to the Junta asking that 20,000 rounds be sent to Tijuana to be ready for us when we arrived. They did not do this, nor did they even reply to the letter. If this had been sent we would have marched directly on to Ensenada before Mayol coluld have started from Bee River. To make a long story short, it disgusted us so much that we decided to quit. Even after Madero had won out and declared us to be filibusterers, etc, the Junta did not visit us. Only through the papers we learned of their intentions. J. K. T. (John Kenneth Turner) visited us while at the fort and said we could not fight both the feds and the Maderistas, as the Junta wanted us to do. We had a meeting with the officers when we got back and practically decided to throw it up.

We were leery of the Mexicans and did not know how to go about it for the best. We were afraid that on account of the Junta still ordering us to continue the fight that if we had a meeting of the boys and declared it all off, the Mexs would call us filibusters etc and start a young civil war amongst us. On the other hand, we figured that if Pryce blew, the bunch would disappear.

June 3,

Just saw James: he tells me you are down there. I didn't think you were ready to leave hospital so soon. I was hoping this letter would reach you in time to prevent you from going down. As far as I can see the game is up, that is the financial end of it, and I don't feel like risking my life for nothing. However, you may look at it in a different light. Would like to see you and have a long talk with you. My next move will be either South America or the South Seas. James says you are all right except for the bullet in the shoulder. Hope you get it out soon.

Well, this is all now. If you wish to keep in touch with me, address me care of Dick Ferris: he is a good fellow and can be trusted. Am looking forward to a letter from you. Au revoir.

Ever your friend,
Melbourne.

Address: C. W. Hopkins, care of Dick Ferris U.S. Grant Hotel, San Diego.

P.S. – When you have read this burn it.

P.P.S. – Will write further when I receive an answer from you. Am working on the 'Pearl proposition.'

Was the 'Pearl proposition' meant to refer to Hopkins's obsession with the lost Treasure of Laguna Salada? As it transpired, Dunn was killed in the next battle for Tijuana.

Pryce's departure was tactical. Desertion would have been wholly uncharacteristic of a man whose life was spent courting danger. By now it would have been clear to just about everyone that once he quit what remained of the Magonista army would disintegrate. The governments in Washington, London and Mexico City could relax. The properties of the Mexican Land and Colonisation Company were safe, and under Madero, Mexico could return to the kind of administration with which America and foreign investors felt most comfortable.

It can only be assumed from all of this the meeting with Flores Magon was unproductive. But Ferris, who had not given up his idea of creating a filibuster state in Lower California, led a rebel delegation to Los Angeles to plead with Pryce to return and resume command of the Magonistas. For a time it seemed Pryce had agreed, and was in fighting mood when he addressed the Los Angeles Press Club on 6 June 1911, promising his audience he would return and establish a new republic in Lower California. Predicting that Mexico's fragile peace would last no longer than three months, after which rival factions would resume hostilities, Pryce boasted that it would require a very large army to drive the *insurrectos* out of Lower California. He told the assembled Press of a telephone call he had made to Madero asking for his support and warning of a hard struggle if the Magonistas were opposed, adding, 'It will be a long time before the government will be in a position to spare a large force to move against Lower California. In the meantime, my army is steadily growing. Recruits are coming in and they are fighters, soldiers of fortune who have served in the American and European armies.'[32]

Since Pryce was never a man noted for bravado, he may well have been planning to continue the revolution. Even though Madero was in Mexico City at the moment Pryce addressed the Los Angeles Press Club, Pancho Villa and Emiliano Zapata remained reluctant to give up the armed struggle, as did many others. Particularly significant about the Welshman's speech to the Press Club was there was no mention this time of defending the interests of the 'poor peons.' But not everyone at Tijuana would have welcomed the return of their commander, some believing the allegations in the Wobbly press and *La Regeneración* that Pryce had 'skipped out with their money'. When rumours reached the Welshman that he and Hopkins had been court-martialed in their absence, the pair headed off for Canada under assumed names.[33]

Arriving in San Francisco they called on an old friend Peter Kyne, the reporter from *Sunshine Magazine* they had last met at Mexicali. At the reunion over beer and cigarettes in a San Francisco café, Kyne was surprised how well and relaxed they looked, commenting on this to Pryce who remarked that the real fighting had been nothing compared to the job of handling his command:

> They began to slip over the border singly and in pairs, and one night Rusty and Bobby Flash and four others beat it with their horses and guns. It was getting so serious that I came up to Los Angeles to see the Junta and find out what they intended doing. They had no money, and we didn't have any ammunition and it was useless to move on Ensenada. So when I found the jig was up, I wrote back to the boys at Tijuana and advised them to disband. Hopkins and I came north to look for something else. Perhaps some day we may go back. I could hold Lower California with a thousand men and a couple of screw guns.[34]

Kyne asked what had become of the men he had met on his first visit to their camp at Mexicali after the Battle of John Little's Ranch. Pryce told how 'Bulldog' Smith had died the day they captured Tijuana. Hit through the jaw, he spat the blood out, grinned at Hopkins lying in the grass beside him, and continued fighting. Fifteen minutes later after he was hit again in the body, he muttered, 'Goodbye Melbourne. I'm finished.' The giant Afro-American Kyne had met sitting under the tree was dead, too. 'Dynamite Bill' had been shot in a fracas at Tijuana, and 'Slim' Dunn's right arm wrecked by a Mauser. 'Doc' Larkins had deserted the night before Tijuana. When the interview ended, the pair slipped quietly away to avoid the Mexican government agents on their tail. They would not stop at kidnapping if that was the only way to get Pryce and Hopkins back to Mexico for their date with the *fusillado*.[35]

NOTES

1. National Archives. Senate Committee Report on 'Revolutions in Cuba and Mexico,' 373-74.
2. *San Francisco Chronicle,* 9 February 1911.
3. ibid., 6 February 1911.
4. National Archives. Senate Committee Report on 'Revolutions in Cuba and Mexico,' 374.
5. *La Regeneración,* 18 February 1911.
6. *San Diego Union,* 6, 13 March 1911; *Los Angeles Herald,* 13 March 1911.
7. ibid., 19 May 1911.
8. Pryce Papers. Letter from Allen Hutchenson, British Vice Counsel San Diego, to British Counsel San Francisco, 19 May 1911.
9. *San Diego Union,* 19 May 1911; *San Diego Sun,* 18 May 1911.
10. ibid.
11. ibid.
12. ibid.
13. *San Diego Union,* 21, 22 May 191; National Archives, U.S. Attorney General George Wickersham to Assistant Secretary of War Robert Shaw Oliver, 27 May 1911, General Records, Department of Justice, Rec. Gp. 74. These, together with correspondence between Secretary of State Knox and Wickersham, show it was only because of a mix up over a legal technicality that the Mexican Government failed in its first attempt to have Pryce extradited.
14. National Archives, Senate Committee, *Foreign Relations, 1911,* 490-91.
15. ibid., 498-99, 500-503, 500.
16. *San Diego Union,* 19 May 1911.
17. ibid.
18. *San Diego Union,* 20 May 1911.
19. National Archives, Washington, United States Senate Committee on Foreign Relations, 1912-1913, *Revolutions in Mexico* (CIS No: S40-3), p. 229.
20. *San Diego Union,* 21 May 1911; for different version of return to Tijuana see *San Diego Sun,* 22 May 1911.
21. Pryce Papers. Letter from Hutchenson to Captain Jones, Commander of HMS *Algerine,* 22 May 1911.
22. *San Diego Union,* 24 May 1911.
23. *La Regeneración,* 20, 27 May, 3 June 1911.
24. *San Diego Union,* 24 May 1911.
25. Public Records Office. Telegram to Mr Hohler, British Consul General Mexico City from British Foreign Office, 16 May 1911, FO 371 1147, 8450/11, No. 24.
26. *San Diego Union,* 24 May 1911.
27. *San Diego Union,* 31 May, 1 June 1911; *San Diego Evening Tribune,* 31 May 1911; *Los Angeles Examiner,* 1 June 1911.
28. *San Diego Sun,* 31 May 1911.
29. *San Diego Union,* 1 June; *San Diego Evening Tribune,* 31 May 1911; *Los Angeles Examiner,* 1 June 1911, 24 September 1911; National Archives, Senate Investigation of Mexican Affairs, II, 2503.

30. *San Diego Union,* 1 June 1911; *San Diego Evening Tribune,* 2 June 1911; *San Francisco Chronicle,* 17 June 1911; Peter Kyne, 'The gringo as insurrecto,' *Sunset Magazine,* XXVII, September 1911.
31. National Archives, Senate Foreign relations Sub-Committee Report, *Revolutions in Cuba and Mexico,* 62 Congress, 2 session (Washington: Government Printing Office, 1913), 99. 197-98.
32. *Los Angeles Times,* 6 June 1911.
33. *Revolutions in Cuba and Mexico,* 379.
34. Peter Kyne, 'The gringo as insurrecto,' *Sunset Magazine,* XXVII, September 1911.
35. ibid.

Chapter 9

El Presidente Dick

The leadership vacuum at Tijuana was filled by Captain Louis James. A shadowy figure, James spent much of his time conspiring around the fringes of the prevailing uncertainty. Claiming to be a 'West Point graduate', he struck a deal with the publicist Dick Ferris to cut out the Liberal Junta and establish Lower California as some kind of 'Gaming Republic.'[1] Even without Pryce, Ferris continued to pursue his plans for a filibuster although still preferring that the Welshman led it. Invited to the rebel camp to discuss the proposition, Dick immediately insisted before any deal was struck that the rebels hauled down the Red Flag. He told them bluntly what it meant to Americans:

> Anarchy in America, and you have got that out in the sight of every American who passes this border. You have got to cut out your socialism, your anarchism, and every other ism that you have got into and form a new government if you hope to do anything right. If you do establish the right kind of government here you can appeal to the young blood of America, and to the Press of America, and there will be no trouble in getting their sympathy and also their money, and I think you can get the better class of Mexicans to join you in this movement. [2]

After Ferris had left, James assembled the increasingly mutinous rebels in front of the *cuartel*, where he delivered a rousing speech and proposed they elected Ferris as president of their new republic. The only way to avoid being 'robbed of the fruits of their victory', James told them, was to tear down the Red Flag, declare a provisional government, and raise above their New Republic the Ferris standard, two straight bars of white and red across a blue field with a big white star in the centre. At that very moment the flag was being stitched together by the publicist's Los Angeles costumier. James told his troops, 'The time has arrived when we must declare to the world that we enlisted in the name of oppressed humanity, willing to serve under any banner as a means to an end, and now that the end has been achieved, we have been left leaderless and thrown upon our own resources.' Their purpose had been noble, and at the very least they deserved Madero's recognition – not forgetting some form of financial consideration – for pinning down 2000 *federales* in Lower California who may

The showman Dick Ferris, close friend of Pryce, was briefly President of the new republic of Lower California.

otherwise have defeated the revolution. 'We have no desire for conquest; we resent the criticism heaped upon us and, as contradiction of this criticism, we propose to establish a New Republic and to claim its recognition for the blood of the white men which has been spilled on the soil of Lower California and Mexico in bringing about the success of the revolution,' said James.[3]

The *insurrectos,* their hopes of being paid raised by James' oratory, cheered wildly, a forest of rifles waved in the air electing Dick Ferris provisional president. Excitedly the men called for *el presidente* to be brought to his republic – but he was nowhere to be found. At that moment, Dick was on his way north on the hope of persuading Pryce to return.[4]

News of Ferris's election as President of a Gaming Republic rang around the world like a great big belly laugh. In Las Vegas, a trainload of gamblers announced they were on their way to San Diego to cheer for Dick Ferris. In Alberta, Canada, Hank Ferris, ex-sheriff of Big Wind, denied he was to become vice-president of Lower California. On Coney Island, Mr Ferris Wheel said he was not in any way connected with the Dick Ferris elected provisional president of Lower California, but was glad to hear of Dick's big doings. At Juarez, where Madero's revolutionary army was camped, his soldiers dropped their cigarettes to wave hats and shout 'Viva Ferris' when told of Dick's coup. In Chicago, Flossie Highkicker, of the 'Gay Maidens' Company, observed, 'Take it from me kid, this man Ferris has got them going. Never saw that new president Dick Ferris, but bet you he is a jim-dandy little official, what!'[5]

With this kind of reaction, Dick began to wonder whether this time he had over-played his hand, especially when it was discovered FBI agents were snooping into the affairs of anyone connected to Pryce and the Liberal Junta. Dick's Los Angeles office was just across the road from the Justice Department and perhaps someone had whispered a warning in his ear. But the bandwagon was rolling and Dick could not resist climbing aboard, allowing friends to organise a Presidential Banquet at the Alexandria Hotel in Los Angeles.[6] The banquet lasted all day, and even in a city accustomed to eccentric extravagance it was something to be remembered, Mrs Ferris making a grand entrance in her specially designed presidential gown. Dick followed with a presidential address in which he was careful not to accept the presidency immediately. But his inherent sense of showmanship was irrepressible, using the occasion to transform what had become a mutinous rabble into an army of 500 stalwart, committed revolutionaries ready to defend his New Republic. If Dick was to be believed, the long-awaited rifles had arrived, so had the machine guns. Around Tijuana the hills crawled with *insurrecto* patrols; there was no way, said Ferris, the *federales* could get within forty miles without being spotted. And almost magically, Dick conjured up a Los Angeles manufacturer itching to invest $12,000 in the campaign.[7]

Pressed to say whether he would accept the presidency, Ferris set out three conditions: firstly, all the Red Flags must be torn down and replaced by his; a constitutional convention called at which Madero would be asked to recognise the *insurrectos* and pay them for their services; and General Pryce persuaded to return. For good measure, Dick, for whom money was never an obstacle, offered Madero $15 million for Lower California, which he promised to re-name the 'Republic of Madero' in honour of Madero's victory.[8] 'The junta,' Ferris concluded, 'offer the *insur-rectos* nothing more than provisions, and they refuse to work any longer with the Junta. General Pryce told them he would not continue in their service if they had nothing better to offer his men.' Newspaper accounts of whether Dick had or had not accepted the offer of the presidency of the New Republic of Lower California were hopelessly confused, one suggesting he had done so at the celebration ball, another that at the end of it he rejected the offer, saying, 'I shall tell the boys on Monday there is nothing doing . . . my election to the presidency of the provisional government of Lower California was without my solicitation or consent, and I have not been officially notified of the fact.'[9] Dick was getting worried.

Meanwhile, there was no improvement in the situation in Tijuana. U.S. Customs were tipped off about a plan to smuggle $50,000 worth of looted goods out of the town once the army disbanded. For a moment, Customs Officers patrolling the border crossing thought the smuggling scam had started when an unusually large number of extremely large women were spotted crossing the border at a point some way along the barbed wire fence. Nothing much was done until one of the women while attempting to crawl beneath the wire became snagged, her corpulence unravelling as she became more entangled, shedding silks, handkerchiefs and other smuggled goods along the fence wire. By the time she was fully unwrapped, and $1,000 of smuggled goods recovered, she was found to be so pitifully thin Customs officers wrapped her in an army blanket. The next coup by U.S. Customs was none other than the ubiquitous Dr James Jackson who had returned to Tijuana to administer to the wounded. When finally he decided to leave, it was not, as previously to see his wife, but to visit his mother in Europe. After a hero's farewell – and now reunited with his two 'nurses' – he set off for the border only to be arrested by U.S. Customs for smuggling a Mexican officer's sabre hidden in his medicine chest.[10]

The new republic's flag was delivered to the rebel camp at Tijuana as a very large pennant flying from the bonnet of Captain Louis James's chauffeur driven auto.[11] But there was no sign of Dick, although he did send a letter addressed to the 'Soldiers and

Citizens of the Republic of Lower California.' If Dick had already decided to reject the presidency, he makes no mention of this, the letter, in fact, created the contrary impression:

> I keenly and sincerely appreciate the great honour you have conferred upon me in electing me your first Presi-dent, and sincerely do regret my inability to be with you in person, but I am detained here on private business of the greatest importance. I hope that each and every one of you will allow nothing but the highest patriotic motives to lead in your future military and governmental actions; that you will forget the different classes that originally constituted your ranks and henceforth become a unit in ideas, hopes, actions, and ambitions. Let your sober second thoughts prevail at all times so that your every step be recognized, approved, and applauded by every liberty-loving nation of the world.
>
> It affords me great pleasure to present to you the new flag of the Republic. The red stripes represent the blood that has been spilled for countless ages in the cause of liberty; the white stripes the purity of your motives, the blue fold, the staunchness of your purpose; and the white star in a dual capacity represents not only the new Republic in the firmament of nations, but like the famous Star of Bethle-hem, your constant guide to victory. May God bless you all, give you strength and courage, and be with you constantly as he always is on the side of right.[12]

At the same time, Dick sent James a personal message regret-fully declining the chance of becoming *el presidente*.[13] Feeling betrayed yet again, the rebels angrily burned the flag and threw James in jail. The Ferris Filibuster had proved a stunt too far. Dick's only concern at a hastily called Press conference was to put as much distance as possible between himself and the rebels, declaring it was all a joke, a great big publicity stunt: 'Tell the public that I have already denied any and all dealings with the *insurrectos*, past, present and future, and if this is not enough I will arrange a schedule for further denials, three times a day and at bedtime!'[14]

But it was too late. The joke seriously misfired, and Ferris was arrested on a Grand Jury indictment for violating U.S. neutrality laws.[15] Released on bail, he quit his job as promotions manager for the San Diego-Panama Exposition to return, so he said, to the stage with his wife in a new play 'The Man from Mexico.' The play performed to packed houses until a year later when Mrs Ferris divorced Dick, resuming her solo theatrical career as Florence Stone.[16]

On the day Ferris was arrested by FBI agents, other agents intercepted Pryce as he headed north out of San Francisco under an assumed name. The Mexican Consul Dr Diaz Prieto had formerly asked the U.S. Government to extradite Pryce to Mexico on charges of arson and murder committed during the fall of Tijuana. He had allegedly shot dead the postmaster and burned the town. In Los Angeles, police were rounding-up Ricardo Flores Magon, his brother Enrique, Librado Rivera, the Liberal Party Secretary, and Anselmo Figuero, editor of the movement's newspaper *La Regeneración,* charging them all with neutrality violations. The four Mexicans, Pryce and Ferris were arraigned to appear before District Judge Wellborn in Los Angeles on 19 June but the hearing was set back when Pryce failed to arrive on time from San Francisco. Only Ricardo Magon and Ferris were granted bail. Unbowed, the Mexican told his *insurrectos* in Tijuana to fight on.[17]

The now leaderless rebels at Tijuana were gripped by internecine warfare. Mexicans fought Americans, and the Indians shot each other. An outbreak of smallpox twelve miles south of the town accelerated the rate of desertions. At last, the Liberal Junta intervened, sending a commission from Los Angeles to supervise the appointment of a new leader, who it was hoped could rescue what remained of their revolutionary force from descending further into anarchy and comic opera.[18] In their hour of greatest need, a new leader stepped forward – none other than the mercurial Jack Mosby, miraculously recovered from the chest wound that caused him to miss the Battle of Tijuana. Now back on the front line, Mosby added to his colourful past by claiming he had also served as an artillery officer in the Boer War. Captains Laflin and Paul Schmidt (alias Smith or Silent) were the other contenders for the doubtful privilege of leading the rebel army. After the customary ballot, Mosby was elected with Laflin as his second-in-command. Schmidt would have none of it and, followed by a group of loyal supporters, stormed out of camp into the arms of U S Customs officers who stopped them as they tried to smuggle a bunch of the Foreign Legion's horses across the border.[19]

Only the hardcore of the Magonistast remained at Tijuana, a mixture of anarchist idealists like the Italians from San Francisco none of whom spoke English, youthful Wobblies hanging on grimly to their dreams of a workers paradise, the soldiers-of-fortune with nowhere else to go, and the brigands, Mexican and American, for whom a retreat across the border meant a place on the hanging tree. Some of the more desperate swore they would die fighting rather than surrender. They had their backs to the wall, not far from every man's mind the certain knowledge that the Mexicans took no prisoners; that their favourite form of execution was the dagger or the garrotte. For some of those crouched in the rifle pits it was all too much, the personal distress obvious. Mosby tried to settle his men with a rousing speech but at the end broke down himself and wept uncontrollably, requiring medical attention, a sorry spectacle for troops preparing for their last stand.[20]

On the advice of Attorney Kirk, Mosby decided to sue for peace but his terms, $100 for each man who enlisted, plus $1 a day and 160 acres of land were too high for Madero. Kirk returned with the Mexican leader's final offer: $10 a head to surrender, take it or leave it, identical terms to those accepted by the sixty American Magonistas who had surrendered in Mexicali. For this, they had laid down their weapons, and then forming themselves into a ragged column, marched across the line into Calexico to surrender to Sheriff Meadows. None of the Mexicali bunch had eaten for days, so after a meal in a Chinese restaurant they were taken two miles out of town and told to keep moving. Wherever they stopped in Imperial Valley, the townspeople drove them out until they had finally left the state.[21] A similar fate now confronted Mosby and his band of surviving insurgents, all the more humiliating because the man offering them surrender terms was none other than the former Magonista leader, Jose Maria Leyva, now an officer with Madero's forces. The rebels answered by threatening to destroy part of the San Diego-Arizona Eastern Railroad as their very last act of rebellion.[22]

They never had the chance. Fingers tightened on triggers in the rebel dugouts after scouts reported that Governor Celso Vega had found the courage to leave his redoubt at Ensenada, and had arrived at the Dupree Ranch a few miles away. Not only had Vega 560 battle-hardened troops, greatly outnumbering the rebels, but also several machine guns and a number of artillery pieces. Even before a shot was fired, General Mosby came close to cashing in his chips. Riding through the town mounted on his white stallion, he was suddenly confronted by a wild-eyed Mexican called Chopo who pointed a revolver at his head and pulled the trigger. As he did so, an American *insurrecto* lunged at the would-be assassin, the bullet just missing its target. Thrown into jail, only the imminent battle saved Chopo from his appointment with the *fusilado*. It was clear from the spectators swarming over the hillsides on the American side of the border, that these were the last days of the Foreign Legion.

By late afternoon on 21 June, the insurgents numbering 155 foreigners and seventy-five Mexicans and Indians, awaited the inevitable attack. All approaches to the town were closely guarded, the hills bristling with rebel scouts. When the San Diego-Arizona Eastern construction train arrived packed with railroad men returning at the end of their day's work, the rebels hi-jacked it. After lengthy negotiations with Conductor Carney, the railroad official agreed to make another train available in case Mosby needed to move his fighters to some other part of the line. Steam up, the train waited all night on a side-track, hitched to it a caboose and a couple of flat tops, two insurgents manning the cab ready to take it out.

Not long after sun up the next morning, it was evident the battle was close at hand when two autos containing Liberal Party official Araujo and eight other Mexicans were spotted leaving Tijuana at speed, bound for the border. The trickle of desertions turned into a tide during the night leaving Mosby's Magonistas outnumbered almost six to one by the morning. What remained of the insurgents, however, still held to the military formation established by Pryce. A Troop led by Captain Stone took the commandeered freight train three miles west to establish a defensive position near Tijuana Hot Springs. Still carrying a bullet in his shoulder, Captain James Dunn and B Troop moved to an advance

position south west of Tijuana, not far from the *federales* lines. C
Troop with Captain Holland in command was held in reserve,
close to the besieged town.

Dunn's company took the brunt of the opening Mexican attack.
The rat-a-tat-tat of their deadly Hotchkiss machine guns froze the
hearts of the insurgents. Dunn had concealed his men in a big,
red barn, hoping to surprise Vega's advancing troops. Barely had
the rebels opened fire on the Mexicans when a stream of machine
gun bullets tore into the flimsy sides of the barn, killing many of
those inside. The survivors fled, leaving behind their dead, and
the giant Afro-American Milton, one time personal bodyguard to
General Pryce. Milton covered the retreat up the hill before
leaping on his horse and joining what remained of B Troop, now
trying to regroup on the ridge. But it was hopeless, the firepower
of the Mexicans so intense the rebels were driven off the ridge
into the ravine below, then across open ground to the border
where they surrendered to the U.S. Army commanded by Captain
E. A. Wilcox.

The greatest slaughter of *insurrectos* occurred among A Troop
when they poured from the rail cars at Hot Springs, the withering
machine gun fire cutting them down like wheat before a sickle as
they leaped out on to the track. Those with the sense to remain
aboard the flat tops, crouched behind bales of hay, with only
cover enough to hold off the attack momentarily, before they were
forced to retreat to a nearby ridge. Pinned down on the ridge with
A Troop, his heart aching for the safety of the U.S. Custom House
only a few hundred yards away across open ground, was Fred V.
Williams, a young reporter from the *Los Angeles Herald:*

> I saw men in that fight cool and deliberate under heavy
> fire, a fire that not only came in front of them but from
> behind, and sometimes criss-crossing in its fury. A young
> fellow named Brown, whom we called 'Slim' because of
> his ability to pick up cigarettes with ease and grace from
> his saddle while riding at a gallop with the troop, attracted
> my attention particularly during the battle. He was a deserter
> from the marine corps of a battleship in the harbour. Dur-
> ing the time 'A Troop was placed on the ridge on the hill,
> after they had left the train, Brown stretched out at full

length in sight of the enemy and went to sleep. Soon their bullets began to sing about him and clip the grass but he only opened his eyes rolled a cigarette and lighted it. When the command came to 'volley fire,' Brown rolled from his perch and dropped easily into action.

As Vega's troops gradually surrounded the rebels on the hill, Mosby rode back and forth on his white stallion, not knowing what to do next. Captain Stone, a veteran of the Spanish-American War, furious at his leader's indecision, rode across to warn that unless they moved quickly they would be cut off and massacred. Mosby finally ordered A Troop on to another hill where the Mexicans surrounded them again. The young reporter from the *Los Angeles Herald* took up the story:

> They pelted away at us and we pelted back. Below the machine guns hammered their tattoo. In front dark forms sprung up on the ridge of the opposite hill and we heard the report of their guns and then the sound of their bullets. I turned to Captain Stone. He looked puzzled. He was swearing. I saw Mosby riding back and forth as if undecided what to do. Then I laid down to escape the hum and dreadful buzz of the bullets above but at my feet and parallel to my body there was still that clipping and sizzling of bullets. Something told us they had the army almost surrounded. The feeling that comes to a man fighting without an exit other than courage when he is in the midst of the hum of bullets and is cut off from escape is nearly akin to calling himself names, forever placing himself in such a dangerous position.
>
> I began to think I would never get back with the news and what was the use of it after all. I assured myself that never again would I step on a battlefield and wished I was back in the Custom House or up on the hill watching the show with the tourists. Then our bugler stood up plain against the skyline and I heard 'retreat'. The thought flashed through my mind that the notes were entirely too tame to suit the occasion. All along the line the rebels ceased firing. Some of us did not know 'mess call' from the 'call to arms',

or any other bugle call, and it was left to some others from the army and navy to shout, "Beat it kids, beat it."

A handful stayed with Captain Stone to cover the retreat. The remainder walked slowly down the hill, exhausted and defeated, stumbling towards the border. Drained of all their fight, the romance of revolution for liberty's sweet sake oozing away, the filibusters' ambitions crushed by the cold reality of war, the *insurrectos* surrendered to Captain Wilcox:

> Mosby: 'Captain we are beaten. We did the best we could but they outnumbered us and their machine guns gave them much the best of it.'

> Wilcox, extending his hand: 'You put up a good fight.'

> Mosby, tears pouring down his cheeks, his voice choking: 'Whatever my own feelings may be, these men are in my care. I am responsible for their lives. If we make a last stand at Tijuana it will be another case of Custer and the Little Big Horn. Every man of us will be shot down. Under these circumstances I feel the best thing for me to do is surrender my command into your hands. Do you think the Government will give us up to the Mexicans?'

> Wilcox: 'No. I don't think you will suffer serious harm. The United States has never given up any prisoners. '

> Mosby: 'What are the conditions under which we surrender?'

> Wilcox: 'You will march your men across the line and lay down your arms in a place designated by me. I will trust you for the good behaviour of your men until those arms are deposited. Of course, my men will be drawn up under arms as you pass through the line not that I believe it to be necessary but because it is the proper thing to do. There would be no excuse should any mishap follow a failure on my part to see that this is done.'

> Mosby: 'I will vouch for the good behaviour of my men.'

After a moment's whispered conversation with Second-in-Command Laflin, the bugler ordered the rebels to assemble for the last time. Mosby stood among them, somewhat taller than most, tanned brown by the sun, a black moustache, dressed in civilian garb with the exception of his military riding boots and cowboy's sombrero. Not the first time that day the General wept as he spoke to his men of their comradeship, of their days and nights together in camp and on the battlefield, of their first victory at Tijuana (which he missed), and of his decision to surrender to the United States rather fall into Mexican hands. 'Some day we may meet again,' he said, 'and when we do, whether it be in the paths of peace or on the fields of battle, we will recognise and remember each other with loyalty and devotion for the comrades we have been.'

'You bet we will!' one insurgent bellowed.

By the time he had finished, Mosby was not the only one in tears, some possibly weeping from sheer relief. Not all agreed to surrender. One group realising it could mean their appointment with the hangman, climbed into their saddles and rode down to Tijuana. Among the fugitives were two of California's most wanted men, Marshall Brooks and Henry Hall, their bodies found some hours later where they were shot down by Vega's *federales*.

Those who surrendered, ejected cartridges from their rifles, then piled their weapons in a heap, a few Winchesters and Marlins among what was largely a collection of antiquated muskets and rifle belts stuffed with cartridges of all sizes. In another pile lay their saddles, the design of these revealing much about the horsemanship of their owners. The straggling line of dejected rebels then climbed aboard two flat tops for the rail ride into San Diego. Eyes bloodshot from sleepless nights, faces caked with desert dust, and with hunger nagging at their bellies, their good-natured exchanges hid how they ached for a plate of pork and beans. Most wore blue overalls, in a few instances with spurs fastened to high-heeled patent leather Oxfords. But the majority had cowhide boots with leggings.

Spectators crowded round for information, a name, a snatch of conversation about the motives that impelled them with their inferior firepower to face Mexican Mausers and machine guns. 'You can't take my picture,' yelled one *insurrecto*, throwing an

Pryce's defeated rebels cross the border to surrender to the U.S. Army. Either this, or face a firing squad in Tijuana. (San Diego Historical Society).

Is this General Caryl ap Rhys Pryce ready for action after capturing Tijuana? He certainly sports the characteristic 'Imperial' moustache popular with fighting men in the early 19th century, especially Boer War veterans.
(San Diego Historical Society).

arm across his face as he heard the click of a camera shutter. 'You are taking them pictures for profit. You are working for a newspaper or some-body and you're getting something out of it but I don't get nothing.' Another rebel with a badly scratched face boasted loudly when questioned by a curious tourist, 'I was fighting for the work-ing man's cause and I am willing to fight again.'

Down below in Tijuana two rebels were sud-denly seen galloping along the main street headed for the hills. 'That's Jim,' cried one of the rebel prisoners shading his eyes with his hand. 'Good boy, he got away.' Others stood up to get a clearer view of the rider. 'No, it ain't. Jim don't ride like that,' said one. 'Who's that other feller?' Nobody seemed to know but all agreed the two had escaped into the hills.

While his hungry men waited on the flat tops for the trip into town, General Mosby and Captain Laflin were eating their first meal in 24 hours in the Red Cross tent. The General lifted the food to his mouth with a trembling hand. Only a week after Pryce had quit his command of the Second Division, Mosby had led the Magonistas to an inglorious defeat. Then a ripple of excitement swept through the hordes of sightseers as a Red Cross ambulance arrived at the border from the battlefield. But it had found no wounded. 'We saw lots of dead horses everywhere,' said one of the ambulance men, 'and we guess a whole lot of wounded are scattered around in the brush. The *federales* told us they did not need any Red Cross help and would *take care* of all the wounded.' The emphasis on these words implied what the speaker thought would be the fate of the survivors.

The last prisoner loaded aboard the flat top before it headed off to San Diego was Lieutenant Bucklow, his arm hanging limply by his side. 'Morgan was near me. His whole face was shot off. He is only a kid,' he said. Lying beside him on the flat top, a wounded rebel with a bloody hole in his leg screamed at a tourist, 'No I won't tell you my name – not by a damn sight.'

As the prisoners left, the Mexicans advance guard was spotted crossing a barley field in two columns. 'There they come,' the

Jack Mosby (left) who succeeded Pryce as general of the Magonistas, and his adjutant Bert Laflin shortly before the Mexicans recaptured Tijuana.

crowd shouted. But the *federales* stopped short of Tijuana, fearing an ambush. That afternoon before Vega entered the town, he spoke to a newspaper reporter at his camp near the Hot Springs. Asked how many men he had lost Vega replied, 'A few'. The *insurrectos,* he said, had lost about sixty, one eyewitness reporting later that 39 were buried in a mass grave. Of all the *federale* officers – among them Lieutenant Guerrero survivor of the First Battle of Tijuana – Vega was the least military in appearance, wearing city clothes, a dark blue coat, grey trousers, fedora hat and glasses. When Tijuana fell at 1.50 on the afternoon of 22 June 1911, the very first thing the Mexican *federales* did was shoot down the Red Flag fluttering above the *cuartel*. Then they raised their own.

At San Diego, 93 rebel prisoners were loaded abroad the government tug *Lieutenant George M. Harris* and transferred to Fort Rosecrans. Held with Laflin on charges of violating U.S. neutrality laws, Mosby finally admitted to being a deserter from the Ninth U.S. Infantry. The remaining *insurrectos,* almost all Americans, were released on 25 June and sent on their way. Before this, Mosby gathered his men together in the camp gymnasium for the last time. Fighting back his emotions as he bade them farewell, his voice quivering, he said:

> I am a United States prisoner now my men. They have brought me from the guardhouse to say goodbye. I want you to think of me sometime as I will think of you. You were brave men and the world recognises it. We put up a good fight. I am mighty glad you are going free. In a few weeks you will probably be scattered over many parts of this country. Wherever you are, remember it is my wish you conduct yourselves with the same honour and integrity you did under me.

Then the camp canon boomed, the shock of the explosion rattling the room. No one moved a muscle. Only the general turned his head, looking over their heads and out through the window. 'I am through,' he said slowly, nodding his head. 'Goodbye, think of me my men as I will think of you.' Pressing closer, each one wrung his hand. Mosby left the room under guard followed by Laflin. Through the barred windows of the guardhouse he watched the departure of his command, thrusting a hand between the bars. His men trudging between two columns of United States soldiers, halted for a moment, and raising their hats waved a silent salute.

Just before 7 o'clock on Sunday morning 25 June, the former rebels scrambled off the tug from Fort Rosecrans at the Navy Wharf at the bottom of H Street. Even two of the wounded had quit the hospital to join the exodus. Waiting were several hundred curious San Diegans anxious for a last look at the men who tried to steal a country, or at least a very large part of one. Police Chief Keno Wilson was also there, first questioning, then detaining several on suspicion of being wanted men. The rest were told to get out of town quickly. After hanging around street corners for a while bidding their farewells, most hitched a ride on the next available caboose singing 'Hallelujah, I'm a Bum.' They were back on the road. Some remained in San Diego for a little longer after Attorney Kirk suggested they make a moving picture about the Magonista Revolution. Nothing came of it and they drifted off to join Wild West shows. Another bunch climbed into an auto to advertise the roomy interior of a car dealer's latest model.

Mosby was charged with desertion and remanded to the penitentiary at Yuma to await trial. On his way there he was shot dead trying to escape. Few believed this but it avoided an embarrassing trial.[23]

NOTES

1. National Archives. Senate Foreign Relations Sub-Committee Report, *Revolutions in Cuba and Mexico*, 62 Congress, 2 session (Washington: Government Printing Office), 378.
2. ibid., 379.
3. *San Diego Union*, 3 June 1911; *Los Angeles Examiner*, 3 June 1911.
4. *Revolutions in Cuba and Mexico*, 379; *Los Angeles Examiner*, 19 June 1911.
5. Close reading of *San Diego Union, San Diego Sun, Los Angeles Times, Los Angeles Herald* accounts of election of Ferris as President of the new republic.
6. *Los Angeles Herald*, 4 June 1911.

7. *Los Angeles Examiner,* 3 June 1911.
8. ibid.
9. *Los Angeles Herald,* 4 June 1911.
10. *San Diego Union,* 4, 5, 6 June 1911.
11. *Revolutions in Cuba and Mexico,* 379; *San Diego Union,* 6 June 1911.
12. *Revolutions in Cuba and Mexico,* 384.
13. ibid., 379.
14. *San Diego Union,* 6 June 1911.
15. *Los Angeles Examiner,* 15, 16, 21 June 1911.
16. *San Diego Union,* 16 June 1911.
17. *Los Angeles Examiner,* 15, 16, 21 June 1911; *San Francisco Chronicle,* 17 June; *Los Angeles Herald,* 20 June 1911.
18. *San Diego Union,* 2, 3 June 1911.
19. ibid., 4, 5, 6 June 1911.
20. ibid., 8, 11 June 1911.
21. Velasco Ceballos, *se apoderará Estados Unidos de Baja California?,* pp. 182-84; *Los Angeles Times,* 18, 19 June 1911; *Los Angeles Examiner,* 18 June 1911.
22. José María Leyva, *Aportaciones a la historia de la revolución* (Mexico City, 1938), pp. 25-28; *The Industrial Worker,* 6 July 1911; *San Diego Union,* 19-21 June 1911.
23. National Archives, Wilcox to Bliss, 23 June 1911; Records of the U.S. A Commands, Department of California and Texas, Record Group 98; close reading of *San Diego Union, Los Angeles Herald, San Diego Sun,* 22-26 June 1911.

Chapter 10

The Trial

General Pryce appeared on extradition charges before Commissioner Van Dyke in the Los Angeles District Court of Southern California on 16 September 1911, after being arrested by a Federal Marshall as he headed for the Canadian border. Hopkins made it across safely and was never heard of again. But Pryce's indecision over whether or not to return to his command in Tijuana seems to have delayed his escape, and with Mexican agents never very far away reporting his every move, his attempt at travelling incognito, on this occasion as a 'Mr Grey,' failed.[1] From his Los Angeles jail cell, Pryce began casting around for help, writing to Hattie Biggs for the first time in almost nine months. The trip to Mexico, he told her, had been exciting but that was the end of his 'revolutionising,' unless next time it was better organised!

In the letter, a copy of which was sent later to his father, Colonel Douglas Pryce, by this time living in retirement in Southsea, Pryce endeavours to explain away his adventure as no more significant than a 'spur of the moment' decision taken because he was 'lonely and off colour.'

> When I got to Seattle I just thought I would keep going, nobody would care "Tuppence" anyhow, so on I went to Los Angeles, and to the end of my money, so I just went on to Mexicali and the joined the *insurrectos*, and here I am back in Los Angeles, but in jail. Well, I had an exciting time anyhow, if nothing else, but no more revolutionizing for me. The next time I go to war it will be with a properly organised and equipped army.
>
> I wrote twice to mother from Mexicali but suppose the men who took my letters across the line, for I could not cross myself, never posted them. I <u>am</u> (Pryce's underscoring)

After Seeing Pryce Trial, Says He Is Real Slayer

SNAPSHOT BY HERALD STAFF PHOTOGRAPHER OF GEN. C. RHYS PRYCE AS HE APPEARS IN JAIL

A confident Pryce poses for photographers while in jail in Los Angeles awaiting trial on extradition charges for murder and arson. "The Los Angeles Herald" artist has embellished the picture for publication with images of a firing squad, which was what Pryce expected to face if he was sent back to Mexico.

194

sorry she never received them, and so did not know where I was, as I did not want her to be anxious on my behalf. I have written Gladys (his sister in Vancouver) since I have been here.

Well, here I am in "chokey," charged with all sorts of horrible crimes, 1, violating the neutrality laws of the U.S. 2, Murder, and 3, Arson. Unless they go to the trouble of manufacturing evidence against me they cannot hold me on No 1 as I was particularly careful not to do anything on U.S. soil in violation of their laws. I never tried to enlist a single man on U.S. territory nor did I purchase any arms or ammunition. When I took San Juana (Tijuana) with my command we had two days fighting in the course of which some casualties naturally occurred. One of the federals Jose Larroque, Lieutenant Governor of Lower California was one of those who went under. Also while we were fighting to clear the town some houses caught fire and were burnt. The Mexican Consul at San Diego was a particular pal of old Larroque. He is also a Diaz man who has not yet been superseded in his office. The Governor of Lower California is also a Diaz man and perfect specimen of the genus "Brute." So the two of them got together, and the consul swore out a warrant for me on charges 2 and 3. I did not kill Larroque, did not kill anyone at all down there being too busy directing to do any shooting myself. These two beasts are trying to get me railroaded across the border into their hands, which would mean a firing squad and an end of C.P., if they were successful. However, as the country was in a state of war at the time and I was properly commissioned by one of the political parties, which were fighting in Mexico, they cannot do it, as the offences charged, if they are offences are political ones, and as such not extraditable. But it is distinctly unpleasant being cooped up here behind all kinds of bars and gratings of steel. [2]

This, the only detailed explanation offered by Pryce for his actions, makes no mention of the 'poor peons' as the reason for his decamping to Los Angeles to join the Magonistas. A curious mixture of bravado and naivety, the letter to Hattie is indicative of a man confident about the outcome of his legal predicament, although a little concerned about prison conditions.

Conditions in the Los Angeles jail were most disagreeable, the cells filthy, the food infrequent and almost inedible. There was, however, another part of the jail, the 'boarders' tank' on the next floor, where for $5 a week inmates could rent themselves a clean cell, and three square meals a day were served off clean table clothes. Hearing that the man who had allegedly run off with the Magonistas' war chest was now penniless, the other inmates clubbed together to pay the cost of transferring the celebrated soldier-of-fortune to the 'tank'.[3]

Although left in the lurch, Hattie Biggs had remained loyal, writing immediately on his behalf to President Taft, urging him to intervene to save the Welshman's neck.[4] Meanwhile, the Mexican Government had re-assured the British Foreign Office that Pryce would be fairly treated by the Mexican courts, if the petition for his extradition was granted.[5] Few Americans believed this. Neither was Pryce encouraged by the support he was receiving from Britain's Vice-Consul in Los Angeles, Charles White Mortimer. Although a lawyer by training, Mortimer had never appeared in a criminal court, and his primary concern was to confirm his client's identity as British. From this, Pryce concluded that it was true what the British community in Los Angeles said about their Vice Consul – that his only interest was 'to make their wills, for that brings a fee into his pocket.'[6] More exasperated than worried by Mortimer's failure to resolve his predicament, Pryce sent a statement explaining his circumstances to Bryce, the British Ambassador in Washington, hoping this might 'get a move on and stir things up a bit.'[7] From his letter to Hattie, Pryce's most pressing concern was clearly the attempt by the Mexican Government to have him extradited for murder and arson:

> My indictment for violating the neutrality laws is not in order for there is no overt act specified in the indictment as called for by the law. They cannot mention an overt act as there is not one to mention. However, I am not bothering to have that indictment set aside just now as I am sparring for time to make a good strong case with which to fight the extradition to Mexico. Cannot afford to take chances on that.[8]

When news of Pryce's arrest reached his parents in Britain, the colonel immediately contacted the Foreign Office. Colonel Pryce was aware of his son's earlier brush with the law in San Diego, but that, he told the Under Secretary of State at the Foreign Office, was a mere 'bagatelle' compared with this new predicament. Since the Mexicans had still probably not paid his son money for his services, the colonel suspected a 'firing file and a blank wall' would be their way of dealing with troublesome claims. As for the cost of providing defence counsel for Caryl, the $5,000 being asked by Mortimer was beyond the colonel's means.[9] Mortimer then wrote to Hattie Biggs explaining Pryce was penniless and if he wanted a first-class criminal lawyer to defend him, his friends would need to raise the cash. 'If this be done I have no doubt that he can be acquitted, but if he is not well represented, he may be convicted of some of the offences charged,' wrote Mortimer.[10] By the end of July, Pryce had obtained the services of attorneys Noleman and Smyser for the extradition hearing on charges of murdering the Tijuana postmaster, Francisco Ceuvas, and arson. Mortimer was still confident there was no serious risk that Pryce would be extradited but he had been instructed, nevertheless, by the British Consul General in San Francisco to stand by in case it was necessary for him to 'take a hand if his extradition becomes probable.'[11]

After several adjournments, Pryce finally appeared for trial on 16 September 1911. By this time he was far less confident of the outcome. Perhaps anticipating the worst, he wrote to his parents begging their forgiveness for all the trouble he had caused them. At this most critical moment in his life, the 'black sheep' sought the succour of his family:

My Dear Father and Mother,

Perhaps you will not read this letter and that is what I deserve. For I have behaved very, very badly towards you and nothing you can think or say would be too harsh to apply to my conduct. You will be quite justified in having nothing more to do with me. I have no excuses to make and have no right to ask for your forgiveness. To say I am sorry seems puerile – but it is true. I have had time to think since I have been held here, and realise what a beast I have been.

But I don't want you to think that I am guilty of these murders and crimes that have been imputed to me by the Mexican Government. I conducted operations according to the rules of civilised warfare and no person met death at my hands except in action with my command. Personally, I killed nobody. One of my own men I court martialled and shot for murdering another man, also under my command. I enclose cuttings from the *Herald* of yesterday, which show you what happened.

The hearing of this case comes off on the 12th prox, and there is no doubt that extradition will be denied, in spite of the efforts of the Mexicans, as the political aspect is so clearly obvious. Gladys and Ken (his sister's husband) have been very good and came down to Los Angeles to help. Ken says he is acting as Secretary to the Towing Co., and that it is doing well. He has probably reported to you. I was a failure at that too but your money is not lost and Ken is making a success out of it.

Gladys will probably have told you that I am going to marry Hattie Biggs in Vancouver when I am freed. I have known, and cared for her, for 4 years now. As she is intensely practical and sensible, she will keep me straight in the future I know. I shall return to Vancouver as soon as possible, after I am freed.

Though with no great claim, I ask your forgiveness and though my actions do not appear to show it, I am still your loving son.

Caryl.'[12]

But his natural self-confidence was soon re-asserting itself, if, indeed, it had ever wavered. Hattie Biggs was not so sure, confiding to Gladys in Vancouver, her fears that Pryce's optimism might be obscuring the very real strength of the Mexican case against him.

By the enclosed extracts from Caryl's letter, you will see it's not all a put-up job, for they have something to go on.

Pryce with his sister Gladys in Los Angeles at the time of his trial.

Caryl seems very hopeful all the way through, and it makes one feel better, tho' the wood is still very dense. It will be all right if the witnesses go on his side, and are not bought over. Let us hope they are not that sort, but one is still nervous about their honour, when so much hangs on it somehow.

Newspapers were full of the story, Hattie assiduously collecting the clippings and photographs of Pryce, one of which depicted him, eyes bandaged, in front of a firing squad![13]

The charges were that Pryce had murdered Ceuvas, the Tijuana postmaster, then set fire to the town after looting it. The alleged violation of U.S. neutrality laws was adjourned to another date. Mysteriously, the official record of the extradition hearing has disappeared. All that survives are newspaper accounts of the trial, and notes made by Commissioner Van Dyke at the time. Virtually indecipherable, the only value of these is to show that Ricardo Flores Magon did give evidence in support of Pryce's contention he was recruited in Mexico and had not transported men and wagons across the border.[14] If the junta leader had suggested anything different, he would have exposed himself to conviction at his own subsequent hearing on charges of infringing the neutrality laws.

The courtroom was packed every day of the week-long trial, former Magonista *insurrectos* and representatives of Madero's new Mexican government glaring at each other across the public benches. Pryce was still a celebrity on the West Coast, most Americans of the opinion that if he, and not Mosby, had been in command during the last days of Tijuana, Vega's *federales* would have been whipped.

Not long after the hearing had started, the Mexican Government case was close to collapse. One of their star witnesses, Mrs C. V. Stick, an employee of Savine's Curio Store, instead of condemning Pryce as a thieving brigand as she was expected to do, complimented him on his courtesy. When at the end of her testimony she walked over and shook him by the hand, wild applause rang around the court, Pryce's delighted attorney jumping up to move for immediate dismissal. This was refused on account of other charges against Pryce.

Chief witness for the Mexican Government was General Sylvio Blanco, commander of a force of volunteers at the First Battle of Tijuana. Reminded by Commissioner Van Dyke that his Government would need to prove Pryce looted Tijuana for personal gain, Blanco admitted that Postmaster Ceuvas was part of his command when killed, that the insurgents were called 'rebels' and that they carried a flag. This, said Pryce's attorney, proved they were organised belligerents, and the postmaster was a combatant whose death was an act of war, not murder. Once again Commissioner Van Dyke refused to dismiss the case because of further larceny charges.

The next witness against Pryce was an old associate, the villainous Francisco Salinas, briefly general of the First Battalion of the Liberal Army at Mexicali, and the man who sat back while Stanley Williams and forty *insurrectos* were shot down by General Mayol's regulars at the Battle of John Little's Ranch. Under cross-examination Salinas admitted he had served time at San Quentin Prison for assault with intent to murder, and was currently wanted dead or alive by the very Mexican Government on whose behalf he was then giving evidence. Besides this, he agreed that while serving with the Magonistas he was paid $5 a week to spy for Madero. But even Salinas was forced to admit that Pryce commanded an army, not a gang of desperadoes, and that there had been an occasion in Tijuana when the rebel leader had personally driven a U.S. Army deserter Frank Hinch out of town after he was caught robbing a Chinese store.

The last witnesses for the Mexican Government, two ranchers Sylvano Preclado and Lorenzo Orera from Tijuana, testified they were held captive at Pryce's camp for three days until they each paid Secretary Araujo of the Liberal Junta $500. Pryce denied any knowledge of this.

Among those in court watching the drama unfold was Captain Monoricus Monterey, an American citizen and a comrade of Pryce throughout the revolt in Lower California. For two days he sat there waiting to give vital evidence in defence of his general. Then when he was called his seat was empty. Some hours later, it was discovered that Monterey had been lured across the border by two Mexicans, bound, gagged and shot to death. Told of this, Pryce covered his face with his hands 'a tear trickled down his cheeks, he clenched his fists and bit his lip in helpless rage.'

> 'A better man than Monterey never lived,' he said later. 'We promoted him from the ranks for bravery. He was educated in an eastern college and just 23 years old. They have murdered him in cold blood for participating in a revolt to bring about better conditions.'

Pryce took the stand on 24 September to prove he led a recognised army in Lower California. As proof the insurgents were a

201

legitimate military force, his attorney produced accounts of the uprising published by the Los Angeles and San Diego newspapers. Almost every statement by Pryce was an assertion that he enforced army regulations from the moment he took up his command at Mexicali, drilling his men according to the U.S. Army drill book, and organising the march from Mexicali to Tijuana in military formation, guards posted at the front, rear and on both flanks of the column. Pryce testified how he had ordered the destruction of all liquor in Tijuana; had posted ordinances forbidding the looting of stores; and had issued written protection to at least one Mexican storeowner. He denied he ordered the burning of the bullring.

Pryce even produced his guest membership card for the San Francisco Press Club as evidence he was not a brigand in flight when arrested by Federal Marshalls. The Welshman admitted he had taken the name of *Grey* while in San Francisco for fear of being hauled back to San Diego by U.S. soldiers. 'My desire to give the *insurrectos* a helping hand was due largely to reading John Kenneth Turner's book,' he said. 'I went into the *insurrecto* army with the idea of helping the Mexicans to a better government.' Whether true or not, it carried weight in court.

Asked to explain why he had deserted the rebel camp in the middle of the night, Pryce said that according to newspaper reports Diaz had fled the country and the war was practically over. When he left, the army war chest contained $600. All that he took was $20 to cover expenses. He had not received a dollar in salary since enlisting at Mexicali. On the basis of this testimony, his attorney submitted Pryce was not a soldier-of-fortune otherwise he would have remained to share the spoils of war on the abdication of President Diaz.

Pryce ended his testimony by declaring he had 'no intentions of rejoining any army in Mexico,' a statement greeted with loud chuckles on the prosecution bench. As the former *insurrecto* General stepped from the stand a supporter rushed forward to present him with a $10 piece, which he promptly handed to his attorney.

The extradition charges against Pryce were all dismissed on 28 September, Commissioner Van Dyke ruling that as Pryce had been

engaged in active warfare, he could not be held criminally responsible for crimes committed while Mexico was in a state of rebellion.
Released on $2,500 bail to await trial on violating the neutrality
laws, Pryce was mobbed as he left the court, jubilant supporters
cheering and slapping his back. In the midst of the celebrations
Pryce announced he was the happiest man in California. His
fiancée, Hattie Biggs, the insurance company typist from Vancouver, was arriving that very day and they were to be married.
They never were.

Apart from the occasional moment of remorse, Pryce remained
generally confident throughout his incarceration and trial. One
explanation for this must have been the eleventh hour confession
published by the *Los Angeles Herald* of a former insurgent, Gordon
Donahue, that it was he who shot the postmaster at Tijuana:

> I dropped him in open fight when a little band of us were
> rushing a breastworks and he and his men were standing
> behind it. The battle was raging all around the town when
> Pryce ordered our little troop to take the trenches in front
> of us. We left the shelter of a clump of bush and advanced
> on a run. They opened up on us. When we got within
> thirty yards of the trenches the Mexicans turned and ran. As
> I stood up I saw the postmaster turn about for a parting
> shot. He was aiming at me. I up and let him have it, drop-
> ped him where he stood and he died.

Although conscious-stricken at the sight of Pryce on trial for the
murder, Donahue was too scared to testify. After his the publication of his confession, Donahue decided the best way to help
Pryce was to take off across the border with a band of former
insurgents, their plan, to size prominent Mexicans as hostages against
the possibility of Pryce's extradition. If Pryce was executed by
the Mexicans the hostages would be shot in retaliation, said
Donahue.[15]

Pryce's confidence during the trial could also have had something to do with the existence of a personal letter sent by Secretary
of State Knox to Mr A. I. McCormick, District Attorney for Southern
California, instructing him that under no circumstances was the

insurgent leader to be extradited without the authority of the State Department. The existence of the letter only came to light a year later, when McCormick and his assistant Dudley Robinson were giving evidence before a Senate Foreign Relations Committee investigating events in Lower California:

> Robinson was asked by Senator Smith inquiring into the composition of the Magonista Army: Were there any other nationalities represented besides Americans and Mexicans?

> Mr Robinson: There was every nationality. We had a Russian who was a star witness for the government and a very intelligent man but he had evidently had nihilistic or anarchistic principles instilled into him. He went down there and they found him very useful in the hospital on account of his intelligence, and he was made a sort of superior nurse. There were Germans. One of their Generals was General Pryce, formerly of the South African mounted police, I believe they called it, who served in the Boer War.

> Senator Smith: On the British side or on the Boer side?

> Mr Robinson: On the British side. He became a general there but according to his story and I believe he told the truth, he went of his own accord and was not sent there by the Magons.

> Senator Smith: A soldier-of-fortune?

> Mr Robinson: He was purely a soldier-of-fortune.

> Mr McCormick: There was an attempt made to extradite him by the Mexican Government for alleged crimes of arson, robbery and murder, involving his operations in Tijuana. He was in command of the rebel army that took Tijuana, in charge of the Custom House, and I believe the evidence of the extradition case showed that he took charge of the various stores and attempted to sell off the goods

and everything else. They charged him also with killing a number of people. They charged him with the murder of those individual people who were killed in the fight, and also charged that his actions in taking the goods from those stores was robbery or larceny or whatever it may be under the treaty.

But the point I want to bring out is that he being a British subject, the British Government took an active interest in this case. The Secretary of State wrote me a personal letter about it, informing me, or instructing me, through the Attorney General, to keep them advised right along, and not to let him be finally extradited until I told them of it.

Senator Smith: Was this an expedition that started from the United States?

Mr McCormick: It started from the United States. They denied the extradition on the ground that the evidence showed everything was political in character and that is not extraditable.

Senator Fall: The British Government interfered on his behalf?

Senator Smith: Was he ever extradited?

Mr McCormick: He was not.

Senator Fall: Our State Department did not interfere with reference to the extradition of the American citizens, did it?

Mr McCormick: No.[16]

Although this session of the Foreign Relations Committee was held in Los Angeles when Pryce was awaiting his second trial on the charge of violating U.S. neutrality, the man who knew most about events in Lower California was never called to testify before the committee.

NOTES

1. Pryce Papers. Unidentified newspaper clipping dated 16 June 1911, quoting Associated Press.
2. ibid. Copy of undated letter from Pryce to Hattie Biggs written at time of his incarceration.
3. ibid.
4. ibid., letter from Pryce to his parents, dated 25 August 1911, written while incarcerated in Los Angeles.
5. ibid., letter from British Foreign Office to Lieutenant Colonel Douglas Davidson Pryce, India Army, dated 21 August 1911, file number 32121/11.
6. ibid., Pryce letter to his father, 3 February 1912.
7. ibid., Pryce letter to Hattie Biggs, written at time of his incarceration.
8. ibid.
9. ibid., letter from British Foreign Office to Lieutenant Colonel Douglas Davidson Pryce, India Army, dated 21 July 1911, file number 29312/11.
10. ibid., letter Charles White Mortimer to Hattie Biggs, 23 June 1911.
11. ibid., letter Mortimer to Colonel Pryce, 25 July 1911.
12. ibid., letter Pryce to father and mother, 25 August 1911.
13. ibid., letter Hattie Biggs to Gladys Hodge, 28 August 1911.
14. National Archives Pacific Southwest Region, RG 21 'Records of the District Courts of the United States – Central District of California,' Los Angeles Division, Commissioners' Records 1888-1915, Van Dyke, W.M. 1911-1913, Box 6.
15. *Los Angeles Herald*, 3 August 1911.
16. National Archives, Washington, United States Senate Committee on Foreign Relations, 1912-1913, *Revolutions in Mexico* (CIS No: S40-3); for U.S. concern over *Shearwater* incident, and related international affairs, also see transcript of official Senate debate, *Affairs in Mexico*, 20 April 1911, pp. 447-452, Congressional record, 62-2.

Chapter 11

The Colonel's Escape!

I cannot talk, I cannot sing,
Nor screech, nor moan, nor anything.
Possessing all these fatal strictures,
What chance, have I in motion pictures.

Photoplay Journal, January 1929.

Pryce had promised Hattie Biggs he would return to Vancouver immediately he was a free man.[1] The spectre of a Mexican firing squad may have disappeared with the dismissal of the extradition warrant by Commissioner Van Dyke, but there remained the second charge of violating U.S. neutrality laws. Pryce was just as confident this would also be dismissed after speaking to the District Attorney and the Secret Service agent involved in the case, both of whom admitted they had nothing on him. Writing to his father, the Welshman claimed that even Van Dyke had said there was no evidence to prove a violation of the neutrality laws.[2] The hearing had, nonetheless, been fixed for 18 April 1912, and in the meantime Pryce moved in with the Ferris's. How he managed to raise the $1,500 bail money is not clear. Penniless and in rags, the Welshman had asked his parents to send him a grey flannel suit, socks and shirt. But when the British Vice Consul, White Mortimer, suggested his father stand surety, the colonel's reply was un-ambiguous, 'I have no money I can send to my son.'[3] Already so frustrated by Mortimer's inaction and incompetence that he had felt it necessary to complain directly to the British Ambassador in Washington, Pryce was even angrier on discovering that his father the colonel, who had already lost heavily on the Vancouver Towing Company, was being asked for bail money. Fresh out of jail, Pryce had no hope of repaying his father when the only work he could find was the occasional odd job with Dick Ferris's latest venture, the California Aviation Society, formed by Dick to organise air shows promoting the latest invention, aeroplanes. In desperation, he fired off a claim to the newly elected Mexican President, Francisco Madero, asking for $10,000 in compensation for 'the persecution his government caused me.' That was the last he heard of it. Not only was Mexico in a state of chaos, but few people, Pryce included, expected Madero 'to last much longer as President.'[4]

Prospects for full-time work improved when a family friend, with contacts among Los Angeles's new golfing community, arrived on holiday from Canada. For a time, it seemed the one time golf champion at Glenalmond College, might be fixed up with a job as a golf instructor. When that came to nothing, the former Magonista general turned to his revolutionary experiences as possible material for short stories. 'A short story writer in San Francisco has offered to put them in shape for me,' he told his father.[5] This was most probably the San Francisco-based journalist-writer Peter Kyne who had twice interviewed Pryce during the uprising in Lower California. The pair were much the same age, in their mid-thirties, Kyne a former newspaper editor struggling to make a living from writing popular, romantic novels. Many of his plots were drawn from western and Mexican culture, with titles like *The Gringo Privateer, Outlaws of Eden, Kindred of the Dust,* and *Webster – Man's Man.* Whatever literary benefit arose from Pryce's experiences it was more likely to have been utilised by Kyne, since Pryce never published anything under his own name.[6]

But his luck was about to change. Los Angeles in 1912 might have been a hot bed for political intrigue and centre for union and socialist agitators like the Wobblies of the Industrial Workers of the World – despite all their setbacks still trying to build a workers paradise – but it also stood at a new frontier: Moving Pictures. The production of 'silent flicks' had up until then been dominated by European filmmakers, what foothold the new form of entertainment had in the United States mostly on the east coast. In those early years Hollywood was not even a suburb of Los Angeles but a desert oasis where retirees went to spend their last days amongst the orange groves, palms and poinsettias. The 120-acre lot had been named Hollywood by the wife of a Kansas prohibitionist, Horace Henderson Wilcox, after he bought it to build his retirement home. Separated from the city by eight miles of desert and scrub, Hollywood was a thirsty place to live, only a few hundred people having settled there by the turn of the century. The water shortage was so desperate that eventually the inhabitants sought the protection of the city fathers, their retirement community thereafter becoming one of LA's six suburbs. As part of a city that promoted itself as having 350 sunny days every year, Hollywood was slow to attract the attention of 'movie people' from the east where production schedules were frequently disrupted by bad weather, and it was not until October 1911 – about the time Pryce was released from jail – that Centaur, an east coast film company owned by two English brothers, William and David Horsley, opened its Nestor Studio in Hollywood. Such was the improvement in their movie output, both quantity and quality, that within a matter of months fifteen companies were shooting in and around Hollywood.[7]

Every morning, all those searching for work as extras on the film sets crowded into the 'bullpens' where movie directors came to pick the ones they needed for that day's shooting. Not only was the movie business new and exciting, it was rapacious, churning out one and two reel 'flicks' by the hundred to entertain the masses in new nickelodeons springing up across the country. The work was very different to what anyone had previously known – and no one needed to know much to break into it! Even those who would only ever play a screen extra were certain of at least one square meal. Each day, which was all it took to make some of the early one-reelers, it was a different story. And for anyone who showed promise, there was the prospect of leapfrogging from extra one moment, to star the next.

The golden rule of movie-making in its golden age was action, because there was little point in making movies that never moved. Acting was secondary to movement, so much so that some directors had reduced the entire process to a series of numbered commands, 'one' for a smile, 'two' for a grimace, and so forth. Stories had to be simple and direct without recourse to mechanical tricks. What an audience saw on film had actually occurred.

It was not uncommon for early movies to have no scripts. The director, whose only qualification at times seemed to be the ability to shout loudest, would have had a rough idea of the story, improvising as he went along. Describing how he started in movies, one of stars of those early days, Joseph Henabery, a former railroad worker, who played Abraham Lincoln in D. W. Griffith's ground-breaking feature film *The Clansman,* later re-titled *The Birth of a Nation,* said, 'In those days, around 1913, no one would tell you what you were doing. They just shoved some clothes at you and said, "Put these on." You were a piece of scenery; that was all. You didn't have to have any talent. All you had to be able to do was move if you were asked to.'8

That was probably not strictly correct. In the absence of make-up artists who had not yet arrived in Hollywood, actors needed the know-how to transform themselves into the characters they portrayed. More often than not in the early days, they were also expected to do their own stunts, which is how Caryl ap Rhys Pryce probably got his first start in the movie business, because he could get on and off a horse faster than most, and was a deadly shot from the saddle. The notoriety of this former revolutionary leader would also have generated publicity, the life-blood of Hollywood success. Pryce, the all-action man, was meat and drink to moviemakers. Still sporting, beneath his patrician nose, the luxuriant moustache cultivated by that daily noggin of whisky and milk during his days on the African veldt with the Imperial Light Horse, he struck a handsome, rugged profile when cast alongside that striking and distinguished beauty of the period, Alice Joyce, the very first 'Madonna of the screen.' It was some-thing of a paradox that a man whose determination to be a player in life rather than a spectator would propel him across three continents in search of adventure, should now embark upon what might easily have become a highly successful acting career.

Pryce most probably started in the 'bullpen' lining up alongside his old Wobbly mates looking for a few dollars work. But it was not long before he made it big time – $25 a film a great deal in those days – starring in at least seven one and two-reelers, with minor roles in others. Two of his most successful was as a sup-porting actor to Alice Joyce in one of the last pictures she made for Kalem at their Glendale Studio in California before returning east. The Glendale Company specialised in westerns and films about Spanish California and Mexican revolutionaries, Pryce

Was the Hollywood movie queen Alice Joyce the 'Alice' Pryce wrote to from the trenches in France?

playing himself, the revolutionary leader. In an interview Joyce gave shortly after returning east, she could have been talking of Pryce when she described how an actor could spring from obscurity to fame, almost overnight:

> Every motion picture stock company must have a number of people who represent distinct types. They must really possess those characteristics, which can be assumed by an actor in the drama through skill at make-up. Often times the eccentricities of one's personality peculiarly adapts him for a desirable type . . . generally speaking, a person is engaged in our profession because of his individuality.[9]

While pictures focussed on the action, dialogue, although not a word was heard until 1927 with the advent of talkies, was still important, because audiences often lip-read what was being said. If in the days without scripts and sound actors were allowed to ad lib a scene, what they said had, nevertheless, to be relevant to the action. Days on the set were long and hard, and very different from the modern Babylon, scandals and hellfire socialising that came later:

> One is obliged to swim, ride, and take part in all manner of athletics, said Joyce. At different times I have run a loco-motive, handled the wheel of a tug, and steered a schooner. These things are all part of the day's occupation, and one must keep in good physical condition to be prepared when called upon for unusual tasks.[10]

A dark-haired woman with an unusual beauty, Joyce, has started life as a telephone operator in Kansa City. Gracious and charming, she had beautiful full eyes and a look most men would die for. By 1913 she was the most popular actress in motion pictures, Pryce able to boast of having starred with her in two films, *The Gun Smugglers: an incident of the Mexican Revolution* (12 June 1912), and *The Colonel's Escape* (24 June, 1912).

The Colonel's Escape, in which Pryce plays a soldier-of-fortune, resonates with incidents drawn from the Welshman's immediate past career. After rescuing a Mexican Customs Officer from brigands, the courageous soldier-of-fortune crosses the border at the head of a band of *insurrectos* to lead the fight for freedom. Hunted by the *federales,* General Pryce is saved by the Customs Officer who in turn is court-martialed and sentenced to death for befriending the leader of the *insurrectos*. On hearing this, his sister, played by Alice Joyce, races to the *insurrectos* camp to raise the alarm, the tale ending with Pryce and his men rescuing the Customs Officer from the firing squad in the nick of time. Only one copy of the film survives and this at the *Nederlands Filmmuseum*, Amsterdam. The lead role of Mexican Customs Officer was played by Carlyle Blackwell, another famous silent star of 171 movies, including the very last silent Sherlock Holmes, before his career died with the screening of the first talkie, Al Jolson's *The Jazz Singer*. Many of these silent stars failed to make the transition, because when they opened their mouths for the first time it sounded as though they were talking through their noses.

Carlyle Blackwell played the lead in most of the films in which Pryce figured in the credits, including another with Alice Joyce,

Pryce's horsemanship won him a role in "The Colonel's Escape", loosely based around his adventures in Mexico and one of the seven Hollywood silent movies in which he starred. Here, he appears with the dark-eyed beauty Alice Joyce, known to picture goers as the 'Madonna of the Screen'.

The Gun Smugglers: an incident of the Mexican Revolution. Blackwell, not Pryce, gets the girl again. On this occasion, Pryce plays a Mexican colonel murdered by a crazed gun smuggler. The only surviving copy of the film in the Library of Congress is so badly deteriorated, and some parts almost un-watchable, that the plot is difficult to follow, except for the end when it seems Joyce is inconsolable on discovering that the Mexican colonel (Pryce) had been murdered. Pryce – credited sometimes as C. Price, Rhys Price, or C. Rhys Pryce – made two other films in 1912, *The Indian Uprising at Sante Fé* when he appeared again as a Mexican, this time as Governor Don Antonio de Otermin, alongside Blackwell as Governor Vargas (was this based on Pryce's real-life adversary Colonel Vega?), and *The Apache Renegade,* starring as himself in a lead role. The following year after Alice Joyce had returned to make films for Kalem on the east coast, her one time insurgent co-star appeared among the credits of certainly three other movies, and considering the huge film output at that time, there may well have been others which are lost. *The Battle for Freedom* is another that sounds as though it might have drawn upon his Mexican adventures, as does *The Last Blockhouse*. His last starring role as far as can be ascertained was in *The Cheyenne Massacre*.[11]

Despite promising Hattie Biggs about returning to Canada, Pryce remained in Hollywood long after the Los Angeles District Attorney dropped the outstanding charge of violating United States neutrality laws. Before he finally left for Vancouver, he made one last screen appearance, according to his great-nephew Brigadier Michael ap Rhys Pryce as a leader of the Ku Klux Klan in D. W. Griffith's epic, though racist masterpiece *The Birth of a Nation*. Lasting three hours, the film caused riots when premiered as *The Clansman* in January 1915. By then, Pryce was back in Canada, and is not listed among the credits of a film that depicted the KKK as southern heroes and the blacks as villains. Griffith, himself a southerner whose father had been ruined by the Civil War, and his film were blamed for the outbreak of racial violence, but nevertheless *The Birth of a Nation* is regarded by film scholars as the single most important film of all time in American movie history, credited with inventing the shot rather than the scene.[12] Whether or not his claim to be part of this groundbreaking motion picture was correct or just bravado, no mention was made of it in

Pryce's 'obituary' when it was published prematurely in *Variety*. The movie magazine could have got this wrong as it did his obituary, killing him off in France as a 'casualty of war' in 1915.[13]

Sniffing a war after the heir to the Hapsburg throne, Franz Ferdinand was assassinated in Sarajevo, Bosnia in 1914, Pryce who had returned to Canada that year, joined the recently formed Fort Garry Horse (motto, 'Deeds Not Words'), at Winnipeg, Manitoba, a thousand miles away from his faithful Hattie Biggs in Vancouver. Britain joined the war when Germany attacked Belgium, and Pryce, now a lieutenant, promptly transferred to the 5th Brigade, Canadian Field Artillery, then assembling at Winnipeg so that he would be part of what would become the Canadian Expeditionary Force. After ten months training, he sailed with the CEF to England aboard the *S.S. Irishman,* transferring again on arrival to the Royal Field Artillery attached to the 38th (Welsh) Division of which his elder brother, Henry, was General Staff Officer.

After twenty years of fighting other people's battles across Africa and North America, the 'black sheep' was back amongst kith and kin, preparing for another war in France, and one from which, this time, he would not escape unscathed. At 38 years of age, his hair already turned a steely grey, Pryce remained a fit, wiry individual, a fraction under six feet tall. His attestation papers on enlistment in Canada states his previous military experience as South Africa, making no mention of Mexico.[14]

The 38th (Welsh) Division, known as Lloyd George's 'Welsh Army,' was recruited in Wales at the instigation of Britain's wartime leader as a vehicle for sending 50,000 Welshmen into the trenches. The corps had its genesis in a perverse appeal made by Lloyd George, then Chancellor of the Exchequer, at the Queen's Hall, London on 19 September 1914:

> I should like to see a Welsh Army in the field. I should like to see the race that faced the Norman for hundreds of years in a struggle for freedom, the race that helped to win Crecy, the race that fought for a generation under Glyndŵr against the greatest Captain in Europe – I should like to see that race give a good taste of their quality in this struggle for Europe; and they are going to do it.

Lloyd George chaired a committee of prominent Welshmen at 11 Downing Street a few days later, following up with a conference to which the good and the great from Wales were invited – Lords Lieutenants, Welsh peers, the Welsh Bishops, Members of Parliament, Mayors and Council Chairmen, trade union secretaries and business leaders. Long before Lloyd George had made his appeal from the platform of Queen's Hall, many thousands of Welshmen had already rushed to the Colours to die in Flanders fields. The Conference at Park Hall, Cardiff, on 29 September under the chairmanship of the Earl of Plymouth, who had lost a son in the first days of the war, was characterised by 'scenes of patriotic fervour' as Wales and Monmouthshire pledged itself to the task of raising the Welsh Army Corps. Within five months, from among an eligible Welsh male population of 720,00 aged 20-40, 20,000 had been recruited in response to Lloyd George's appeal to 'stand manfully by the flag of freedom, fair-play, honest-dealing, progress of Europe.'

Pryce's brother Henry was instrumental in helping recruit the Welsh Army Corps. Instead of returning to India in 1914, Lieutenant Colonel Henry ap Rhys Pryce had remained in England to re-organise the British Army's chaotic transport support for the troops at the front. Having completed the planning side of the operation – its implementation was to prove much harder – the colonel was appointed by Lloyd George as liaison officer for the recruitment of the Welsh Army, which meant working with scores of high-profile recruiting committees, fronted by prominent local dignitaries waving the flag across the length and breadth of Wales.[15] By the time Caryl arrived with the Canadian Expeditionary Force, the Welsh Corps was in place, and ready for action, its artillery support, the 'Welsh Gunners' needing a commander for A Battery 119th Field Artillery Brigade. Caryl transferred, and on completion of training in England moved his Battery into position directly opposite the Saxon and Prussian Guards in November 1915, where they dug in for the next seven months.[16] Throughout this period, Pryce kept a war diary, the entries testifying to his escalating disdain for the conduct of the war by his superior officers. Pryce clearly expected from others the same high standards he had set himself. When this failed to materialise, he said so with the rapier thrust of a sardonic wit.[17]

*Major Pryce, commander of D Battery 119th Royal Field Artillery
with his officers and sergeants at Aldershot before
being sent to the trenches in World War I.*

A battery brigade spent much of its time maintaining its lines in readiness for the order from battalion headquarters to unleash a ferocious bombardment in support of the infantry, or at some enemy position. Between these thunderous and murderous exchanges, the bombardiers were mostly employed repairing trenches around their gun emplacements, building fortifications and draining the quagmire that became synonymous with trench warfare. Artillery was hauled around the battlefields by horses whose dung accumulated around the wagon lines where, unless it was removed was washed into the trenches by heavy train. If his battery was not to be caught napping by a snap inspection, the battery commander depended upon his subalterns to ensure the lines were kept clean, and the elaborate infrastructure of duckboard paths and drainage canals properly maintained. Reflecting on the dodges to which the rank and file resorted to avoid what was monotonous, dirty and exhausting work, Pryce,

His War Diary, damaged by a piece of shrapnel.

now promoted to Captain, noted in his Diary 'Tips for Generals,' an amusing mixture of practical advice and observation:

> Battery commanders should receive the maximum of attention. They delight to throw all blame for their wagon lines on to subalterns and hide away in OPs (observation posts) and the trenches where, if found, they are invariably drinking with the infantry. Every effort should be made to get these officers down to their wagon lines and to disabuse them of the idea that their battery is the best in the division.

> Remember that your greatest enemy is the subaltern in charge of a wagon line. With every self-assurance possible he will try to deceive you, and when remonstrated with, will immediately plead ignorance . . . it is sound policy to strafe all subalterns thoroughly and continually.

A good time to visit a wagon line is the first fine day after several days continuous rain. The probability of finding dung mixed with mud is not then remote; imperfect drainage will, or should, begin then to assert itself, and the absence of roads, paths, canals, and aqueducts becomes painfully apparent. Sometimes everything may appear satisfactory, and then an exhaustive and serious search should be made of latrines, cookhouse, billets, dining hall and the gun park. If everything still appears satisfactory it is safe to assume there is a flaw somewhere in the inspection and it is well to start again.

Never on any account offer a word of encouragement, or automatically a feeling of self-satisfaction will set in, which will result in slackness, and men, instead of feverishly putting up roofs, or putting down brick standings, will, before long, loaf about gambling, and murmur discontentedly about leave.

Insist on every subaltern quickly acquiring a knowledge of engineering, sanitation, architecture, haulage, interior and exterior economy and, in view of the approach of the wet season, navigation. Finally, if your wagon lines are somewhat scattered, remember that the establishment has provided you with useful subordinates to whom too sedentary a life is not to be recommended.

Battery Sergeant Majors are only the confederates and confidants of subalterns and should be dealt with accordingly. It is useful to bear in mind that whenever a BSM explains away the absence of his offices by saying he has gone to the R.E. Yard (Royal Engineers) be certain he means to Poperinghe (*sic*). The wisdom of putting that town out of bounds cannot be too strongly insisted upon and will ensure increased efficiency in all wagon lines.

Pryce concluded his 'Tips to Generals' by proposing they should be read to all Generals at the Corps School of Instruction on three successive parades.[18]

219

Despite his general criticism of Battery Sergeant Majors for conspiring against him with negligent subalterns, Pryce could not have been more than satisfied with the one eventually posted to A Battery. Sgt Major Horlock had already won the Victoria Cross for his bravery, and no sooner had he reported for duty than he was sent down to the wagon lines 'to jock things up there as much as possible.' Pryce expressed himself well pleased with Horlick's efforts, describing his new BSM as a 'treasure.'

While many of the entries in the war diary are pretty mundane, when pieced together they provide a perceptive account of a year in the trenches during World War I. When the battery moved into position, latrines were the very first things constructed, one for the officers, and another for the men. Then came a fireplace for the officers' mess. And when the men needed a bath, Pryce would form them up during a lull in the fighting and march off to the nearest bath complex behind the lines.

Not all engagements were sustained bombardments. If the Observation Post concealed in one of the few trees left standing reported a potential enemy target Pryce ordered his guns into action:

> 3 February 1916: Fixed at 7.20 a.m. on enemy carrying planks; very good shooting. Shells fell on either side of Doll's House, right in the thick of them. Hope we got a few. Huns did not retaliate. Infantry very pleased with our shooting yesterday.

Even though the battery was hidden among trees behind the infantry trenches, Pryce's bombardiers still had to contend with incoming enemy fire, the German artillery finding the range to repay in kind for the earlier attack:

> 23 February: Bosches got a direct hit on the tree from which observation is done. Lucky none of us got strafed.

> 20 March: My batman nearly walked into a shell. It landed just in front of him, the concussion knocking him down. Just as he was getting up again a clod of earth hit him in the back and put him on his face. A narrow squeak.

8 April: Was going to the battery when Fitzgerald hailed me from the butcher's shop. Was standing in the middle of the road talking to him when a shell landed just behind him and, as it were, blew him into the butcher's shop.

Besides enemy bombardments, the artillery were constantly troubled by what Captain Pryce euphemistically noted in his diary as 'prematures.' These were his battery's own shells, or those of a neighbouring British artillery unit which showered shrapnel in all directions when they exploded prematurely. The only ones to blame for this were the manufacturers of the ammunition and Pryce said so, forcibly:

1 February: Battery in rear had a premature today, which spattered my battery, without doing any damage.

11 March: Had three prematures. Wounded a man in the infantry out in front, rotten luck, but nobody to blame but the people who made the ammunition. Of course, Rudkin talks as if we had done it purposely and says that something is radically wrong with our shooting – instead of being decent and commiserating with us on the bad luck of having such a mishap; he tries to make us out as black as possible – damn him!

Colonel Rudkin, the group commander, was a 'bally pen pusher' and not one of Pryce's favourites. When Rudkin caught the 'flu, Pryce noted in his diary, 'Wish he would go home to England or die or something.' He was no less critical of junior and senior officers alike, describing one who was leaving him to join another battery as 'a miserable little beast,' another as an 'uncouth sort of animal,' and an inspecting General and Colonel as 'blighters expecting you to make bricks without straw . . . strafed the colonel about that.' Frustration with his superiors is evident from his first days at the front, the exasperation showing itself in one particularly animated entry: 'Bally limit the way they will tell you to do this and that, and cancel the orders after you have started work – playing on the men for nothing.'

As a World War I officer, Pryce was something of a paradox, a curious mixture of disciplined authoritarian, and as such very much part of the officer corps, while remaining querulous, almost defiant, as though still wedded to his revolutionary tendencies. He could also be bigoted, the arrival of a new officer causing him to observe, 'Bernstein is a very keen, hardworking sort of chap – if only he was not so servile. Like all his race, he cow tows to anybody in authority over him. It is a 'sir' every fourth word with him which annoys and disgusts me.'

But there was time for moments of relaxation at the front, which usually meant lunch with other commanders at their mess, and occasionally with his brother Henry, a staff officer at Divisional Headquarters. The brothers were worried about their sister Gladys and how to get her safely back to England from Vancouver after the collapse of her marriage. The meetings with his elder brother were also useful because Henry was able to brief him on 'the whole shooting match – gun positions, telephones, OP, and every-thing . . . some useful tips as to what the general likes to see.' The officer Pryce wanted to impress most was Major General C. G. Blackadder, 'a decent sort, a soldier and not a politician.' At the end of the war, Blackadder provided Pryce with a testimonial, describing the Welshman as a man 'possessing strength of char-acter, determination, tact, and power of command . . . who under-stands thoroughly the handling of men and can get the best out of them without any friction,' adding, that previously, he had long experience as a policeman. No mention of his revolutionary adventures![19]

Then there were the letters to his father, one a request for a cake and some pencils, another giving instructions to invest a legacy from an uncle in 5% Exchequer Bonds. The cake arrived, so did a pair of warm Norwegian boots costing six guineas from Faulkner and Son. The diary entries were momentarily inter-rupted on 11 July 1916 when a piece of shrapnel from a German shell blew the corner off it. And again a few weeks later when Pryce was rushed to hospital to have his gall bladder removed, not an experience he enjoyed very much, on account of the 'filthy sheets on the beds' and because the hospital was generally a 'very sloppy place.' Before this however he did get a spot of leave back in England, describing his stay at the Grosvenor Hotel as 'blessed peace,' 'calm and tranquil,' and 'just quiet.'

All entries in the diary are self-explanatory apart from two. These mention a woman called 'Alice':

13 February: 'Letter from Alice with photo of nephews.'

11 September: 'Wrote letter to Alice.'

Who was Alice? The only person of that name in his immediate family was a maiden aunt, and Caryl and his brother Henry were her nephews, the letter from Alice containing a photograph of two young children. Alice might have been Hattie Biggs, because one newspaper account during Pryce's trial in Los Angeles refers to 'Alice Biggs.' Not only had Pryce never used this name when writing to her, Hattie was the manner by which she was addressed in all official correspondence relating to the general's arrest and trial after the collapse of the Magoinsta revolution. Could it then have been his co-star from silent movies, Alice Joyce? It just might have been, because just a few days after mentioning he had written to 'Alice,' Pryce saw an old Bronco Bill film which caused him to write in his diary, 'Was taken at Pine Crest I should think and certainly got me back two years ago or more.' Whoever Alice was, and how meaningful the relationship, it never survived the end of the war, which for Pryce was not that far away.[20]

At the beginning of July 1916 Pryce was ordered to move his guns into position behind Fricourt, not far from Mametz Wood, one of the objectives of the bloody Somme offensive. The day before part of his diary was blown away by a piece of German shrapnel, he and two other officers were reconnoitring the German positions at Contalmaison when they stumbled upon an enemy machine gun position held by seventeen Germans all of whom surrendered to the three British officers after a furious exchange of fire.[21]

Pryce's battery had been moved from the Somme into the reserve by the time of the final diary entry, 15 November 1916. The Allied forces were preparing for the Flanders Campaign for which the battery would move back into line north of Ypres as part of the Fifth Army. The Fifth Army was the one most men feared to serve with on account of its reputation for almost always taking the brunt of any German offensive and suffering the highest casualty rate.[22] Pryce's battery was in position in late May 1917 awaiting the assault on Messines. But shortly before this began Pryce was hit in the shoulder by a shrapnel burst on 3 June, sufficiently badly wounded to be invalided home, spending the remainder of the war in command of a reserve artillery brigade at Aldershot.[23] The lump of shrapnel surgeons removed from his shoulder he wore on his watch chain for the rest of his life.[24] On the day after he was wounded, the *London Gazette* announced that Pryce, now a Major, had been made a Member of the Distinguished Service Order for the courage shown in tackling the nest of German machine gunners.[25] Released from hospital, and posted to Waterloo Barracks, Aldershot, the 42-year-old soldier-of-fortune met Ellen Mary Morkill, the widow of Lieutenant R. F. Morkill, West Yorkshire Regiment, and fifteen years his junior.[26] They were married at All Saints Church, Eastbourne, Sussex, on 20 November 1918, the week following the Armistice, and retired to what was expected to be a quiet life in the country.[27] His adventures over, it was thought Pryce would devote the rest of his days to his favourite pastimes, fishing and shooting.

NOTES

1. Pryce Papers. Copy of undated letter from Pryce to Hattie Biggs written at time of his incarceration in Los Angeles.
2. ibid., letter from Pryce to his father Colonel Douglas Davidson Pryce, 3 February 1912.
3. ibid., letter from Mortimer to Colonel Pryce, 7 November 1911.
4. Pryce Papers. Letter from Pryce to his father Colonel Douglas Davidson Pryce, 3 February 1912.
5. ibid.
6. Bancroft Library, Peter B.Kyne Papers, 1914-1957, four cartons, BANC MSS C-H 29; copy of *The Gringo Privateer* (1931, New York Cosmopolitan Book Corporation), Bancroft Library, BANC: F855.1.K99gri.
7. Kevin Brownlow, *The Parade's Gone By . . .* (London, 1968, Secker and Warburg), pp. 30-31.
8. ibid., pp. 42-64.
9. *The New York Dramatic Mirror,* 18 June 1913.
10. ibid.
11. *The Internet Movie Data Base*, www.imbd.com.
12. Brigadier M. H. ap Rhys Pryce, 'Major Caryl ap Rhys pryce, D.S.O., late RA,' p. 2.

13. *The Internet Movie Data Base*, www.imbd.com.
14. Pryce Papers. Caryl ap Rhys Pryce 'Statement of Service in the Canadian Armed Forces,' National Personnel Records, Public Archives, Canada.
15. Newport Public Library, 'Report on the work of raising the Welsh Army Corps,' September 1921.
16. *Great Britain, History of the Great War, order of battle of divisions (38th Welsh Division)*, London, HMSO, 1945.
17. Caryl ap Rhys Pryce, '1916 Diary,' Royal Artillery Library, Royal Artillery Institution, Woolwich, RAI/A/C 8105-6, Military Document 1518; Colin Hughes, 'Lloyd George's Welsh Army and the battle of Mametz,' (unpublished transcript), Imperial War Museum, London, p. 7.
18. ibid., Caryl ap Rhys Pryce, '1916 Diary.'
19. Testimonial. Copy, Royal Artillery Library, Woolwich, RAI/A/C 8105-6, Box 1518.
20. ibid., Caryl ap Rhys Pryce, '1916 Diary.'
21. ibid., 10 July 1916.
22. Leon Wolff, *In Flanders Field, the 1917 Campaign* (New York, 1963, Time Inc.,), pp. 188-189.
23. Pryce Papers. Date of Caryl's wound is mentioned in a testimonial letter written by the Commanding Officer of the 38th (Welsh) Division, Major General C. G. Blackadder, 27 April, 1920.
24. From interview given the author by Pryce's great nephew, Brigadier Meyric ap Rhys Pryce.
25. Pryce Papers. Copy of Record of Service.
26. ibid., copy of testimonial letter written 3 September 1925, in which Mr John W.Morkill says he had known Pryce for seven years.
27. ibid., Copy of Marriage Certificate.

Chapter 12

From the Ku Klux Klan to the Black and Tans

What became of Caryl ap Rhys Pryce between his marriage to Ellen Morkill in November 1918 and March 1922 is not clear. The only clues to those missing years are no more than straws in the wind. It might well be that he settled down to a quiet life in the country with his new wife. But would that have been possible? At the end of World War I, Pryce was without work, and with no visible means of support, apart from the legacy inherited from his 'Uncle Alick.'[1] Much of what was of value at the family's home at Penn's Rock at Withyham in Sussex, formerly owned by William Penn, Quaker founder of Pennsylvania, had already been snaffled by a spinster aunt and carried off by her to Jersey.[2] Pryce's marriage to Ellen Morkill could have been one of convenience, her late father, Thomas Wilkinson, having had interests in the iron and steel industry of the north east England. But if there had been a dowry, then is it likely that Pryce on reaching middle age would have still been seeking gainful employment? All that is known for certain is that while the Great War in Europe might have ended, another had broken out – in Ireland – and, if nothing else, Pryce was an expert at sniffing out trouble.

At the conclusion of the peacemaking process at Versailles in 1919, the British Empire found itself in a situation of imperial over-stretch. The Empire's subjects were restless, the most persistent demand for freedom coming from Ireland, an integral part of the United Kingdom since the 1800 Act of Union dissolved the Irish Parliament. The war had presented Irish nationalists with the opportunity to seize power but their attempt to do so in the Easter Monday Rising in Dublin in 1916 had been brutally suppressed, many of their leaders executed and 1,850 political prisoners interned at Frongoch Camp, near Bala, Merionethshire in Wales. There had been other British internment camps, the most notorious of these in southern Africa in which 26,000 men, women and children died during the Boer War. Frongoch was the first on British soil and was originally set up to hold German aliens at the outbreak of World War I. When Michael Collins, Terrence MacSwinney, Dick Mulcahy, J. J. O'Connell, Sean T. O'Kelly, Tomas MacCurtain, and other Irish patriots arrived in June 1916 at what had once been an old whisky distillery, they immediately set about transforming it into a training camp for those who would renew the struggle for freedom on their eventual return to Ireland. It was here at what became known as the 'ollscoil na reabhloide' ('university of revolution') that Michael Collins and his senior aides plotted the Anglo-Irish War. When it came in 1919, it would not be a conventional one of pitched battles, the Irish having learned from the Easter Rising that while that sacrifice stirred the patriotic conscience, they would always be numerically outnumbered. Next time around, Collins and his supporters would fight a guerrilla war, adopting the hit-and-run tactics of the Boers. Although interned at Frongoch for little more than six months, the foundations of the Sinn Fein policy of resistance in jails and internment camps were laid, many a lad entering as 'a harmless gossoon and leaving with the seeds of Fenianism deep in his heart.'[3]

On their arrival, Michael Collins and his fellow prisoners were inspired on hearing the Welsh language. After their arrest in Ireland, they had been dispersed among a number of mainland prisons, until transferred to Frongoch in batches as soon it was cleared of Germans. About two and a half miles from Bala, the camp could not have been more remote, one of the Irish internees observing as he arrived, 'It's so like Ireland,' and another, 'They're so different to the English who look at you in the way a cow looks over a hedge.' Collins, who spent much of his time preparing his men for the fight to come, did, evidently, make some effort to learn Welsh by acquiring a Welsh dictionary from one of the Welsh staff at the camp.[4]

Just fourteen months after the Easter Rising, the last of the republican prisoners returned home from Frongoch via Holyhead to an enthusiastic reception, and the beginning in January 1919 of what was in effect an undeclared war between guerrilla units of the Irish Republican Army (IRA) and the forces of the Crown charged with restoring order. Since the military were to play only a supporting role, it was left to the Royal Irish Constabulary (RIC) to deal with the nationalist insurgents. Consequently, the IRA took the view that RIC officers were English collaborators opposed to the struggle for Irish freedom, and as such were legitimate targets in a remorseless campaign of intimidation. By the end of 1919, the IRA had killed 18 policemen, this increasing to 55 six months later, clear evidence of how IRA violence had escalated by early 1920. The response of the British Government to this was to create as part of the RIC a special force recruited, firstly, from ex-servicemen – the Black and Tans – and later, ex-officers, the Auxiliaries, the new recruits with their experience of weapons and warfare adding a new dimension to the conflict. While Lloyd George was persuaded by the Irish, and not London as some assumed, to recruit the Black and Tans – even the sobriquet was Irish, their dark green RIC caps and tunics with khaki trousers reminding the Irish of a pack of hounds from Limerick with a similar name – the first seeds of the plan for 'Auxiliaries' were planted by Sir Winston Churchill as Secretary of State for War.[5]

But the British Government's approach to the recruitment of both was extraordinary – it advertised in newspapers for men prepared to 'face a tough and dangerous task.'[6] Recruiting stations were opened in London, Glasgow, Liverpool and Birmingham, and by March 1920 the Black and Tans, often accompanied by their wives and girlfriends, began arriving at the RIC's Phoenix Park depot in Dublin, and from there were distributed as small detachments attached to police barracks around the country. On the advice of Churchill, a former Royal Artillery officer, Major-General Hugh Tudor was appointed as the new Chief of Police in Ireland, and while the Tans and the Auxiliaries were supposed to be subordinate to police authority, they were often undisciplined, terrorising the civilian population, especially the Catholic majority. But Tudor appeared to support the policy of random terror, to the extent that IRA atrocities met with violent and destructive reprisals from the Tans, towns sacked and set ablaze, and suspects shot without ceremony. One Irish observer commented at the time:

> They had neither religion nor morals, they used foul lan-
> guage, they had the old soldier's talent for dodging and

scrounging, they spoke in strange accents, called the Irish "natives," associated with low company, stole from each other, sneered at the customs of the country, drank to excess and put sugar on their porridge.[7]

The outrages of the 'Tan War' inflamed public opinion in England and overseas, especially in the United States. Most feared by the Irish insurgents were the Auxiliaries with whom the Tans were often confused. In the early days of they looked much the same, wore the same Glengarry caps, carried .45 Webley pistols in open black leather holsters and had bandoliers for their ammunition slung across their shoulders. But the Auxiliaries were distinguished by their officer-style khaki tunics and trousers – later replaced with a dark blue uniform – worn with high leather boots or leggings. Organised into companies of up to one hundred men led by a colonel or major, and equipped with Crossley tenders for mobility, they constituted a rapid response force capable of mounting raids on suspects, and searches for IRA weapons caches at a moment's notice.[8] Known as 'Tudor's toughs,' the Auxiliaries are remembered by Tom Barry of the IRA's No. 3 Cork Brigade for the vigour of their policing:

'They had a special technique. Fast lorries of them would come roaring into a village; the occupants would jump out, firing shots and ordering all the inhabitants out of doors. No exceptions were allowed. Men and women, old and young, the sick and the decrepit were lined up against the walls with their hands up, questioned and searched. No raid was ever carried out by these ex-officers without their beating up with the butt ends of their revolvers, at least half-dozen people. They were no respecters of persons and seemed to particularly dislike the Catholic priests.'[9]

Of all the atrocities committed by the Auxiliaries, the attack on the crowd at the Croke Park football match was one of the worst outrages. The Auxiliaries were supposed to assist the RIC in searching the crowd, but it turned into an indiscriminate reprisal for the assassination by the IRA of twelve suspected British Intelligence Officers. Arriving at the park early, I Company of the

Auxiliary Division of the RIC, its passions inflamed by the loss of two its own men that very same day, proceeded to fire at random into the crowd, killing twelve and wounding dozens. A few weeks later, the Auxiliaries' outrageous behaviour culminated in the destruction of a substantial part of Cork City centre in another orgy of looting and burning, an event so devastating that Lloyd George ordered an inquiry which, in turn, compelled the Prime Minister to order a cessation of reprisals.[10] Peace eventually broke out with the truce of July 1921. The RIC was disbanded the following year and so also, the Tans and Auxiliaries. While there is no official record of Pryce having served with either the Tans or Auxiliaries in Ireland during the Anglo-Irish War, he might have been one of the many intelligence officers whose names still remain on the 'Secret' list, because the next occasion he emerges into the daylight it is as commander of a company comprised largely of former Black and Tans!

In 1922 Britain was given the mandate by the fledgling League of Nations to govern Palestine. The Arabs, whose numbers at that time dwarfed the tiny resident Jewish population, suspected that the Balfour Declaration, which the British at first refused to admit the existence of, was intended to promote the emergence of a Jewish homeland for the tens of thousands of Jews that Theodor Herzl's Zionist movement were encouraging to migrate to Palestine. The Arabs believed that Palestine had been sold out to the Jews and that they themselves were about to be sacrificed. Except for the Palestinians themselves, everyone seems to have known it was the British Government's intention to settle Jews in Palestine, although it had never planned to create a Jewish homeland at the expense of the Arabs. Very quickly, a formerly friendly Arab people became violently anti-British, Arabs and Jews rioting in the streets of Jaffa where the largely Arab police was either unable or reluctant to maintain order.[11]

A new force was needed. So Winston Churchill sent his friend and 'super cop' from Ireland, Major General Sir Hugh (Owen) Tudor, together with the now disgraced Black and Tans, to crush another rebellion. But as was the case in Ireland, all they ever succeeded in achieving was an escalation in the violence, which continues to this day, the so-called terrorists still undefeated. At the time, however, the recruitment of this special militia force to

The area of the mandated territory designated as a Jewish homeland
by the San Remo Conference in 1920 covered a much larger area
than what has become known as Palestine. But the creation of a
Jewish homeland by the British was never supposed to be
at the expense of the Arabs already living there.

support the Palestine police was a stroke of luck for 'Tudor's Toughs.' The disbandment of the RIC meant there would be no place in the new Garda Siochana for anyone who was not Irish. As for the Tans, fearing reprisals once the Irish Free State became a reality, they were getting out as fast as possible. Walter Harrison, one of those who made the transition from the RIC to the British Section of the Palestine Gendarmerie, wrote:

'Word came round the canteen by word of mouth, and later by notices. Many of us were interested. After all, our job was disappearing, and what other employment was there? Most of us knew no other occupation, except military, or para-military service of some sort. The more we thought about it, the more the whole adventure appealed to us. It all seemed very attractive so I volunteered. If one was a loyalist, that is, if one was non-Irish, then one must get out. It was rather like the time the Romans left Britain, or so it seemed to us at the time. Then word went around Limerick that a new force was to be formed for service overseas as a sort of police force. If enough of my comrades were to join me, it would not be so bad. We all needed a job, for which we were trained and here was a wonderful opportunity.'[12]

Seven hundred men, mostly ex-Black and Tans or Auxiliaries, assembled for training in a sea of mud at Fort Tregantle, an old Napoleonic fort that once formed part of the defences around Plymouth Sound. Apart from the pay, exceedingly generous for those days – ranging from 20 shillings a day for platoon officers to 10 shillings for constables – the project was dogged by problems. The new recruits never really knew whether they were supposed to be army or police. From their uniforms, it seemed they were a para-military force with policing duties. The most unusual feature of the uniform was a Stetson hat, as worn by New Zealand troops during the Great War, but in some ways appropriate in view of the wild-west approach to policing that the Tans took with them to Palestine from Ireland. Around each Stetson was a thin red and green pugri, the green reminding them of the RIC still dear to many.[13]

March, April 1922 was cold and wet on Plymouth Sound. Because the old fort had no heating whatsoever, the greatcoats with which the recruits were issued never left their backs as they drilled in the mud and perfected their marksmanship on the firing range. Shortly, as one of their number observed, they would leave for the Holy Land, the first police to do so since the Crusaders.[14]

Major Pryce joined the Palestine Gendarmerie at Fort Tregantle in March, after providing a glowing testimonial from Lieutenant General R. S. S. Baden-Powell. Baden-Powell, who was at Seige of Mafeking and later founded the Scout Movement, was confident Pryce would be of 'special value for organising and administering Gendarmerie in Palestine.' Together with 762 officers and men, Pryce left Plymouth – and his new wife – for the Middle East on 13 April aboard an ageing troopship, the *S.S. City of Oxford*.[15] The old soldier it seemed had one last shot in his locker! And once again, he had joined a company of ruffians, albeit British Army trained, whose job would be to patrol the arid wilderness along Palestine's borders with Trans-Jordan and French-administered Syria. Palestine was then bounded in the north by French Syria, in the west by the Mediterranean, in the south by Egyptian and Hezaz territory, with Trans-Jordan in the east included as part of the British Mandate. The 13,724 square miles of mandate territory became a British responsibility at the end of World War I when the Turks were defeated and the Ottoman Empire broken up. A country of mountains and plains, of desert and pleasant valleys, Palestine has, from the desolation of its barren hills to its broad stretches of deep, fruitful oases, excited the interest of east and west from Biblical times. Its most important geographical feature has always been the deep fissure that is the Jordan Valley, dividing Palestine proper (now Israel and the West Bank) from Trans-Jordan (now the Kingdom of Jordan). The Valley through which the River Jordan flows is remarkable for its descent from its headwaters at 3,000 feet, through a chain of lakes as it drops into the Dead Sea, 1,292 feet below sea level. After this, the generally mountainous country loses itself in the desert of the Sinai Peninsular. In 1922 when Britain assumed responsibility for its governance, there were more Christians than Jews, and ten times as many Moslems. Immigration in the 19th and 20th centuries accounted for the bulk of the Jewish population, the only surviving representatives of ancient Israel continuously in occupation being a small remnant of Samaritans. The British population, excluding the garrison, numbered only 1,100 souls.[16]

That the *S.S. City of Oxford* ever made it to Jaffa amazed most on board: seven hundred men crammed on to vessel that should only have taken 200, and experiencing one of the worst ever crossings of the Bay of Biscay. Within hours of leaving port, the vessel plunged into a violent storm that lasted three days, flooding the companionways, washing away hammocks and clothing, and smashing some of the lifeboats beyond repair. The crew were close to mutiny as conditions worsened, the master forced to put two cooks under lock and key. At one point such was his concern the ship might founder, that he sent a wireless message giving its position. Men lay everywhere in their own vomit as the *City of Oxford* was buffeted by the high seas. No one was allowed on deck and there was no fresh air. Lights had failed in some parts of the ship and since both cooks were in the brig there was no cooked food either. Men, who when they enlisted were told they were civilians, found themselves subjected to military discipline. Those who had formerly held commissions in the British Army began to question why they had been sent to sea at all aboard a vessel that was clearly unfit for the voyage. It was, indeed, the *City of Oxford's* very last voyage, her next destination after Jaffa, the breaker's yard. Grievances were not addressed, the men even refused permission to see either the master or their own commanding officer, Brigadier General Angus McNeill, who disappeared from sight for a large part of the voyage. Some order was restored out of the chaos and misery when a small group of officers took charge of the situation and volunteers took over the galley. Even after the ship limped into Gibraltar, the men were denied the opportunity for respite and the chance to stretch their legs. For whatever reason – perhaps he thought they might desert – McNeill decided they would remain aboard while he and his fellow officers went ashore for tennis parties and, generally, to enjoy Gibraltar's hospitality. But with mutiny in the air, McNeill was forced to rescind his order.[17] Once in the Mediterranean the weather improved, and McNeill, now recovered from his seasickness, reappeared to join his fellow officers in planning how the Palestine Gendarmerie could best keep the peace between Arabs and Jews. Besides headquarters company at Sarafand, there would be six others, Major Pryce given command of No. 6 Company at Nazareth.[18]

From the moment they arrived, the new gendarmes were known to the local population as the 'Irish Police.' Using the same aggressive tactics as the Black and Tans had employed in Ireland, buildings were commandeered for billets without any concern for the welfare of the Arabs they ejected from their homes. There was friction immediately between the police and those they dispossessed. Besides the law, they also administered rough justice, many a chase through Palestine's barren hills ending in the execution, rather than apprehension, of the alleged villain. Off duty, McNeill's men were belligerent, usually drunk, swaggering and arguing as they crowded into Herman's and Sherman's, their favourite drinking haunts in Jaffa. Helen Bentwich, wife of the Attorney General of Palestine wrote of the new arrivals: 'Our Irish Constabulary have arrived, and a rough looking lot they are. Already it's rumoured they are painting Jaffa red. They don't fit in with our scheme for a moral Utopia.'[19] Soon, the shopkeepers in Jaffa were locking and bolting their stores immediately they heard the Irish Police were on a night out.

If some of the behaviour could be excused as high spirits, other actions were reminiscent of Black and Tan patrols at the height of the Irish troubles. When the gendarmerie suffered its first casualty – a dispatch rider shot and wounded by Arabs – two of the gang were killed in a running battle, this incident establishing the corps reputation for taking instant reprisals. After this, the local population knew that if any member of the Irish Police was harmed it could expect immediate retaliation, in some ways not so bad a reputation for a small force often called upon to deal with rioting Arabs and Jews.

Generally well-disciplined while under orders, even then the gendarmerie had its share of eccentric troublemakers ready to test authority to the limit. One major, who insisted on wearing his polo helmet on parade, and refused McNeill's order to remove it, ordered his entire company to 'Shoulder Arms' defiantly, before marching them off the parade ground. Another went on parade wearing belt, regulation kit and side arm, but otherwise stark naked. One of Pryce's brother officers at Nazareth, Captain Laidman, with rather too many fond memories of his service with the

As commander of a mounted squadron in Palestine, Pryce was responsible for patrolling the borders against Arab slave traders and smugglers.

Royal Irish Constabulary, instructed his entire command to blacken their belts and webbing RIC-style. Platoon Officer Bankier always appeared on parade wearing solid gold spurs, while an Irish Protestant officer Lieutenant Stafford had to contend with a Roman Catholic company that insisted singing Irish rebel songs on church parade.

Soon after the gendarmes arrived, McNeill realised the need of a mounted unit to deal with the gangs of Arab highwaymen infesting the roads of Palestine, and also to patrol the borders across which slave traders and smugglers continued to operate from Syria and Trans-Jordan. There were more than enough ex-cavalrymen in the ranks for such a unit, and Pryce was given command of the new squadron towards the end of 1922. For the remainder of his service in Palestine, when not mounting border patrols, he could have expected to supervise the gangs of convict labour building a new road and rail network. But as peacekeepers the gendarmerie's reputation continued to suffer from the activities of an undesirable element that refused to shed the aggressive policing methods they had brought from Ireland. McNeill, finally, decided to deal with the problem, and by the middle of 1923 had discharged and sent home one quarter of all those off the *City of Bristol*. New recruits would be more carefully selected, and be drawn mostly from Scotland and England. The improvement in the intake had its effect, and Palestine enjoyed a relatively peaceful four years. But criticism of policing tactics did not go away. Neither did the escalating cost of maintaining the force. In April 1925 Pryce's mounted squadron was disbanded, followed the next year by the entire British Section of the Palestine Gendarmerie, some of the para-militaries absorbed into the civilian police, others forming a new corps, the Trans Jordan Frontier Force.[20] Those who opted for neither returned to Britain, among them Major Pryce.[21] The 'super cop,' Major-General Sir Hugh Tudor, had already been re-called. But the man who had also previously been Chief of Police in Ireland during the Tan War dared not risk a return to Britain. With the help of his friend, Winston Churchill, Tudor was given a new home and new life in the British colony of Newfoundland, spending the last forty years of his life as an exile, moving from place to place, cared for all this time by a live-in-nurse, Monica McCarthy.

NOTES

1. Caryl ap Rhys Pryce, '1916 Diary.'
2. From author's conversation with great nephew John ap Rhys Pryce, Weybridge, Surrey, England.
3. McGowan, Seumas, *Captain Irish Citizen Army:* orders and correspondence concerning his imprisonment in Frongoch Camp, Wales, Reading Gaol, Kilmainham Gaol and Gormanstown Internment Camp (1916-23).
4. Edwards, Elwyn, *Y Casglwr,* No. 60, Summer (1997). The recollections of two former staff at Frongoch have been tape recorded for posterity by Mel Edwards, Editor, *Y Casglwr.*
5. Townshead, Charles, *The British Campaign in Ireland,* pp. 45-46; Bennett, Richard, *The Black and Tans,* p. 24.
6. Diary of Sir Henry Wilson, 11 May 1919, Papers of Sir Henry Wilson, Imperial War Museum, DS/MISC/80.
7. O'Shea, Patrick, *Voices and the Sound of Drums* (1981, Belfast), quoted in Peter Somerville-Large's, *Irish Voices: an informal history 1916-1966,* 2nd Edn. (2000, London, Pimlico).
8. For background on the Auxiliaries, see Bennett, *The Black and Tans.*
9. Barry, Tom, *Guerrilla Days in Ireland,* 4th Edn. (1989, Dublin, Anvil), p. 37.
10. Lloyd George to Sir Hamar Greenwood, 25 February 1921, Lloyd George Papers, House of Lords Records Office, F19/3/4.
11. Public Record Office, The Palin Report, FO 371/23229.
12. Walter Harrison interviewed in 1972 by Edward Horne, author, *A job well done – a history of the Palestine Police Force 1920-1948* (1982, Palestine Police), pp. 76-78.
13. ibid., p. 79.
14. Douglas V. Duff, author of many books about his life in the Palestine Gendarmerie.
15. Pryce Papers. Testimonial letter written by Lieutenant General R. S. S. Baden-Powell, 9 February 1922.
16. Luke, Harry Charles, *The Handbook of Palestine* (1922, London, Macmillan).
17. Horne, Edward Horne, *A job well done – a history of the Palestine Police Force 1920-1948* (1982, Palestine Police), pp. 80-83.
18. ibid., p. 85.
19. Bentwich, Norman and Helen, *Mandate Memoirs 1918-1924.*
20. Horne, Edward Horne, *A job well done – a history of the Palestine Police Force 1920-1948* (1982, Palestine Police), pp. 85-96.
21. Great Britain, Colonial Office, Report by H.M. Government to the Council of the League of Nations on the administration of Palestine and Trans-Jordan (1926, London, HMSO).

Epilogue

Mexicans and Wobbly friends

The rout of the *insurrectos* at the Second Battle of Tijuana failed to deter Ricardo Flores Magon even after he was arrested with other leading members of the junta. The only Magonista of importance to escape the U.S. Marshalls was Party Secretary Antonio Araujo who fled Tijuana just before the battle. Although there were reported sightings of Araujo all over the United States, it is thought he disappeared into obscurity on reaching the Canadian border.

On bail awaiting trial, Magon tried to rally the remnants of his army by confirming the appointment of Tirza de la Toba as his new general in the field. Toba, who had returned with his bandits from raiding ranches on either side of the border, had already promoted himself after Mosby surrendered, offering the Liberal Junta's revolution just a flicker of life. But it was seized upon, Magothe issuing fresh orders to their new general to abandon any thought of re-capturing Tijuana and, instead, to head south to Santa Rosalia, the most important industrial centre in Lower California. Santa Rosalia owed its existence to a powerful French syndicate, El Boleo Copper Company, which owned most of the large mines in the region. The company had imported thousands of Indians from Sonora Province across the Sea of Cortez to work the mines, where the giant smelters belched smoke and fumes day and night, burying the surrounding area in a grubby, chocolate-brown dust. Magon calculated that within the ranks of the exploited miners Toba might find willing recruits for a new Magonista Army. But to reach Santa Rosalia meant a daunting trek 400 miles along the *camino real,* the trail cut through the inhospitable interior by Jesuit missionaries two hundred years earlier and still the only route south. Toba decided not to bother, leading his desperadoes on further raids on ranchers in the neighbourhood of El Campo until they were all either shot or dispersed.

Flores Magon blamed Pryce for the collapse of the Revolution, referring to this in his instructions to Toba:

> The Assembly (his Mexican Liberty Party) is in a desperate condition financially at this time. Unfortunately, Pryce has not sent money to this city for the support of the revolution and, as you know, he went with the funds. If it were not for this, we would aid the assembly. However, you can secure protection so you will lack nothing.
>
> Do not be discouraged. We hope soon that we will have the news that you have captured a place of importance. You are a small number but on your road you can go raising fights until you reach Santa Rosalia, which is the most important place.
>
> I am your esteemed companion in social revolution.
>
> R. Flores Magon.
>
> PS. I neglected to say that the members of the Junta were arrested. I went in liberty under caution, however. They want to take the rest of the companions but the persecutions are of no importance to us as long as there are always brave companions who are ready to continue the fight.[1]

The trial of Magon and other members of the Liberal Junta for alleged neutrality violations took place in Los Angeles before Judge Wellborn in June 1912. As in Pryce's case, all official transcripts have disappeared from the public records, which means the only account of the trial is that pieced together from a close reading of the Los Angeles press.[2] For the three weeks of the hearing, the court was in almost constant pandemonium, the participants often close to violence. Assistant District Attorney Dudley Robinson prosecuted the junta members with an intimidating phalanx of Magonistas and Wobblies at his back, hissing and barracking his every move from the well of the court. Extra police drafted in to evict the more threatening of Magon's supporters made little difference, the corridors outside the courtroom overflowing with noisy demonstrators.

Because Mexican witnesses refused to co-operate, Robinson had great difficulty preparing a case against the junta. Paul Schmidt (alias Paul Smith or Paul Silent), one-time captain with General Pryce, was one of the few persuaded to testify against Magon, in return for which he was promised immunity from prosecution for smuggling stolen horses across the border when, in high dudgeon, he deserted the rebel camp at Tijuana after Mosby's election as leader. Schmidt was later, however, to repudiate his statement to the prosecution, claiming he had been bribed with the offer of a government job and $10 a day if he could recruit former *insurrectos* to testify against the accused.[3] The strongest evidence against Magon was a sworn statement from General Pryce. But that has also disappeared along with the official record of the trial. All that is known, is that Pryce was asked to make his statement a second time after the notebook containing his original affidavit was stolen from the District Attorney's office, allegedly by agents acting for Madero's secret police.

Much of the evidence of witnesses from both sides dealt with allegations that certain American business interests were financing Pryce and his insurrecto army. The Spreckles family who were financing the construction of the San Diego-Arizona Eastern Railroad were frequently mentioned as having backed the revolution in Lower California by secretly providing the rebels with provisions. Witnesses stopped short, however, of implicating Spreckles too deeply for fear of recriminations.[4]

On 22 June 1912, a year after the Magonistas were defeated at Tijuana, Magon and his three junta comrades were convicted of neutrality violations and sentencing was set for the following Monday. That weekend, the Industrial Workers of the World rallied all their members in Los Angeles instructing them to besiege the courtroom, promising that the four Magonista leaders would never be jailed. On the Monday morning, police restricted admission, forcing a huge crowd to form on the stairs and out into the street. When Judge Wellborn sentenced the four to 23 months each in the penitentiary on McNeil's Island, the crowd rioted, the police just managing to hold the demonstrators off while the prisoners were hustled out through a back door, down an alley to the county jail next door. In the melee, Magon's stepdaughter, Lucille Norman Guidera, slapped Schmidt across the face and 'with eyes flashing scorn, lips trembling with anger and calling out the word coward' threatened to kill him. Surrounded and abused by a dozen Wobblies, the hapless Schmidt fought his way to an exit.[5]

Pouring out on to the plaza, the demonstrators were joined by several hundred others waiting outside for the verdicts. At the height of the riot, Wobblies and other Magonista supporters forced their way back into the court building in a desperate effort to rescue the jailed junta members. On the stairs they were met by police brandishing clubs and swiping at heads with the butts of their heavy-duty revolvers, the rioters drawing pistols and knives in retaliation. Lucile Guidera, her young daughter clinging to her legs, charged into the thick of it, clawing at the face of a police officer before she and eighteen ringleaders were dragged from the crush and flung into police cars.[6]

And so it was that the very last battle of the Magonistas was fought on the streets of Los Angeles. Released from jail in January 1914 after completing his sentence, Magon, still the indefatigable revolutionary, resumed his verbal onslaught on the Mexican leadership through the columns of his resurrected mouthpiece, *La Regeneración*. Twice again his extremist sentiments ran foul of U.S. authorities and he was jailed for short periods.[7] Then came the final act. After the United States entered World War I in 1917, Congress passed an Espionage Act to discourage radicals from interfering with the war effort. Inspired by the Bolshevik Revolution in Russia, Magon defied the sanction by publishing a manifesto predicting the imminent demise of capitalist society, and appealing to anarchists and workers throughout the world to rise up. References to workers roaring their vengeance in dynamite, and to the heroes of world revolution caressing their rifles, were sufficient to convict him and Librado Rivera for violating the Espionage Act. This time there would be no trifling sentence of one or two years. Not for the last time were Americans seeing reds under the bed. Ricardo Flores Magon and Rivera were each jailed for 22 years.[8]

Behind the iron bars of Leavenworth, the ageing revolutionary mellowed, his brief flirtation with the Russian Revolution not lasting long. Increasingly wary of Lenin and Trotsky, he accused them of murdering revolutionary principles: that 'the dictatorship of the proletariat is in reality the dictatorship of Lenin and Trotsky over the proletariat.'[9] From a direct-action anarchist of the most dedicated kind, he changed into a kind-hearted pacifist advocating a world ruled by goodwill. After 1920 efforts were made to obtain his release, the Mexican Congress offering him and Librado Rivera pensions to ease in some small way their imprisonment. But the old rebel remained stubborn to the end, refusing to seek a pardon, or a pension, replying:

> I do not believe in the state . . . I fight for the universal brotherhood of man. I consider the State an institution created by capitalism to guarantee the exploitation and subjugation of the masses. Consequently, all the money derived from the state represents the sweat, anguish, and sacrifice of the workers. Were the money to come directly from the workers, I should accept it with pleasure and pride, because they are my brothers. But coming by intervention of the State . . . it is the money that would burn my hands and fill my heart with remorse.[10]

If he had requested a pardon, it would almost certainly have been granted. But as this meant denying his convictions, he preferred instead to resign himself to dying in prison. On 21 November 1922 by which time Magon was almost blind, he was found dead at the door of his cell in Leavenworth, murdered, according to Rivera, but in the view of his Wobbly cell mate 'just a broken man.'[11] His body was returned to Mexico for burial, the old rebel, reviled by the establishment, now immortalised, hailed by the poor peons as a martyr. It would be another twenty-four years before the establishment acquiesced and his remains were interred in the Rotunda of Illustrious Men in Mexico City.[12]

Dick Ferris and the Actress

While Magon had no hesitation in blaming the Welsh adventurer Caryl ap Rhys Pryce for the failure of his great revolutionary enterprise, the showman Dick Ferris did much to undermine it by his farcical exploitation of the situation.[13] Almost everything Dick ever touched was enveloped by the burlesque, its players transformed into music hall caricatures. This is not to say the Ferris Filibuster was always intended to be a gag: isolated in Tijuana and deserted by the junta, Pryce had warmed to Dick's scheme for the Republic of Lower California. By then, the Ferris Filibuster was the only realistic hope the insurgents had of a payday. Whatever were Pryce's motives for involving himself with the Magonistas in the first place, he had led the revolution to within one victory of creating either a new republic or the 51st State of the Union. If Ensenada had fallen to the insurgents, Madero, and following his assassination a year later, subsequent Mexican presidents, would have been hard pressed to recover their lost territory. All that Dick Ferris achieved was to wreck the revolution by persuading the only man then capable of taking it to a successful conclusion to desert his *insurrecto* army at the critical moment. That is, unless Pryce already had desertion in mind.

Ferris more or less admitted this to the Senate Foreign Relations Sub-Committee investigating revolutions in Cuba and Mexico when called upon to defend himself against an allegation that he financed the uprising: by passing a cheque for $2,000 to Pryce to buy rifles.[14] The Senate hearing was held in the Justice Department at Los Angeles, just across the road from the Ferris office in the Security Building. After Senator Smith told District Attorney McCormick he had absolute affirmation from an unnamed source that Ferris bankrolled Pryce, McCormick replied:

> Dick Ferris is an actor and has been for a great many years. I have gained the impression the reason Dick went into this was to get money out of it in the way of advertising in the theatrical business. Within a week after he was arrested in his neutrality case, he commenced the production of a play, Willie Collier's old play, 'The Man from Mexico', and because of the part he was supposed to have taken in the revolution he had full houses. That has always been my candid opinion as to why Dick Ferris went into this thing. I think Dick will tell the truth about it. It is possible that while these things were at a focus Dick may have deceived these people into believing he was an ardent and sincere revolutionist, and they might have passed over to him $2,000 or more, and told him to do so and so with it, and he might have done it. He is right across the street, if you want him.

After consulting among themselves, the Senate Committee said Ferris should be called, despite a warning from Assistant District Attorney Dudley Robinson that:

> The only thing about Dick is that he will turn us into an advertisement, too. Our department made a careful investigation of some advertisements that were put into the New York papers (advertising for recruits). He had millions of dollars that he was going to spend here. He sent a telegram saying he was going to buy Lower California, and Madero very seriously declined the offer.

The consummate showman, for whom fact and fiction merged to suit whatever end he had in mind, Dick was unable to resist the temptation of being seen as part of the conspiracy in Lower California. He had been interested in the area for some years, he told the Senate Committee, admitting that on one occasion he had expressed the opinion to the *Los Angeles Examiner* that 'somebody was going to go in there and take it away from Mexico.' And yes, when Diaz was on the way out he had offered to buy it, but purely as a business proposition, adding hastily, 'In other words, to make it a commercial Utopia with an invitation to young Americans to come down there and locate – but it would have to be done in a legal way.'

Dick denied advertising for recruits in the New York newspapers, although he believed there had been a huge response. 'The first thing I knew about it all was a flood of mail that I received, containing copies of discharges of foreigners from foreign armies, and so on, and also the discharge papers of many United States Army volunteers. I don't know what they were driving at,' he said.

Asked by Senator Smith whether he had given Pryce cheques totalling $2,000, Ferris replied, 'Absolutely not. The only check that ever passed between Pryce and myself was a check for $100, given under the following circumstances. The very thing that won me to Pryce was this incident.' Dick then explained that when the Welshman was released from prison after his first arrest and detention at Fort Rosecrans he had taken him some shirts and collars, because he had nothing:

I said to him, 'Pryce you are wrong over there (Tijuana). You want to leave that bunch. It is possible to get a lot of real men over there. The possibilities are wonderful. I am going to Los Angeles tonight and if you need some little things here is a check.' I gave him my check for $100, and what won me to him was this. He said, 'If I need it I will use it. If I don't I will return it.' So the next time I saw him he said, 'Here is that check. I do not have any use for it', and gave it back to me, and I still have the un-cashed check. My checks were on the Central National Bank over here. I have a very odd check, a peculiar check; one that I have especially made and easily identified. My bank account over there is open to inspection, and the president of the bank will gladly tell you whether any $2,000 check from me to Pryce ever passed through the bank. If anyone has sworn that he saw such a check passed to me by Pryce, that statement is absolutely untrue.

Asked by the Committee why he was interested in Lower California, Dick said it was the only appendage left in the world and he thought he might as well amputate it.

Ferris: If you were to find an uninhabited island some-where it would be the spirit of young Americans to want to go out and leave their homes and live there. There is no doubt that a government established down there along the right lines would attract hundreds of thousands of young Americans. There is some beautiful land down there in the northern part of the country. For fifty miles it is beautiful. You could not find anything more pretty. As you go down into the bare mountains it is horrible.

Senator Smith: But the valleys are all right?

Ferris: The valleys are all right. There is plenty of water in the northern part. Admiral Phelps told me that the Indians used to bring him down nuggets of gold but they would not let a white man go up there: and he said that outside Ensenada and Tijuana you would never know that the

Mexican Government had anything to do with it. It is practically a wilderness. There is no coast in the world that is
so important as Lower California, considering the Panama
Canal.[15]

After his filibuster fiasco, Dick capitalised on his notoriety,
playing to packed-houses with his actress wife Florence in 'The
Man from Mexico', a performance that contained such memorable
lines as, 'There are bars all around me but I can't get a drink.'
When the play folded so did the Ferris marriage, and the couple
divorced in 1913, his wife returning to her stage career as Florence
Stone.

As the years passed, Dick slipped out of the headlines although
he continued to dream dreams about Lower California, in the late
1920s taking a lease on 14,000 acres of land between Tijuana and
Ensenada on which he planned to develop a luxury resort, the
Paradise Beach Club. But the flamboyant showman is probably
best remembered not for his clumsy attempt to steal Lower
California from the Mexicans but for his most successful ever
promotion – the Los Angeles Yellow Taxi Cab Service.

Dick Ferris died in 1933 at the age of 66. Showman to the end,
he still announced on every birthday that he had 'just turned 38.'
Before his death he gave one last interview to a Mexican newspaper about his part in the Magonista Revolution in which he
alleged that General Pryce was a British secret agent. Never before
had he mentioned this, not even when cross-examined by the
Senate Foreign Relations Committee. But if anyone knew, it would
have been Dick Ferris.[16]

Although there is only Ferris's word for this, it would explain
the involvement in the anarcho-syndicalist Magonista uprising in
Mexico of a man from an otherwise unimpeachable upper middle
class background; a man who appeared not to have a radical
bone in his body. A son of the British Raj, Pryce had devoted his
life to defending the Empire, both before and after the affair in
Mexico. A policeman by training and inclination, he would seem
a most unlikely candidate to lead an army of cutthroat mercenaries,
unless, of course, he had some covert objective. There are co-
incidences that suggest this could have been the case, most
important of these the *Shearwater* incident, and the landing of

British marines at San Quintin. Britain, through the privately owned Mexican Land and Colonization Company, had massive interests in Baja California, which could have expanded into a *de facto* colonial presence during the chaos created by revolution, in spite of the Monroe Doctrine. Coincidentally, Pryce's brother-in-law, Lieutentant Graham, was serving aboard the *Shearwater's* sister-ship, *H.M.S. Algerine*, as part of the Royal Navy's Pacific West Coast Fleet, its orders from the Admiralty to protect British interests during Mexico's revolutionary upheaval. Did Pryce have any contact with his brother-in-law during this difficult period when the *Algerine* was docked in San Diego, and its crew playing cricket against the locals in Balbao Park? According to his nephew Brigadier Meyric Pryce, he did. Even if this is correct, there could be a simple explanation: the opportunity for a reunion with his sister who was visiting her husband aboard the *Algerine* in San Diego. But was it just convenience that Pryce passed himself off as 'Mr Graham' when he checked into San Diego's Grant Hotel? Or was Lieutenant Graham also there for a clandestine meeting with the *Generalissimo*?

The frontier between the United States and Mexico was awash with foreign agents seeking to capitalise on the revolutionary turmoil for their respective governments. Britain was no exception. Perversely, Pryce's greatest contribution to a Mexican Revolution that by June 1911 appeared to have been won by the combined forces of Francisco Madero, Pancho Villa and Emiliano Zapata was his decision to desert his army in Tijuana. Without his leadership the Magonistas collapsed in chaos. With it, they could have taken the whole of Baja California and held it for the foreseeable future, especially as the Mexican Revolution had not ended, but was set to drag on for many years after Madero was assassinated.

Gringo Revolutionary

By the time Pryce returned to England from Palestine in 1925 he was at 49, too old for further active service. Still not inclined to retire, the former revolutionary general of an anarchist army considered embarking on a political career as a Conservative Member of Parliament. In the end he decided not to expose himself to public scrutiny, opting instead to become the party's agent in Chesterfield, almost certainly concealing from his new employers his previous political affiliations.[17] For them, he would have pointed to his squeaky-clean entry in *Who's Who,* the most prestigious publication in the country of the achievements of the great and the good. There he listed his Distinguished Service Order for bravery in France, the medals won during the Mashonaland Rebellion and Boer War, and his service in Palestine, but not a word about Mexico, nor his trial in Los Angeles, nor his flirtation with Hollywood.

On 17 October 1927 he was appointed full-time political agent of the Chesterfield Conservative and Unionist Association, taking care of all its official correspondence and working closely with its Member of Parliament. After filling this position for two years, Pryce suddenly resigned, although he was to remain a Conservative supporter all his life, subscribing to policies fundamentally different to the extreme Magonista ideology he had, supposedly, embraced in Mexico.[18]

The old soldier made a last attempt to secure yet another military position, this time a secretarial post with the Territorials. When he failed to get it, and now aged 55, he accepted retirement, moving with his wife to Harrogate.[19] But this was only a base, the couple spending a large part of their time travelling the country as the Major indulged his passion for angling. On one of these trips to Scotland in 1941 his wife was taken seriously ill and died soon afterwards in a Glasgow hospital.[20]

Two years later Pryce moved to Cockermouth in the Lake District, an area he had grown to love during his fishing expeditions. The last twelve years of his life were spent living in one room in the Lakes Hotel, while angling for salmon on the Derwent River, and writing film scripts based upon the novels of Sir Walter Scott.[21] As far as is known none was accepted, the rejected scripts, and other written material belonging to the major lying forgotten for many years in a packing case in a repository in Harrogate. A second packing case with his effects was stored in another repository in Southsea.[22] When not fishing or writing, Pryce devoted his still boundless energy to researching his family genealogy, and became a frequent visitor to the National Library of Wales at Aberystwyth. The information obtained from these trips enabled him to begin the construction of an elaborate family tree, which traced the family's descent from John Pryce (1553), Member of Parliament for Cardigan in the First Parliament of Queen Mary, through to Sir Carbery Pryse, the lord of Gogerddan and owner of the fabulously rich lead mines at Esgair Hir in 1694. It was at about that time, that one of six brothers in the family crossed the border into England, settling at Wearmouth in Durham as a Customs Officer, and from whom Caryl ap Rhys Pryce was directly descended. Several centuries later when the major's nephew, Brigadier Meyric Home ap Rhys Pryce was continuing the family research he met Lady Pryse, widow of Sir Lewis Pryse, on the steps of the National Library at Aberystwyth in April 1980. Before he had a chance to introduce himself, Lady Pryse said, 'You look just like my brother-in-law.' Deeper still in the family history was the connection with Owain Glyndŵr in the 15th century, and beyond that Gwaethfod, Lord of Cardigan, who ruled two decades before the battle of Hastings. The Magonista *generalissimo* could invoke a pedigree stretching back for almost a thousand years.[23]

With his 'thumbstick' in his hand, Major Pryce was a familiar sight in the countryside around Cockermouth until 20 November 1955 when he died, aged 79, after a short illness at the Cottage Hospital. That day, before their match at Laithwaite, members of the Cockermouth Rugby Club of which he was vice-president, stood together with their opponents from Carlisle in silent tribute to an old revolutionary who had made his home amongst them but whose amazing life remained a mystery to most.[24] Pryce's ashes were interred in his wife's grave at Erylhome, near Darlington, County Durham the following Wednesday.[25]

The major was not a rich man although according to his will he did share a Trust Fund established by the family when his spinster aunt Alice Maud Pryce died intestate in Jersey. It was she who had seized a large part of the effects from the family home at Penns Rock and took them off to Jersey. Caryl's most precious possessions, a 12-bore Holland and Holland shotgun and his fishing rods and tackle, he bequeathed to his great nephew John Henry ap Rhys Pryce on his fifteenth birthday. Two hundred and fifty pounds he left to John Henry's father with instructions that when the boy reached fifteen, it and the interest accrued should be devoted to giving his great nephew a 'thorough training and

Caryl ap Rhys Pryce knew all about billiards from an early age . . .
In 1953 he fires his last shot across the table at Cockermouth Rugby Club.
Two years later he had died.

instruction in the arts of shooting and angling as I think a man misses a great deal of enjoyment and good fellowship by not engaging in field sports.'[26]

While many questions remain unanswered about a man who declined to talk about his Mexican adventure – and certainly never wrote a word about it – Caryl ap Rhys Pryce was, undoubtedly, at his most confident in the company of other men in a war situation. On the balance of the evidence, his role in the Mexican Revolution was not as a political activist fighting for the 'poor peons' but neither was it strictly speaking as a soldier-of-fortune, although a fine line divides the two. Penniless and alone in Los Angeles in 1911, with warfare his only real qualification, and finding himself tempted by the offer of mercenary work, it seems highly likely he may have joined the wrong revolution, signing on with the Magonistas – who were by then financially and morally bankrupt – instead of Madero, the eventual victor. Following his arrest in Los Angles, the British Foreign Office when it became involved on his behalf actually believed Pryce was fighting on behalf of Madero's forces![27] Whatever the explanation, Pryce's lack of political commitment was more than compensated by leadership qualities that pitched him into the cockpit of revolution, and pivotal to its success or failure. While he may have been ideally placed to sabotage, by intent or accident, the entire Magonista campaign, which was what he eventually did by deserting his command, the ramifications of the revolution in Baja California would have gradually dawned upon a man familiar with the Jameson Raid and Britain's Imperial designs in Africa. Pryce could not but have failed to have seen the analogy between the situation in Baja California and Rhodesia. Even if were true that he had blundered into the wrong revolutionary camp, the opportunity for a filibuster nonetheless remained. So why should the adventurer not take advantage of it? Speaking of his intentions, Pryce was invariably enigmatic, one moment talking only of helping the 'poor peons,' the next assuring the manager of San Diego's Brewster Hotel that his property interests in the Baja Peninsula would be a 'whole let better off' once it was controlled by his insurgents.[28] And while the Red Flag flew over Tijuana, Pryce was not averse to the suggestion it might be replaced by the Stars and Stripes.

To what extent the arrival of Pryce's brother-in-law Lieutenant Graham aboard the *Algerine* influenced his actions we will never know for sure. The likelihood is that it was entirely coincidental. But the landing of marines at San Quintin by the *Shearwater* was probably not: more of a marker by Britain of its continuing interest in Central America as Mexico tottered on the brink of disintegration under the pressure of violent revolt. In fact, the Mexican Revolution was not one (the Maderistas), not even two (the Magonistas), but several uprisings, ripping the country apart like a series of prairie fires that burned until 1921, generally accepted as the year widespread armed revolt ended. The peasant struggle for agrarian reform would, however, last even longer. It is only because Ricardo Flores Magon, and his Mexican Liberal Party with its banner proclaiming 'Land and Liberty' are perceived to have been part of that struggle that today they are acclaimed as heroes of the revolution. On the other hand, Pryce – the man who might well have realised Mexico's dream of agrarian reform decades earlier had he only the nerve to persevere – is reviled by Mexicans as the filibusterer who in partnership with the clown Dick Ferris tried to steal a large part of their country. In fairness to Pryce, the Magonista Revolution was doomed from the outset, because it had no clear and realistic political agenda, while Magon's professed support for the poor *peons* was shown to be smoke and mirrors, no more than a cover for his wild anarchist ambitions. The result was that Pryce, Magon's only true general, was starved of the military and financial support necessary to conduct a successful revolution. As for the adventurer who lived life on the edge, the revolution was probably just another event in a lifetime of infinite curiosity. But he would feel deeply wounded to discover that history had cast him as the villain of the piece.

NOTES

1. National Archives, Ricardo Flores Magon to Tirzo de la Toba, 26 June, 1911, U.S. Senate Committee report, 'Investigations of Mexican Affairs,' II, 2516-17.
2. Lowell Blaisdell, *The Desert Revolution: Baja California 1911* (Madison, 1962, University of Wisconsin Press), p. 189. According to Blaisdell who requested a search in 1952 from the U.S. District Court for the Southern

District of California, nothing could be found. There were indications at that time the records may have found their way into private hands.

3. National Archives, Wilson Papers, James A. Finch, Pardon Attorney, U.S. Dept., of Justice, to U.S. Attorney General James C. McReynolds, 30 June 1913; Edith Turner, *The Revolution in Lower California,* pp. 84-88.

4. *Los Angeles Examiner,* 6 June 1912; *Los Angeles Express,* 25 June 1912; 'Investigation of Mexican Affairs,' II, 2518.

5. *Los Angeles Express,* 25 June 1912; *Los Angeles Examiner,* 26 June 1912.

6. ibid.

7. National Archives, 'Congressional Record, 67 Congress, 4 Session, LX1V' (19 December 1922), p. 682; Abad de Santillan, *Ricardo Flores Magon,* pp. 109-12.

8. ibid., *Congressional Record,* pp. 682-91; ibid., Santillan, pp. 109-12.

9. Nicolas Bernal, *R.F.M., vida y obra* (1920), II, p. 30.

10. Rafael Carillo, *Ricardo Flores Magon* (Mexico City, 1945), p. 47.

11. ibid., III, p. 83.

12. Teodoro Hernandez, *La historia de la revolution debe hacerse* (Mexico City, 1950), pp. 123-24.

13. National Archives, letter Ricardo Flores Magon to Tirzo de la Toba, 26 June, 1911, Senate Committee hearing report, 'Investigations of Mexican Affairs', II, 2516-17; *La Regeneracion,* 10 June, 1 July 1911.

14. National Archives, Senate Committee hearing report, 'Revolutions in Cuba and Mexico,' pp. 231-33, 377, 381-83.

15. ibid.

16. *Los Angeles Times,* 6 March 1926, 23 August 1927, 5 December 1930, 13 March 1933; *San Diego Union,* 24 August 1927.

17. D. C. Dabbs, 'The Clarion Calls' (unpublished biographical sketch of Caryl ap Rhys Pryce), 24, personal correspondence with Mr F. G. Evans, Chairman, Chesterfield Division Conservative Association, 1 April 1982.

18. ibid.

19. Dabbs, interview with Brigadier Meyrick Home ap Rhys Pryce, Weybridge, Surrey, 1982.

20. Pryce Papers. Unidentified newspaper clipping.

21. Interview author with Brigadier Meyric Home ap Rhys Pryce, Weybridge, Surrey, 1998.

22. Pryce Papers. Draft will of Major Caryl ap Rhys Pryce.

23. Interview author with Brigadier Meyric Home ap Rhys Pryce, 1998.

24. *Cumberland Evening Star,* 'Death of Major Caryl Pryce – world traveller who chose Cockermouth,' 28 November 1955.

25. *West Cumberland Times,* 30 November 1955.

26. Pryce Papers. Last will and testament of Caryl ap Rhys Pryce, 27 August 1945.

27. Public Record Office. Foreign Office to Colonel Douglas Davidson Pryce, 25 August 1911, No. 33162/11.

28. *San Diego Sun,* 10 May 1911.

Selected Bibliography

Carleton Beals, *Porfirio Diaz, Dictator of Mexico* (Philadelphia, 1932).

Norman and Helen Bentwich, *Mandate Memoirs 1918-1948*.

Lowell Blaisdell, *Desert Revolution: Baja California 1911* (1962, University of Wisconsin Press).

Edgar H. Brooks, and Colin de B Webb, *A History of Natal* (Pietermaritzburg, 1965, University of Natal Press).

Kevin Brownlow, *The Parade's Gone By . . . . . . a vivid affectionate portrait of the golden days of Hollywood* (London, 1968, London, Secker and Warburg).

Velasco Ceballos, *se apoderará Estados Unidos de Baja California?*

L. H. Gann, *A history of Southern Rhodesia, early days to 1933* (1965).

Peter Gibbs, *The History of the British South Africa Police* (Salisbury, 1972, Mardon Printers), two vols.

G. F. Gibson, *The story of the Imperial Light Horse in the South African War, 1899-1902.* (Central News Agency, 1937).

Great Britain, *History of the Great War, Order of Battle Divisions, 38th Welsh Division* (London, 1945, HMSO).

Maurice Harbord, *Froth and Bubble* (London, 1915).

Teodoro Hernandez, *La Historia de la revolucion debe hacerse* (Mexico, 1950).

H. P. Holt, *The Mounted Police of Natal* (London, 1913, John Murray).

José María Leyva, *Aportaciones a la historia de la revolución* (Mexico City, 1938).

Joyce L. Kornbluh, *Rebel Voices, an I.W.W. Anthology* (Ann Arbor, University of Michigan Press).

Colin M. Maclachlan, *Anarchism and the Mexican Revolution: the political trials of Ricardo Flores Magon in the United States* (1991, University of California Press).

D. Martin, and P. Johnson, *The Struggle for Zimbabwe: The Chimurenga War,* (Harare, 1981, Zimbabwe Publishing House).

Thomas Pakenham, *The Boer War* (New York, 1979, Random House).

Terence Ranger, *Revolt in Southern Rhodesia* (1967).

Patrick Renshaw, *The Wobblies: the story of syndicalism in the United States* (New York, 1967, Doubleday and Co, Inc.).

Victor Sampson and Ian Hamilton, *Anti-Commando* (London, 1931, Faber and Faber).

F. C. Selous, *Sunshine and Storm in Rhodesia* (1896).

Olive Schreiner, *Trooper Peter Halket of Mashonaland, 1897.*

Vere Stent, *A personal record of some incidents in the life of Cecil Rhodes* (Cape Town, 1924).

Grace Heilman Stimson, *Rise of the Labor Movement in Los Angeles* (1955, University of California Press).

F. W. Sykes, *With Plumer in Mashonaland, 1897.*

Leon Wolff, *In Flanders Field, the 1917 Campaign* (New York, 1963, Time Inc., Book Division).

Index

OTHER BOOKS FROM GLYNDŴR PUBLISHING
www.walesbooks.com

Full Reviews appear on the website

By John Humphries:

The Man from the Alamo: Why the Welsh Chartist Uprising of 1839 Ended in a Massacre – John Humphries
(ISBN 190352914X Glyndŵr Publishing 2004)
'*one of the fastest-selling books in Welsh publishing history*', '*the remarkable story of two men sentenced to hanging, drawing and quartering. Zephaniah Williams ended up a respectable businessman after being transported to hard labour in Tasmania. John Rees ('Jack the Fifer' escaped from the Alamo to probably fire the first shot at the Westgate Hotel, before escaping back to join the great California Gold Rush*', '*an amazing story, full of meticulously researched new facts, from the former editor of the Western Mail.*' £9.99

Books by Terry Breverton

An A to Z of Wales and the Welsh
ISBN 0715407341 296pp (Christopher Davies Ltd. 2000)
the first Welsh encyclopaedia!' '*an important addition to the Welsh reference bookshelf*', '*A massive treasure chest of facts and figures covering thousands of years of history, which no collector of books on Wales can overlook*', '*the A-Z has many surprising as well as predictable entries and is clearly the result of a passionate interest in post-devolution Wales combined with impeccable research . . . an important addition to the Welsh reference bookshelf*', '*this book is great fun*', '*a comprehensive anthology and compendium of Welshness*', '*the author wants the world to know what Wales has to offer . . . alongside the Cool Cymru actors and pop stars, there is a wealth of information on more traditional Welsh culture, history, legend, art, literature and so on.*' £14.99

The Secret Vale of Glamorgan
ISBN 190352900X 230pp (Glyndŵr Publishing 2000) **Millennium Award**
'Terry Breverton belongs to that rare breed of Welshmen who stake their livelihood on trying to publish books in which they passionately believe.

His imprint Glyndŵr Publishing/Wales Books has already made its mark on the Welsh publishing scene by bringing out substantial and hand-somely produced books on Welsh subjects, particularly local history. He was born in the Vale of Glamorgan, to which he has returned after many years as a management consultant in Britain and overseas. He is the author of several useful books such as An A-Z of Wales and the Welsh and One Hundred Great Welshmen. What drives him as a publisher is the belief that the Welsh people have been deprived of their own history. He aims to provide the information that will make them proud of their country. If that means he has to lose some money, he thinks it's well worth It. Among his most recent books is The Secret Vale of Glamorgan which shows a local man's pride in the history and culture of his native patch, combined with a historian's delight in tracing the past and relating it to the present. For anyone born or living in the Vale, this book should be essential reading. There are chapters on Cowbridge, St Athan, Gileston, Aberthaw, Flemingston, and all the places in between, together with a wealth of information about the area's most famous son, the wayward genius Iolo Morganwg' £13.99 OUT OF PRINT.

The Book of Welsh Saints
ISBN 1903529018 606pp hardback (Glyndŵr Publishing 2000)
*'this book is **a really extraordinary achievement**: a compilation of tradition, topography and literary detective work that can have few rivals. I have enjoyed browsing it immensely, and have picked up all sorts of new lines to follow up' – Rowan Williams, Archbishop of Canter-bury; 'impressive', 'the book is full of fascinating information . . . a must for anyone interested in the history of the Church in Wales, indeed for anyone interested in learning the glorious heritage bequeathed to them from the time when Wales was the only Christian country in the world,' 'Another work from the prolific pen of Terry Breverton who is blazing a trail in producing bodies of knowledge about Welsh heritage and history. The Book of Welsh Saints is **an enormous work of research and will provide a welcome and ready book of reference** to the men and women who in Tad Deiniol's words "created Wales". The much-bandied term "The Dark Ages" may well have meant just that east of the Severn, but to us this period is the Age of Saints. And there are hundreds of them – over 900 in fact – monks, scholars, warriors, missionaries. Breverton places Arthur firmly in the context of Welsh history and shows how the seminal folk legends of European romance and literature originate in Wales. We see Wales at the very heart and very root of western Christian civilisation, a pre-eminent position from which it was thrown down by greedy, rapacious invaders who not only usurped its legacy but traduced*

*its memory with sickening arrogance and chilling contempt', 'An **impressive** work', 'Wales certainly seems to have not only the oldest surviving language in Europe, but also the oldest Christian heritage; for in the first millennium it was accepted by Rome as the "cradle of the Christian Church". The unique historical importance of Wales has for too long been neglected until now. An important book in putting the record straight is "The Book of Welsh Saints", 'The book is **a veritable gold mine of information**, 'The Book of Welsh Saints' is an excellent publication – conscientious, clear, intelligent and, where necessary, modern', a lovely book', 'The Book of Welsh Saints is more than a compendium of folk tradition and mythology. Like all books, it has an agenda: it is just that Breverton is more explicit about his aims than most. What he is imploring us to undertake is nothing less than a revitalisation of our spiritual culture. His programme spirals out from the revival of the cults and feast days to encompass farmers' markets, Welsh kilts, locally produced crisps and Welsh theme pubs. He directs his anger against the bland 'MacDonaldisation' of our popular culture and the corrosive political neglect which has pushed Wales to the margins of democratic life and the bottom of the UK household income statistics', 'a remarkable achievement. The amount of work and study you have put into it almost beggars belief, and I found it **utterly absorbing**', 'The book also confirms that King Arthur was Welsh, despite many claims from other parts of the UK that the legendary king is part of their folklore. Mr Breverton said more than 100 Welsh saints from the 5th and 6th centuries were associated with King Arthur and the Knights of the Round Table. The book reveals that the legends of the Holy Grail, Tristan and Isolde, The Fisher King, the Black Knight, Camelot, Sir Gawain, Sir Lancelot, Avalon and Queen Guinevere stem from Wales. Mr Breverton says "The book sets Arthur absolutely into his Welsh context, with direct links to over 100 6th century saints, predating the medieval romances, and I wish to explore this subject further." £24.99*

100 Great Welshmen (First Edition) ISBN 1903529034 376pp (Glyndŵr Publishing 2001) Welsh Books Council **Book of the Month** '
a revealing volume illustrating the great and good with Welsh connection . . . painstaking research', 'Now he (Breverton) wants to ensure that his discoveries are shared by releasing a fascinating compendium of short biographies celebrating some of Wales' most venerable sons. 100 Great Welshmen is a revealing volume illustrating the great and the good with Welsh connections, either by birth or family ancestry . . . From heroes of Waterloo and computer engineers to lethal pirates and golf champions, Breverton has attempted to include them all, and that's no

mean feat given our colourful heritage,' 'Now and again a book comes along that answers most, if not all your questions about your Welsh heritage. Who are the Welsh, who are their military heroes, political leaders, writers, poets, kings, princes, saints, historians, explorers, men of industry, famous actors, athletes and religious leaders? The amount of research that went into the making of this book is astounding, it seems the author left no stone unturned in order to ferret out information concerning his subjects. He has produced a veritable gold mine of a book that you can dip into again and again. 100 Great Welshmen will make you proud of your Welsh heritage by reminding you that the little country of Wales has contributed so much to the modern world in so many areas,' 'Hwyl and Hiraeth, heritage and history, people and places, myths and imagination all come together in Terry Breverton's comprehensive anthology and compendium of Welshness. He starts by asking the question "What is Wales?" and then goes on to show us. The book is, as Breverton says, a sort of "Hitchhiker's Guide to the Galaxy" that is Wales and declares modestly that his background is more modest than academic. We have just what's needed in this unashamedly proud-to-be-Welsh work. Everythin from "Assassination" (Owain Llawgoch) to "Zulu Wars" (Rorke's Drift) is covered with few stones unturned. A massive treasure chest of facts and figures covering thousands of years of history, which no collector of books on Wales can overlook,' 'This book is great fun . . . 'Letter to Author – 'I hope you don't mind me writing to you, but I was compelled to. I have just brought the book '100 Great Welshmen'. I have been unable to put it down and have read every last word in the Appendix. Astounding and inspiring work that put me to shame. I had very little knowledge of my heritage, but I have now vowed to re-educate myself. With such associations now being set up, I hope that our future in Wales and our language is about to flourish. Thank you for inspiring hope. Diolch yn fawr, Mared' £18.99 **Second edition is ISBN 1903529158 – £14.99**

100 Great Welsh Women

ISBN 1903529042 304pp (Glyndŵr Publishing 2001)

'Perhaps the most prolific Welsh author today is T. D. Breverton, of Glyndŵr Publishing, in the Vale of Glamorgan, South Wales. This astonishing worker has recently produced such practical reference books as 'An A-Z of Wales and the Welsh', 'The Secret Vale of Glamorgan', 'The Book of Welsh Saints' and '100 Great Welshmen' (Volume I of Eminent Britons), as well as published important books by other Welsh authors. Now Terry has done it again. His latest book has finally arrive to fulfil the enormous gap in our knowledge of the enormously important, but

sadly unheralded contribution of women, not only to Welsh society and Welsh history, but to Western civilisation itself. Titled '100 Great Welsh Women' (Part II of Eminent Britons), it gives short biographies to those of the fairer sex who deserve to be added to out pantheon of Welsh heroes', 'These (referring also to '100 Great Welshmen') are not necessarily books that you want to read from cover to cover, but to browse in, following your nose, as one section leads to another in a serendipitous sequence that throws up some pleasant surprises. Both are really extraordinary achievements by a single author whose industry and enterprise seem to show no bounds . . . Terry Breverton is to be congratulated', 'This most invaluable addition to every bookshelf and library begins with the little-known Saint Almedha (5th-6th century) and ends with Jane Williams (19th century). In between, you can read of such modern notable Welsh women as singers Charlotte Church, Shirley Bassey, and Petula Clark; of world-class athletes such as Tanni Grey-Thompson; of such historical characters as Nell Gwynn, mistress of Charles II, or Saint Helena, the mother of Constantine the Great; of Catherine Zeta Jones, whose recent wedding to Michael Douglas caused such a stir; and so on. The book is an absolute must for all those who value their Welsh heritage, and for all those who wish to see Welsh women accorded their rightful place in history . . .', 'Famous figures stand alongside equally illustrious but lesser-known names. Entrants enjoy a detailed biography, which flags up their links to Wales, and it is a fascinating read. His list includes the obvious, such as Shirley Bassey and Catherine Zeta Jones, alongside the more surprising, such as Kylie Minogue, and the obscure, such as Princess Nest, and Helen of Wales', 'Breverton's breadth, generosity and sheer enthusiasm about Wales are compelling. However, one is left feeling that his potential readership may be confined to the Welsh, those with Welsh ancestry, Kylie-obsessives or someone like myself, about to marry a hugely accomplished Welsh museum director – come to think of it, quite a large potential readership after all!' 'The result of another extensive trawl through time, it celebrates the history and achievements of Welsh women through the ages', 'Breverton's two well researched and entertaining volumes are a delightful tour-de-force and an astounding achievement by a writer who seems to be ever so prolific. It was a huge task even in its contemplation'. £16.99

The Welsh Almanac
ISBN 1903529107 320pp hardback (Glyndŵr Publishing 2002) Welsh Books Council **'Book of the Month'**
'Terry Breverton's ongoing series of Welsh history books continue to enthuse as my library steadily increases with his work. And the latest,

The Welsh Almanac is one of the most enjoyable to date. In fact, I'll go so far as to say it's a must for anyone with a drop of Welsh blood in them. Continuing his solo mission to make Wales' proud history more accessible or for that matter readable, in comparison to the huge dusty tomes hidden in darkened libraries, The Welsh Almanac is yet another success. Filled with fascinating facts and figures, Breverton explains that the rationale behind the publication is two-fold. On the surface it is for Welsh people to remember their loved ones' birthdays, anniversaries, important dates and events. There is also an A-Z section annexed, so that addresses and telephone numbers can be entered. But on the other hand it is to record information about famous Welsh people and events upon each of these days. For each day there is also a quotation, usually from a Welsh source, tying in with people and events of the day,' *'A tremendous undertaking and a very worthwhile and absolutely fascinating addition to the library of Welsh history,' 'Every day has space for the reader's own notes and a few apt quotations to add interest to the page. So this is a Book of Days in which people can record important dates in their personal histories and see them in the context of Welsh history. It's useful for jotting down birthdays and anniversaries, especially those one tends to forget, and will take its place on the shelf with other works of reference', 'All in all, it is a prodigious work, chock full of facts and figures from every age of Welsh history. One example will hint at the wealth of information contained within this fascinating book. On the 1st of January, Welsh people can celebrate not only Dydd Calan (New Year's Day), no fewer than six saints, the birth of the first Welsh language newspaper, a Welsh defeat of a Norman army, and Welsh team victories in rugby football and so on. The entries for each day are accompanied by a quotation that ties in with the people and events of the day. This wonderful book, attractively priced at £16.99 . . .'* £8.49 (**Special Offer**, from £16.99)

The Path to Inexperience

ISBN 1903529077 160pp (Glyndŵr Publishing 2002)

'Terry Breverton is well known as a tireless recorder of welsh achievements in many fields. In this poetry collection, he allows us a glimpse of the tumultuous feelings that drive him. A tortured energy rushes through this book. There is bitter anger, a keen sense of injustice, national pride, compassion, fear of loss. The images whirl. He jokes and parodies, he gets drunk on words; and there are quieter moments too. Sometimes he gives us a long 'found poem' like his 'inventory' of statistics about the suffering of the miners of South Wales, where the plainly stated facts are the agonised poem; or his final 'partial list of endangered species' with

their evocative and often musical names. It is good to know that out of this turmoil have come – and are still coming – books so positive in their celebration of Wales, its people, history religion and arts,' 'magnificent, compassionate and moving . . . **"Chalice" will surely help Aberfan to stay in our memories.** *'* £5.99 (Special Offer, **from £10.99)**

Glamorgan Seascape Pathways – 52 Walks in the Southern Vale of Glamorgan

ISBN 1903529115 144pp (Glyndŵr Publishing 2003) **ARWAIN Award**
Fascinating *. . . useful to anybody interested in the topography, geography and history of the southern Vale of Glamorgan,' 'Yet another publication to add to the ever-growing Breverton library of Welsh history – this time a very interesting ramble across the South coastline . . . Ramblers will love it, and armchair devotees can easily imagine the beauty from the descriptive passages, or maybe it will be enough to inspire them to drop the TV dinner and take a stroll', 'Terry Breverton believes in giving value for money, but it is still amazing how much info he crams into a slim book like this. There are practical details about the main walks, which stretch west from the Gwent levels to Cardiff Bay and on to Gileston. But there are also stacks of local history, ancient and modern, about the buildings and landscapes you see along the way, which makes this good for armchair travellers too. This coastline deserves more recognition.'* (Special Offer, **£6.99 from £10.99**)

The Book of Welsh Pirates and Buccaneers

ISBN 1903529093 388pp (Glyndŵr Publishing 2003) Welsh Books Council
'Book of the Month *'*
'an immense work of great scholarship *. . . effectively, a study of the whole genre of piracy . . . exemplary, yet the writing is light and accessible . . . wonderful, fascinating detail and essential reading' . . . 'absolutely fascinating.'* £17.99 OUT OF PRINT

The Pirate Handbook – A Dictionary of Pirate Terms and Places

ISBN 1903529131 388pp (Glyndŵr Publishing 2004) Welsh Books Council
'Book of the Month *'*
'This **wonderful source book** *is an absolute "must" for anyone who is interested in nautical matters . . . if you ever wondered where phrases like "hit the deck" and "let the cat out of the bag" come from, then this is undoubtedly the place to look . . . the amount of detail and depth is* **phenomenal** *. . . this book is a vitally important addition to the canon of literature about naval history,' 'a lot of fun.'* **£9.99**

Black Bart Roberts – 'The Greatest Pirate of Them All'

ISBN 1903529123 254pp (Glyndŵr Publishing 2004)

'the true story of John Robert, the most successful pirate of all time, who took over 400 ships in just three years, and brought transatlantic shipping to a standstill', **a must reading** *for anyone interested in pirates and American nautical history – first-hand accounts, court documents and maps accompany* **a fascinating story** *of piratical history on the High Seas,' 'based on an impressive list of books to tell the story of Black Bart. If you like pirate stories and tales of the High Seas, get a copy!' 'Long ago just the whisper of his name was enough to strike terror into the hearts of all who sailed the high seas. Dressed in his crimson jacket and hat, bloodthirsty Black Bart was a terrifying figure that ruled the oceans from the West Indies to the coast of North Africa. So why is it that no one has heard of the Pembrokeshire pirate who took 400 ships and had half the British navy determined to hunt him down and hang him? Historian and author Terry Breverton is about to put the record straight with his latest book, which chronicles the Welsh pirate's lost history. "Blackbeard, who is much more well known, was nothing but a rank amateur compared to Black Bart," said Mr Breverton, a lecturer at the University of Wales Institute of Cardiff. "He was the most successful pirate in history. He would attack anything – he basically declared war against the world."* £8.99

Admiral Sir Henry Morgan – The Greatest Buccaneer of Them All

ISBN 1903529174 174pp (Glyndŵr Publishing 2005) Welsh Books Council **'Book of the Month'**

This book has been made into a three-part TV series by ITV/S4C (The Welsh Pirates), shown in 2005. The portrait we have of Henry Morgan is that of a brutal and sadistic criminal, who indiscriminately pillaged and sacked ships that stood between him and greater glory. The facts have been obscured by a 17th-century book upon pirates that not only served as source material for later biographies, but was also the subject of the first recorded successful libel suit – in 1684, brought by Morgan himself. In fact Admiral Sir Henry Morgan was scrupulously honest in the legality of his leadership of the buccaneers in the Caribbean. He personally organised and led campagn after campaign against the greatest military power in the world, Spain, in his service to the English Crown. Most of his greatest successes, over a fifteen-year period of un-paralleled bravery, were the result of his superb grasp of military tactics and strategy – he is Britain's forgoten general, known at the time as 'the sword of England.' This biography of the undefeated Sir Henry Morgan, general, admiral, lieutenant-governor of Jamaica, and above all, leader of a superb fighting force, explodes the myths surrounding his career. Admiral Sir Henry Morgan deserves to take his place alongside Sir Francis Drake, Nelson and the Duke of Wellington in the panoply of history's greatest heroes. £11.99

OTHER AUTHORS WITH GLYNDŴR PUBLISHING

The Dragon Entertains – 100 Welsh Stars – Alan Roderick
ISBN 1903529026 230pp (Glyndŵr Publishing 2001)
*'a **celebration of Welsh talent** in all its vibrany variety', 'this is the book to reach for the next time someone tells you that Wales has not nurtured any great talent in the worlds of entertainment or show-biz.'* £5.99 (**Special Offer**, from £11.99)

A Rhondda Boy: The Memoirs of Ivor Howells – Ivor Howells, edited by Owen Vernon Jones
ISBN 1903529050 144pp (Glyndŵr Publishing 2001)
'a charming evocation of the childhood of a 93-year-old Welshman. Son of a miner, Rhondda born and bred, Rhondda educated apart from his degree years at Aberystwyth, Ivor Howells spent all his professional life as teacher and headmaster in Rhondda schools.' £6.99

From Wales to Pennsylvania: The David Thomas Story – Dr Peter N. Williams 2003
ISBN 1903529085 112pp (Glyndŵr Publishing 2002)
'the story of the man who emigrated from Ystradgynlais, to transform the American iron industry and make America an economic superpower . . . Dr Peter Williams takes us back to the days of mass emigration to the United States. The terrible conditions at home, which sparked the Chartist Riots, are described, to put into context the reasons for this difficult transatlantic flight. Through Dr Thomas's correspondence with Wales, Dr Williams shows us the Welshman's immense contribution to the industrialisation and economic growth of America.' £8.99

Glyn Dŵr's War: The Campaigns of the Last Prince of Wales – Gideon Brough
(ISBN 1903529069 Glyndŵr Publishing 2002)
'The Great Liberation War is THE defining moment of our nation's history. Had it not been for Owain Glyndŵr and the men and women who stood at his side against overwhelming odds, there would be no Welhs nation today. You will find all the details here,' **'A massive**

undertaking *indeed for a 30-year-old, first-time author, but one which Brough, who himself boasts an impressive military background, has tackled with immense confidence and success.'* £13.99

Heroic Science: Swansea and the Royal Institution of South Wales 1835-1865 – Ronald Rees

ISBN 1903529166 Glyndŵr Publishing 2005

Who knows that at one time Swansea's scientists were at the centre of the Scientific Revolution, and the great men of the day made their way by carriage and boat to the Royal Institution? The book covers three remarkable decades when Swansea, as well as leading the Industrial Revolution, was at the forefront of European scientific investigation. It features the interlinking biographies of eminent scientists, revolving around the great meeting of 1848 at the Royal Institution of South Wales. £9.99

FORTHCOMING BOOKS

William Williams and the First American Novel – Terry Breverton (2006) *– Breverton went to Indiana to transcribe the original 'The Journal of Penrose, Seaman' and has appended a biography of its author, the amazing yet unknown William Williams, polymath, marooned buccaneer, artist, theatre-builder, poet, writer of America's first novel, who taught Benjamin West to paint. Williams has been called* the first flower of American culture' *and the factional novel based upon his being marooned on the Miskito Coast is probably the first anti-slavery book.*

Cave of Heroes – Various Writers, edited by Terry Breverton with Rhys Parry (2006) *– a children's featuring all of Wales' greatest heroes, their stories told by the best Welsh writers of the day. Hopefully a Welsh edition will appear in 2006.*

Wales at War at Sea: Memories of World War II – Terry Breverton with Phil Carradice (2006) *– at last the untold contribution of those who served at sea and in Welsh docks – to be followed by books recounting the stories of those who served in the air and on land.*

Ramblings of a Patagonian: 'When You Going Back, Then?' – Rene Griffiths (2006) *– if you like off-the-wall reminiscences, this is the biography of a Patagonian troubadour and film actor who spends half his life in Cardiff and half on his ranch in the foothills of the Andes.*

Very humorous, and utterly absorbing in his perspective of two vastly different cultures.

A Patagonian Diary – **W. C. Rhys (2006)** – *the remarkable story of one of the first Welsh settlers in Patagonia, translated and updated from the previous Spanish edition.*

Another 100 Great Welshmen – **Terry Breverton (2006)** – *featuring many men who should have been in the original* 100 Great Welshmen.

WHERE TO BUY

*All of the Above Books are Available from The Welsh Books Council, Unit 16, Parc Menter Glanyrafon, Llanbadarn Fawr, Ceredigion SY23 3AQ, or from its **website www.gwales.com**, or from **any good bookseller**. If your bookseller states that it cannot get any of these books, they are on all the relevant ordering databases, so please take your custom elsewhere. Alternatively, **send a cheque** with order to Wales Books (Glyndŵr Publishing) at Porth Glyndŵr, Higher End, Sain Tathan, Bro Morganwg CF62 4LW. There is no postage on orders in the British Isles, but £6 per book is charged for overseas orders. Visit our **website www.walesbooks.com** to download an order form, if you wish. The web pages feature a Welsh Quiz, addresses for over 400 Welsh Societies around the world, and reviews on all our books. The site is in process of updating, so please let us know any additions or alterations to societies.*

Our American Publishing Partners are **Pelican Publishing Company**, PO Box 3110, Gretna, New Orleans LA 70054, with the **website www.pelicanpub.com**. In process of publication is John Humphries' *'The Man from the Alamo'* (Fall 2005). In 2004 Pelican published Terry Breverton's *'Black Bart Roberts'* and *'The Pirate Dictionary'*, and in 2005 *'Admiral Sir Henry Morgan'*, and it is hoped that all of Glyndŵr Publishing's output will be available in the USA via Pelican over the forthcoming years. However, at the moment of printing, it is unknown whether Pelican has been badly affected by Hurricane Katrina.